of a complex and often frust
Gercik has helped hundreds o
"win-win" situations and buil
turing relationships with the .
an extended period of time.

Thousands of people consider a good relationship with Japan vital to success in business today. For business people, and those who simply want to learn more about the web of psychological relationships that lie at the core of Japanese society, *On Track with the Japanese* is the golden key to making cross-cultural communications work.

Rosalie Post

Patricia Gercik spent the first twenty years of her life in Tokyo. Since 1985 she has been coordinating internships for students traveling to Japan, as well as conducting Japan-related business workshops. Ms. Gercik, currently the Managing Director of the M.I.T.-Japan Program, lives in Cambridge, Massachusetts.

ON TRACK
WITH THE
JAPANESE

ON TRACK
WITH THE
JAPANESE

A CASE-BY-CASE
APPROACH TO
BUILDING SUCCESSFUL
RELATIONSHIPS

PATRICIA GERCIK

KODANSHA INTERNATIONAL
NEW YORK • TOKYO • LONDON

Kodansha America, Inc.,
114 Fifth Avenue,
New York, New York 10011, U.S.A.

Kodansha International Ltd.,
17-14 Otowa 1-chome,
Bunkyo-ku, Tokyo 112, Japan

First published in 1992 by Kodansha America, Inc.

Printed in the United States of America

First edition, 1992

93   94   95   6   5   4   3   2

Library of Congress Cataloging-in-Publication Data

Gercik, Patricia
    On track with the Japanese : a case-by-case approach to building
successful relationships / Patricia Gercik. — 1st ed.
        p. cm.
    ISBN 4-7700-1602-6
        1. Business etiquette—Japan. 2. Negotiation in business—Japan.
3. Business entertaining—Japan. 4. National characteristics, Japanese.
5. Corporate culture—Japan. 6. Americans—Japan.
I. Title.
HF5387.G47 1992
395′.52′0952—dc20   92-11939
                                                              CIP

Book design by Louise B. Young

The text of this book was set in Century Old Style.
Composed by Haddon Craftsmen
Scranton, Pennsylvania.

Printed and bound by R.R. Donnelley
Harrisonburg, Virginia.

To Alexander and Mara

CONTENTS

INTRODUCTION

Two days before I was to leave Tokyo during a recent business trip, I called my father's business associate, an old friend of the family. It was an important call for me. I hadn't seen him for twenty-five years, yet when I recall the history of my family's connection to Japan—which dates back to the 1920s—he always comes to mind. My memories of childhood and young adulthood in Tokyo are filled with images of him sitting in our living room, drinking whiskey and talking politics with my parents. At eighty-three, he is still very much involved in business, and had just recently received an award from the emperor for his service to Japan. "Quite a man," as my father says.

He laughed when I reintroduced myself over the phone. Immediately he wanted to know if I preferred Japanese or Western cuisine, and I felt his pleasure when I answered "Japanese." The night I arrived, he met me at my hotel in downtown Tokyo. I recognized him right away as he rose to greet me. His eyes were bright and warm; he was delighted that I still remembered how to speak Japanese, insisted I hadn't changed a bit since I was twenty-two, and asked after my parents. During dinner we spoke of prewar Japan and of how his uncle brought my father's eventual business partner out of Hitler's Germany in the Thirties, and later retired to a Shinto shrine. As he spoke of the past, our web of connections grew, and he repeatedly lifted the sake bottle to fill my cup.

The waitress brought the customary dessert melon, and there was a lull in the conversation. Then he reached into his bag, took out two neatly wrapped packages, and placed them on the table. "For your father," he said quickly. "Hot rice crackers—he likes them with his whiskey." He nodded at the second package and said, "Christmas light-bulb set—make sure you point out the adjustable blinkers."

I packed the gifts carefully, remembering long evenings of whiskey, hot crackers, and political discussions in my parents' home, especially when we held our annual party to celebrate the successful export to America of that year's Christmas lights. The thoughtfulness of the gifts were a token of his knowledge of and history with my father: they were intimate symbols of mutual understanding and trust.

My interest in the process of negotiating and communicating with the Japanese springs from my long history with that country. For the past fifteen years, I have taught and developed Japanese history and culture classes in companies such as GE and Motorola, and in association with cultural institutions like the Japan Society of Boston. In 1986, I began working in the MIT–Japan Program, the largest, most comprehensive program of applied Japanese studies in the world, where I continued to develop courses on cultural awareness as well as teach a series of seminars on Japanese history, culture, and society for our program's interns. As part of our curriculum, interns must take two years of language and culture classes, and participate in an orientation retreat before leaving for Japan. Though my seminars were popular and the students attentive, I began to notice that, within the context of "hands on" interactions such as exchanging letters and interviewing, students were failing to pick up on some of the obvious cues in Japanese culture.

Simultaneously, I had also been debriefing students who had recently returned from yearlong internships with some of the most prestigious university and corporate laboratories in Japan. During these discussions, I spent many hours listening as they described how they had coped with everything from the confusing first day to the inevitable good-bye party. As I listened, I realized that they too suffered from a lack of understanding about Japanese ethics and society. I decided to make our training program more interactive and started reviewing the classic business case studies usually used in cross-cultural programs, but soon realized that they were formal, dry, and lacked insight. I began to write short problem-solving case studies and found them to be an enormous classroom aid: the students' interest level soared and so did their ability to extract and identify specific behavioral cues. Abroad, interns found that interaction with their co-workers began to improve and many of them wrote to say that our problem-solving sessions had been a valuable preparation tool and a real boon to their experience in Japan.

As I collected information from my students, I saw patterns of interaction emerging. The stories they shared encouraged me to venture outside the academic arena to interview other professionals and gather their impressions and experiences of negotiating with the Japanese. Unlike the MIT interns, my newest subjects had had no intense preparation for their dealings with Japan, yet almost all had managed to develop a good rapport with their contacts in that country. I discovered that the dynamics they described paralleled the experiences of my students: in every case, the Japanese concentrated on building trust by following intricate cultural rituals, and cultivating an intimate knowledge of their counterparts—personally as well as their business backgrounds—over a period of time. This sort of relationship, which relies equally on factual and emotional knowledge, is what American businessmen typically find unusual and uncomfortable. Nonetheless, each person I spoke with felt that dealing with Japan was vital to their business interests. Interns and businessmen alike emphasized the long, slow journey from being an outsider in Japan to becoming a trusted member of a working group.

These cases are narrated almost entirely from a non-Japanese point of view, and I have tried to analyze them from a Japanese perspective as best I can, based on my knowledge of and experience with Japanese culture. Those who have found success in Japan have often had to learn to openly acknowledge problems without prejudging the Japanese and, in some cases, make hard choices in order to come to terms with certain issues of gender, race, and family commitments. It is often the case that expectations in Japan run counter to what many American professionals have become accustomed to in this country, and displaying an understanding of and a willingness to work within the system, rather than reacting on an emotional level, goes a long way toward reaching business goals. Throughout my research, I found that success in Japan is largely based upon reaching mutual understanding and building trust.

In Japan, trust is a powerful, sophisticated concept encouraged and codified by traditional institutions and respected throughout society. Trust is based on knowledge and backed by careful scrutiny. Making a good first impression is vital to conveying commitment to a project. Lawyers may not be present at initial meetings, but all parties should have access to solid legal counsel. Trust is built gradually, and is the result of meticulous advance preparation and a certain knowledge of intricate rituals. Considerable patience is necessary in order to acquire sufficient information about a situation or potential business partner. With shared history come expanded networks, which reflect mutual commitment and confidence, and enable all parties to focus on a common goal. In Japan, the rules that guide business and social behavior alter as an individual blends into a working group, as do the expectations and responsibilities of everyone involved. Trust paves the way to individualization. In order to be successful in Japan, Westerners must understand the meaning of trust, how to interpret behavior, and how to recognize each stage in the process of building relationships.

On Track with the Japanese is the culmination of three years of interviews with MIT interns and professionals who have worked closely with Japanese executives. After participating directly in negotiation sessions and assembling countless interviews, I have developed a theory that organizes the Japanese approach to building relationships into four basic stages: Know Me, Trust Me, Believe Me, and Marry Me.

All of the case studies presented here stress the difficulty of entering into Japanese society. My staged model begins in the "know me" phase, in which preparation prior to and including early meetings demonstrates commitment to a relationship; the next is "trust me," the stage that addresses the subtle politics and tests of commitment to a project or group within the workplace (often this stage is the most frustrating to Westerners, as little of consequence seems to happen); followed by "believe me," in which hard negotiating tactics are accompanied by opportunities to network with specific inside groups and participate in some of the bonding rituals of Japanese society, thereby elevating trust; and finally "marry me," in which we examine how to nurture and sustain relationships once they have been established. Each case is followed by an in-depth analysis of the characters' situation and, though each section highlights the key elements of that stage, in many instances it incorporates traits from other stages. The characteristics of each stage apply to all variations of negotiating with the Japanese, whether here or overseas.

The students and professionals with whom I have worked report that, once they understood the Japanese way of establishing a certain negotiation ritual, they were able to target a specific phase of interaction and modify their behavior to ensure that their negotiations progressed efficiently. Businessmen, trainees, students of Japan, and professionals working or negotiating with the Japanese will, I hope, find this book useful in defining concepts fundamental to business everywhere, and vital to any relationship with Japan.

On Track with the Japanese would not have been possible without the support of the many professionals who generously gave their time and energy to this project. In particular, I would also like to thank Professor Richard Samuels, director of the MIT-Japan Program, for his support and guidance. His early recognition of the value of this case method of teaching about Japan, and the staged model for describing communication in Japan, created a dialogue that has been enormously supportive throughout this project. I would also like to thank Professor Philip J. Stone of the Department of Psychology at Harvard University for his advice and comments. Finally, I would like to thank Janice Welch for her support and enthusiasm.

KNOW ME

"Knowing" the Japanese starts before initial face-to-face contact is made. It begins with extensive research and proceeds through participation in the first formal meetings. The "know me" stage involves preparation through use of effective networking, documentation to answer questions about the project and the company involved, and understanding the purpose of the formalities of the initial meetings.

This stage is the crucial foundation for developing trust. The Japanese need to "know you" for two reasons. First, they feel entitled and committed to understanding the overall situation of your company, the proposed project, and the reputation of key players and their past performance. The Japanese study the documentation you give them during this stage carefully to ensure reliability and so they might develop an internal consensus and strategy. More traditional societies that are used to this kind of preparation and scrutiny will have an easier time doing business with the Japanese. In Moto's case, Moto comes to America having not only researched Allmack, but also Allmack's president. His choice of a gift reflects this. Moto is ready to do business with Allmack. Second, Japanese expect the foreign company to have done their homework. The extent of your research and understanding of the Japanese company is considered an important criteria in measuring your company's commitment to the project. In Peter's case, he bases his business strategy on vague notions of Japanese business, thereby constantly revealing his ignorance of the immediate situation. Peter is not taken seriously. A foreigner must work to establish credibility in Japan. Knowledge, in short, is credibility.

The initial meeting is ritualized and formal in tone. Ceremonial introductory speeches provide a brief history of the project and outline general expectations. Carefully wrapped gifts codify the degree of interaction and subtly reveal the extent of the preparation. A harmonious tone is established for further business. Commitment is measured by the degree of preparation and understanding of the situation. The groundwork of ideas should be carefully laid through go-betweens, before the actual ideas are introduced.

Together, these ceremonies set the stage for further obligations. The meetings that follow will also be formal. Japanese tend to listen rather than talk, and at this early stage, there may be little productive interaction by foreign standards.

Where a relationship is initiated by Japanese, the situation can be somewhat different. Often, there has been a great deal of study and internal discussion before the approach is made, and foreigners are often amazed by the speed with which deals are concluded.

Japanese society and norms are complex, especially for a foreigner who may indeed need help in figuring things out. Often, a Japanese colleague will assume the role of a mentor. Mentor/student relationships are common in Japanese life. Japanese institutions routinely assign mentors to their new hires. Young people are judged on their ability to network and find a protective relationship. Obligation plays an important role in these situations, even though the relationship will equalize over time. Business relationships and friendships usually begin through obligation. In Ann's case, her help is requested by a Japanese woman who is trying to survive in America. The initial ties of obligation eventually result in a friendship. For foreigners in Japan, the mentor relationship can be a critical path through a bewildering world. It can also be limiting in that foreigners become excessively dependent on single informants.

Although the cases in this section transverse many stages, they emphasize the role of preparation in the first contacts and introductory meetings with Japanese.

MOTO: Coming to America

Moto arrived in Chicago in the middle of winter, unprepared for the raw wind that swept off the lake. The first day he bought a new coat and fur-lined boots. He was cheered by a helpful salesgirl who smiled as she packed his lined raincoat into a box. Americans were nice, Moto decided. He was not worried about his assignment in America. The land had been purchased, and Moto's responsibility was to hire a contracting company and check on the pricing details. The job seemed straightforward.

Moto's firm, KKD, an auto parts supplier, had spent 1½ years researching American building contractors. Allmack had the best record in terms of timely delivery and liaisons with good architects and the best suppliers of raw materials. That night Moto called Mr. Crowell of Allmack, who confirmed the appointment for the next morning. His tone was amiable.

Moto arrived at the Allmack office at nine sharp. He had brought a set of *kokeshi* dolls for Crowell. The dolls, which his wife had spent a good part of a day picking out, were made from a special maple in the mountains near his family home in Niigata. He would explain that to Crowell later, when they knew each other. Crowell also came from a hilly, snowy place, which was called Vermont.

When the secretary ushered him in, Crowell stood immediately and rounded the desk with an outstretched hand. Squeezing Moto's hand, he roared, "How are you? Long trip from Tokyo. Please sit down, please."

Moto smiled. He reached in his jacket for his card. By the time he presented it, Crowell was back on the other side of the desk. "My card," Moto said seriously.

"Yes, yes," Crowell answered. He put Moto's card in his pocket without a glance.

Moto stared at the floor. This couldn't be happening, he thought. Everything was on that card: KKD, Moto, Michio, Project Director.

KKD meant University of Tokyo and years of hard work to earn a high recommendation from Dr. Iwasa's laboratory. Crowell had simply put it away.

"Here." Crowell handed his card.

"Oh, John Crowell, Allmack, President," Moto read aloud, slowly trying to recover his equilibrium. "Allmack is famous in Japan."

"You know me," Crowell replied and grinned. "All those faxes. Pleased to meet you, Moto. I have a good feeling about this deal."

Moto smiled and lay Crowell's card on the table in front of him.

"KKD is pleased to do business with Allmack," Moto spoke slowly. He was proud of his English. Not only had he been a top English student in high school and university, but he had also studied English in a *juku* (an afterschool class) for five years. As soon as he received this assignment, he took an intensive six-week course taught by Ms. Black, an American, who also instructed him in American history and customs.

Crowell looked impatient. Moto tried to think of Ms. Black's etiquette lessons as he continued talking about KKD and Allmack's history. "We are the best in the business," Crowell interrupted. "Ask anyone. We build the biggest and best shopping malls in the country."

Moto hesitated. He knew Allmack's record—that's why he was in the room. Surely Crowell knew that. The box of *kokeshi* dolls pressed against his knees. Maybe he should give the gift now. No, he thought, Crowell was still talking about Allmack's achievements. Now Crowell had switched to his own achievements. Moto felt desperate.

"You'll have to come to my house," Crowell continued. "I live in a fantastic house. I had an architect from California build it. He builds for all the stars, and for me." Crowell chuckled. "Built it for my wife. She's the best wife, the very best. I call her my little sweetheart. Gave the wife the house on her birthday. Took her right up to the front door and carried her inside."

Moto shifted his weight. Perhaps if he were quiet, Crowell would change the subject. Then they could pretend the conversation never happened. "Moto-san, what's your first name. Here, we like to be on a first-name basis."

"Michio," Moto whispered.

"Michio-san, you won't get a better price than from me. You can go down the block to Zimmer or Casey, but you got the best deal right here."

"I brought you a present," Moto said, handing him the box of *kokeshi* dolls.

"Thanks," Crowell answered. He looked genuinely pleased as he tore open the paper. Moto looked away while Crowell picked up a *kokeshi* doll in each hand. "They look like Russian dolls. Hey, thanks a lot, my daughter will love them."

Moto pretended that he hadn't heard. I'll help by ignoring him, Moto thought, deeply embarrassed.

Crowell pushed the *kokeshi* dolls aside and pressed a buzzer. "Send George in," he said.

The door opened and a tall, heavyset man with a dark crew cut stepped inside the room.

"George Kubushevsky, this is Moto-san. Michio . . ."

"How do you do?" Kubushevsky's handshake was firm.

Moto took out his card.

"Thanks," Kubushevsky said. "Never carry those." He laughed and hooked his thumbs in his belt buckle. Moto nodded. He was curious. Kubushevsky must be a Jewish name—or was it Polish, or maybe even German? In Japan he'd read books about all three groups. He looked at Kubushevsky's bone structure. It was impossible to tell. He was too fat.

"George, make sure you show Michio everything. We want him to see all the suppliers, meet the right people, you understand?"

"Sure." George grinned and left the room.

Moto turned to Crowell. "Is he a real American?" Moto asked.

"A real American? What's that?"

Moto flushed. "Is he first generation?" Moto finished lamely. He remembered reading that Jews, Lebanese, and Armenians were often first generation.

"How do I know? He's just Kubushevsky."

During the next few weeks Moto saw a great deal of Kubushevsky. Each morning he was picked up at nine and taken to a round of suppliers. Kubushevsky gave him a rundown on each supplier before they met. He was amiable and polite, but never really intimate. Moto's response was also to be polite. Once he suggested that they go drinking after work, but Kubushevsky flatly refused, saying that he had to work early the next morning. Moto sighed, remembering briefly his favorite bar and his favorite hostess in Tokyo. Yuko-san must be nearly fifty now, he thought affectionately. She could make him laugh. He wished he was barhopping with his colleagues from his *ringi* group at KKD. Moto regretted that he had not brought more *kokeshi* dolls, since Kubushevsky had not seemed delighted with the present of the KKD pen.

One morning they were driving to a cement outlet.

"George."

"Yes, Michio-san."

Moto paused. He still found it difficult to call Kubushevsky by his first name. "Do you think I could have some papers?"

"What kind of papers?" Kubushevsky's voice was friendly. Unlike Crowell, he kept an even tone. Moto liked that.

"I need papers on the past sales of these people."

"We're the best."

"I need records for the past five years on the cement place we are going to visit."

"I told you, Michio-san, I'm taking you to the best! What do you want?"

"I need some records."

"Trust me, I know what I'm doing."

Moto was silent. He didn't know what to say. What did trust have to do with anything? His *ringi* group in Tokyo needed documentation so they could discuss the issues and be involved in the decision. If the decision to go with one supplier or the other was correct, that should be reflected in the figures.

"Just look at what's going on now," George said. "Charts for the last five years, that's history."

Moto remained silent. George pressed his foot to the gas. The car passed one truck, and then another. Moto looked nervously at the climbing speedometer. Suddenly Kubushevsky whistled and released his foot. "All right, Michio-san, I'll get you the damned figures."

"Thanks," Moto said softly.

"After we see the cement people, let's go for a drink."

. . .

Moto looked uneasily at the soft red light bulb that lit the bar. He sipped his beer and ate a few peanuts. Kubushevsky was staring at a tall blonde at the other end of the bar. She seemed to notice him also. Her fingers moved across the rim of the glass.

"George," Moto said gently. "Where are you from, George."

"Here and there," Kubushevsky said idly, still eyeing the blonde.

Moto laughed. "Here and there."

Kubushevsky nodded. "Here and there," he repeated.

"You Americans," Moto said. "You must have a home."

"No home, Michio-san."

The blonde slid her drink down the bar and slipped into the next seat. Kubushevsky turned more toward her.

Moto felt desperate. Last week Crowell had also acted rudely. When Imai, KKD's vice president, was visiting from Japan, Crowell had dropped them both off at a golf course. What was the point?

He drained his beer. Immediately the familiar warmth of the alcohol made him buoyant. "George," he said intimately. "You need a wife. You need a wife like Crowell has."

Kubushevsky turned slowly on his seat. He stared hard at Moto. "You need a muzzle," he said quietly.

"You need a wife," Moto repeated. He had Kubushevsky's full attention now. He poured Kubushevsky another beer. "Drink," he commanded.

Kubushevsky drank. In fact they both drank. Then suddenly Kubushevsky's voice changed. He put his arm around Moto and purred in his ear. "Let me tell you a secret, Moto-san. Crowell's wife is a dog. Crowell is a dog. I'm going to leave Allmack, just as soon as possible. Want to join me, Michio-san?"

Moto's insides froze. Leave Crowell. What was Kubushevsky talking about? He was just getting to know him. They were a team. All those hours in the car together, all those hours staring at cornfields and concrete. What was Kubushevsky talking about? Did Crowell know? What was Kubushevsky insinuating about joining him? "You're drunk, George."

"I know."

"You're very drunk."

"I know."

Moto smiled. The blonde got restless and left the bar. Kubushevsky didn't seem to notice. For the rest of the night he talked
about his first wife and his two children, whom he barely saw. He
spoke of his job at Allmack and his hopes for a better job in California. They sat at a low table. Moto spoke of his children and distant
wife. It felt good to talk. Almost as good as having Yuko next to him.

As they left the bar, Kubushevsky leaned heavily on him. They
peed against a stone wall before getting in the car. All the way home
Kubushevsky sang a song about a folk hero named Davy Crockett,
who "killed himself a bear when he was only three." Moto sang a
song from Niigata about the beauty of the snow on the rooftops in
winter. Kubushevsky hummed along.

They worked as a team for the next four months. Kubushevsky
provided whatever detailed documentation Moto asked for. They
went drinking a lot. Sometimes they both felt a little sad, sometimes
happy, but Moto mostly felt entirely comfortable. Kubushevsky introduced him to Porter, a large, good-natured man in the steel business who liked to hunt and cook gourmet food; to Andrews, a tiny
man who danced the polka as if it were a waltz; and to many others.

Just before the closing, Kubushevsky took him to a bar and told
him of a job offer in California. He had tears in his eyes and hugged
Moto good-bye. Moto had long since accepted the fact that Kubushevsky would leave.

Two weeks later Moto looked around the conference room at
Allmack. Ishii, KKD's president, and Imai had flown in from Tokyo
for the signing of the contract for the shopping mall, the culmination
of three years of research and months of negotiation. John Crowell
stood by his lawyer, Sue Smith. Sue had been on her feet for five
hours. Mike Apple, Moto's lawyer, slammed his fist on the table and
pointed at the item in question. The lawyers argued a timing detail
that Moto was sure had been worked out weeks before. Moto glanced
nervously at Ishii and Imai. Ishii's eyes were closed. Imai stared at
the table.

Moto shifted uneasily in his seat. Sue was smarter than Mike, he
thought. Perhaps a female lawyer wouldn't have been so terrible.
While it was not usual to see females in professional positions in
Japan, this was America. Tokyo might have understood. After all,
this was America, he repeated to himself. Internationalization re-

quired some adjustment. A year ago he would have had total loss of
face if confronted with this prolonged, argumentative closing. Today
he did not care. He could not explain to Tokyo all he'd learned in that
time, all the friends he'd made. When he tried to communicate about
business in America, the home office sent him terse notes by fax.

Now the lawyers stood back. President Ishii opened his eyes.
Crowell handed a pen to Ishii. They signed the document together.
The lawyers smiled. Sue Smith looked satisfied. She should be
pleased, Moto thought. Her extensive preparation for the case made
him realize again that the Japanese stereotype of the "lazy" American was false. Sue's knowledge of the case was perfect in all details.
I'll have to use her next time, Moto thought. She's the smart one. Yes,
he thought, his friend Kubushevsky had taught him many things.
Suddenly he felt Kubushevsky's large presence. Moto lowered his
head in gratitude.

Analysis:

*This case underlines the critical importance preparation, bonding,
and documentation have in the initial "know me" and "trust me"
stages of Japanese business practice.*

*Moto has come prepared to do business with Allmack. However,
because early stages of communication are often indirect in Japan,
this is not immediately apparent to Crowell. In the initial meeting,
which Moto carefully designed to set a harmonious business tone
(aisatsu), Moto attempts to communicate KKD's knowledge of Allmack and KKD's serious intent through language and gesture. In
Moto's point of view, this formal meeting is a chance for Crowell and
Moto to become acquainted with each other.*

*Moto begins the meeting by presenting his name card. Crowell
ignores the card, which implies all Moto's achievements. An employee
of KKD in a position like Moto's has most likely graduated from a
prestigious university. The difficulty of the entrance exam to such a
university is common knowledge in Japan. It is also common knowledge that only students from elite schools are accepted into the best
companies in Japan. In addition, Japanese companies send their fast-
track managers to work overseas. Moto can't say all this directly to
Crowell, so his card becomes an important transmitter of information
that must be looked at, pondered over, and remarked on.*

Moto starts to discuss the relationship of KKD and Allmack in the

*hope that this will reveal Moto's commitment to Allmack and provide
a sound basis for future business, but it does not go well. Instead of
waiting patiently and responding in kind, Crowell replies with an
update on Allmack's current status in the competitive marketplace.
For Crowell, the history of relations between the two companies is
secondary to the immediate situation. Crowell's informality is both
puzzling and offensive to Moto.*

*At this point Moto is upset and hopes his gift will establish a
connection with Crowell, deepening and solidifying their relationship.
Armed with the knowledge that Crowell is from Vermont, Moto has
purchased a box of* kokeshi *dolls, made from maple common to
Moto's hometown, which is in a mountainous region comparable to
Vermont. Moto hopes the dolls will provide a link between them. They
will discover they are from similar villages and this will establish a
harmonious tone* (wa). *Japanese often initiate conversations among
themselves and with foreigners by searching for a connection, such as
similarity in size of their towns of residence.*

*Instead of admiring and questioning Moto on this unusual present,
Crowell puts the gift aside. He prefers to communicate directly with
Moto by boasting about Allmack's achievements, his house built by a
famous architect, and even his "best" wife.*

*Deeply embarrassed, Moto ignores Crowell's boasts. From Moto's
point of view, any exposure of Crowell's behavior would humiliate both
Crowell and himself and cause loss of face. Unpleasant situations are
often ignored in Japan, especially at the early stages of a relationship.
Reference to shortcomings in others—either through jest or in ear-
nest—is a serious breach of etiquette. Also, mentioning a competitor—in this case, saying that Moto will get the best price at Allmack—
shows Crowell's lack of respect for Allmack's reputation and for
KKD's diligent research. Only through saving face can the friendly
professional tone be maintained. In Japanese culture, the subtext of a
situation (or what really is happening) is quite distinct from surface
behavior (or the formal, outward trappings). Crowell, of course, is
oblivious to either the real situation* (honne) *or the situation as it is
being constructed formally by Moto* (tatemae).

*The purpose of this meeting in Moto's mind is to help his "group"
or company establish a connection to a commercial enterprise through
good human relations* (ningen kankei). *Japanese refer to their own*

company as their house (uchi). *People are either labeled as outsiders (soto) or insiders (naka) in relation to the company. To facilitate this process of "connections," Moto categorizes people so that he can identify with the right person who belongs to the right group. It is quite natural for Moto to group Kubushevsky in terms of religion or race: Japanese are self-consciously aware of their homogeneity and thus tend to categorize other people in such terms.*

Moto's early attempts at bonding also fail with Kubushevsky. Kubushevsky at first refuses to go drinking, and he dismisses Moto's need for documentation. Moto is frantic. Under similar circumstances in Japan, Moto and the client would spend an evening at a small bar. They would learn something about each other and let their guard down. From Moto's point of view, neither Crowell nor Kubushevsky understands the subtleties of human relations.

Similarly, Moto loses face with KKD's Vice President Imai when Crowell drops them off at a golf course. From Imai's point of view, Moto isn't yet on the inside with Crowell.

Determined to rectify the situation, Moto insists that Kubushevsky provide documentation for his group in Japan, and although resentful, Kubushevsky agrees. Then Moto uses the atmosphere at the bar to initiate a mentor/student (sempai/kohai) relationship by advising Kubushevsky to get married. Initially, relationships often begin in this manner of adviser/advisee and equalize over time.

Kubushevsky responds by criticizing Crowell, insisting he will leave Allmack and inviting Moto to join him. Moto is shocked. It is unheard of to criticize one's company and boss so openly, especially to an outsider. Like most Japanese, used to lifelong employment, Moto identifies with and feels obligated to his company. A typical Japanese employee of a large company spends the first two years working in the company factory, traveling with salesmen, and taking courses to learn the company and its culture.

Moto is angered by Kubushevsky's unorthodox behavior, but he is also desperate for Kubushevsky's help. Moto pragmatically excuses Kubushevsky's lack of tact, attributing it to his drunkenness (the Japanese believe that inebriation relieves an individual from responsibility). Moto then also uses the freedom that drink and the atmosphere of a small bar provides to discuss his own personal life. By the end of the evening Kubushevsky and Moto are comrades. Personal relation-

ships that provide a basis of trust in business often begin in such settings. The alcohol provides a freedom for an intimate dependency (amae). With this friendship, Moto feels successful. Kubushevsky is part of Moto's working group. By the time KKD signs the contract with Allmack, Moto accepts the fact that in order to internationalize, Japanese must learn the American system; the last-minute bargaining bothers his superiors but does not bother Moto, and Moto considers using a female lawyer in the future, although he will have to convince Tokyo of the wisdom of this idea. Kubushevsky has become his window (madoguchi) to America. Moto lowers his head in obligation (on) to his teacher Kubushevsky. Unlike normally incurred debts, on can never be repaid.

ALLEN: Knowing Your Group

Allen stood next to the window in the crowded train. The heat and the smell of pomade made him ill. He glanced at his watch: another hour before he got home. His Japanese colleagues said 1½ hours was a normal commuting time. He wiped his brow: the train was stifling, it was already nine o'clock, and he hadn't eaten supper. The *mushi pan* (Chinese bread) he'd bought at the station felt warm in his hand. Slowly he opened the package and began to nibble. He broke off one large piece, then another. Finally he opened the package and stuffed half the bread in his mouth. He looked up. The man next to him, and several others nearby, were frowning. One man stepped toward him and pointed at the food. "No," he said in English. Allen felt the blood drain from his face. He turned away, stuffed the wrapper in his pocket, and tried to compose himself.

By the time he got off the train he was shaking. He, Allen, a grown man, an engineer, could not walk. He hated himself. He was nothing—empty—a hollow drum. In the past he'd never thought about himself. Professors and classmates described him as a "doer." After three months in Japan he thought about himself continually and felt only the pain of being nothing. He held on to his upbringing and the values he'd been taught as a boy. They were his beacon.

He grabbed the railing, slowly made his way to the landing, and began the walk to his small apartment. He turned a corner, and suddenly he saw an open field in front of him; he had never noticed it before. In the moonlight the green gray grass reminded him of Argyle, Virginia—his hometown. He took a deep breath. As the trembling in his legs stopped, he straightened his back and felt the slight breeze against his face. He began to run toward the field, blood rushing to his face. He spread his hands and hooted his football cry. The sound echoed in the night. He hooted again and again, until suddenly the hoots turned to sobs. His chest hurt, his cheeks felt raw, and his shirt was wet. His legs moved faster until he stumbled on a root and fell.

Allen slowly raised his head. He expected half the town to be gazing at him, but the field was empty. He rubbed his hands and spat dirt from his mouth. He was on a slight hill. Using the root to balance himself, he sat cross-legged and took a deep breath. Where had it all gone wrong? His world was upside down. Just three months ago he'd been so confident, so sure of everything. He'd been a straight A student, Phi Beta Kappa, and he'd done everything right. The internship program demanded two years of Japanese, so he'd taken three. The program encouraged Japanese history, so he'd taken a minor in Japanese culture. When Monta Company accepted him, he'd written that he was fluent in Japanese. Now nothing fit—he was not sure of anything. He thought back to his first week in Japan.

When he'd arrived in June, the rainy season was late and the moisture in the air gave him headaches. On his first night he was invited to a banquet where, because of jet lag and lack of food, he became so drunk he was late for work the next day. The Japanese engineers were polite and joked about his lateness, but he did not think much of the incident because his American roommate, with whom he'd been placed by Monta, was routinely a half hour late. They often came to the office together at first.

Two weeks after he started working at Monta he was given his current apartment, and though it was farther away he was glad to be living alone. However, he remained tired and often felt overwhelmed. He spoke Japanese nearly all the time, but many of his Japanese colleagues answered him in English and seemed disgusted with his level of Japanese. The secretaries stared blankly at him. Although discouraged, Allen was stubborn about his achievements and dug in his heels. He lowered his eyes as he continued to speak Japanese. The fact that he stumbled over words did not matter. The fact that no one answered also did not matter. The more insistent he became, the more hollow he felt. One day after making a particularly long speech in Japanese, he ran to the bathroom and vomited.

He was slow to have his business card made up, rationalizing he could not get used to the importance placed on cards. In fact Allen had deliberately shunted aside all the information he had learned in his Japanese history and culture courses. In his own stubborn way, he wanted the Japanese to know him firsthand. Every day he was presented with at least ten cards, which he tried to ignore by immediately stuffing in his pocket; he preferred to greet his Japanese visitors directly. He also employed this direct approach with other aspects of etiquette: he often showed his self-reliance and a precise, business-like manner by pouring his own beer; he gave departing visitors precise directions to the elevator, instead of escorting them. He was upset when colleagues reported that his boss felt he wasn't working hard enough. Subsequently he had several confrontations with his boss.

Two months after he arrived the Monta Company held a retreat where he was openly accused by the president of not being more able in Japanese, and of often being lazy. The company felt they were not getting their money's worth. From the time of this retreat Allen began to have daily fantasies of going back to America. Sometimes in the middle of a conference he would daydream about purchasing a ticket home or even boarding Northwest.

Most Monta employees didn't leave the office until seven-thirty or eight. Several times colleagues asked him to join them for drinks, but he excused himself, saying he was too exhausted and the 1½ hour commute to his apartment made afterwork activities difficult. The Japanese joked with him about Americans' inability to hold liquor, and he agreed in all seriousness that Americans were weak in that respect.

In mid-August Monta had an enormous work load and Allen felt swamped. Increasingly he became dependent on the help of Emiko, a secretary in the office. He put in long hours and went on several trips. He saw that people brought small gifts back after trips and although he was on a tight budget he decided to buy his secretary a gift the next time he went away. He thought about the gift a great deal and finally chose an expensive mother-of-pearl necklace because he'd noticed Emiko liked jewelry. The morning he returned from his trip, he proudly presented the box to Emiko. The colleagues in his group stopped talking, and several secretaries leaned forward—the room was deathly quiet. Emiko stared at the box for what seemed like several minutes. Her face paled and she looked around the room. Then, she pushed the box back across the desk.

"I can't accept this," she said in a barely audible voice. "How much was it? I'll pay you."

"Pay me?" His voice sounded agitated. "It's a gift."

The Japanese resumed their conversation. Allen walked hurriedly from the room. When he returned, he found the box on his desk. That evening Kyoshi, a Japanese colleague, invited him to a bar. He was feeling so low he decided to accept.

Kyoshi took him to a small, intimate place where he was well known, and soon they were surrounded by girls. The cheap perfume and superficial banter alienated Allen further. He felt he was floating. When Kyoshi brought up the current elections, Allen was at a loss for words. Although in America he prided himself on reading Japanese newspapers, he realized he hadn't picked up a newspaper here for weeks. The girls finally left and Allen glumly stared at the table. Finally, Kyoshi suggested they leave. Allen did not take the train home immediately. He began to walk and was soon lost. Although he passed several people he was reluctant to ask for help. After all, he reasoned, he was brought up to be independent, to solve his own problems, to stand straight like a man, and he was not going to give in now on some narrow street in the center of Tokyo.

He finally reached home at three in the morning. The next day he was hung over and did not go to work. Although he came to work the following morning, he felt distanced from everything, as if he were floating. That evening he'd boarded the train, perspired heavily, and several times hyperventilated and felt dizzy.

Three weeks later Allen left Japan.

Analysis:

Preparation is considered a measure of the seriousness of intent in Japan. Japanese think research and preparation for a project are essential for the smooth running of a group. This is especially true at the "know me" stage of interaction with a Japanese company.

Before joining Monta, Allen has prepared himself with three years of Japanese language and many courses on Japanese history and culture. However, once he is actually in the country, Allen becomes overwhelmed and dissociated. He exhibits many symptoms typical of "culture shock": anger, paranoia, stubbornness, and obsessiveness, among others.

He is understandably proud of his accomplishments and has told Monta he is fluent in Japanese. Most experts agree that it takes at least four years of Japanese-language training to read a newspaper with some fluency and even longer to read without the use of a dictionary. At the retreat, the president of Monta confronts Allen directly on this issue and uses the situation as a basis for a conversation on Allen's commitment to the "group" in general.

Direct confrontation is appropriate to Japanese in a setting such as a retreat where work issues are being discussed. Retreats provide a time for reflection and self-evaluation without loss of face. The openness of the conversation will, it is hoped, eventually enhance the working relations of the group, and in this spirit the president of Monta is incredibly blunt. Thus, the Japanese code of ethics is situation dependent. In the office setting the same criticism could not be voiced directly without loss of face to both the president and Allen.

Commitment to the group is essential for an employee working in a Japanese company or, in fact, in any situation involving the Japanese. At the "know me" phase of the relationship, the individual will be watched and tested as to his sincerity and respect for smooth group dynamics. Allen underestimates his colleagues' discomfort about his tardiness and, in so doing, ignores the indirect way Japanese communicate. Allen misreads other efforts to communicate as well. He refuses to go drinking with his colleagues from the office because he is concerned about fatigue and commuting time. Missed opportunities for friendship and for informal communication set up impenetrable boundaries for him. The small bar and alcohol are opportunities to let off steam and have off-the-record conversations, which would help establish Allen's network. Allen lives alone in an apartment located some distance from his work, which makes casual interactions with office mates more difficult.

Allen's boyhood values of individualism and self-reliance inhibit his understanding of the situation at Monta. The more frustrated and isolated he feels, the less he depends on his preparation or common-sense observations (this is a common occurrence when people undergo culture shock). Allen's reliance on American values of independence only exacerbates an already tense situation. Thus, he is slow about making up a business card, reasoning that he should become acquainted with Japanese by introducing himself and his accomplishments directly. At best, this transgression is confusing to the Japanese, who depend on the information on a business card to inform them of a person's status. Allen even refuses to acknowledge the business cards his visitors present him with; instead he expects his visitors to inform him of their background and status directly.

Allen's self-reliance is also at odds with other aspects of Japanese etiquette. He refuses to admit the Japanese concept of dependency (amae) and its use in social situations. Dependency supports the vertical organization of Japanese society. It encourages human ties (ningen kankei) and obligation (on/giri), which together provide a framework for Japanese values. Allen's refusal to understand the dependent nature of Japanese relations puts him on the outside in a society governed by these values. His self-sufficiency makes him a poor guest and a poor host. By pouring his own beer and expecting others to do likewise, Allen is discarding the outward manifestations of dependency. When he fails to escort guests to the elevator, let alone remain there until the doors close, Allen creates emotional distance.

Although Allen works long hours, his boss complains that Allen is not working hard enough. Allen's reaction is to withdraw even more. He further reveals his lack of understanding of the Japanese by stating that foreigners are "weak" in respect to holding liquor. Here, in addition to insulting his own group, Allen refuses to acknowledge the role drink plays in Japanese society.

Allen also shows his alienation and misunderstandings through his gift-giving. At this point Allen is working hard and feels some sense of accomplishment and wants to reward his secretary for her help while showing the work group his knowledge of Japanese customs. Allen presents his secretary with an expensive, inappropriate gift in front of the group. This causes the secretary to be singled out and lose face. She reacts by returning the gift, thus making clear to the group that she is not in league with Allen. Defeated and feeling hopeless, Allen nonetheless holds on to his own notions of individualism and independence in a culture that nurtures trust as part of an ongoing, formalized process.

ANN: Obligation as the Beginning of Friendship

One morning in the dead of winter, Ann, an American who'd been raised in Japan and moved to the United States at the age of twenty, looked out through the tiny, star-shaped frost patterns on her windows. She'd had an exhausting week at the Institute. Ann was glad to be indoors and relieved it was Saturday.

When the phone rang, she picked up the receiver eagerly, expecting a familiar voice.

"Sorry to bother you," a woman said in Japanese. "I am Matsukata Fumiko. Do you remember me?"

"That's okay," Ann answered, trying to place the voice. Her work brought her into contact with the wives of Japanese researchers. The wives helped with cultural activities, and in turn Ann provided practical advice on adjustment to American living.

"I'm sorry to bother you," Fumiko said more urgently.

"I remember you, of course," Ann answered. Ann could not place the voice. She waited.

Fumiko apologized a third time for disturbing Ann on the weekend. Her voice had an edge of desperation. "My apartment has flooded. Water is coming through the ceiling and all our furniture is wet."

"That's terrible," Ann replied. She began flipping the pages of her phone book for the name of a plumber.

"My son has a cold," Fumiko continued. "He has a fever and a cough. His bed is wet. Our refrigerator is broken. Something must have happened to the wire."

Ann scribbled down the numbers of two plumbers and a family doctor. "Have you called the plumber?" she asked.

"No," Fumiko answered in a hesitant tone, "no plumbers." Her voice suddenly went soft. Its vulnerability put a catch on the last syllable. There was a pause.

Ann closed her eyes. She didn't want to leave the warm house and the smell of popovers. Her family would be down for a late breakfast soon. The table was set with a blue-and-white tablecloth with matching napkins. Her children, Sarah and Sam (eight and ten respectively), loved the morning ritual. Her husband, Tim, had smiled softly at the frost on the window that morning and said, "I guess it's a popover morning."

"Well now," Ann kept her voice bright and cheerful. "We must find you a good plumber."

The line was silent. Ann cleared her throat. Suddenly she remembered Fumiko. She was small and delicate with round cheeks and bright eyes. Ann had noticed her first because of her refinement and later because of her clear mind and abrupt wit. At the last meeting of the Japanese wives, Fumiko had sat in the front row and followed Ann's welcome speech eagerly.

But I still can't sit in a wet apartment on my day off, Ann thought. What I really mean is, I won't. After all, under the circumstances, I wouldn't expect Fumiko or anyone for that matter to sit with me. She's over twenty-one, she has a child, a husband. She's been to university. Ann cleared her throat and continued. "I will give you the names and numbers of two plumbers and a good doctor. If you have any trouble just call me, okay?"

There was a long pause. "Taro-chan's so sick," Fumiko said softly. "The refrigerator doesn't work. There must have been an electrical short . . ." Fumiko's voice trailed off.

Ann was about to suggest an all-purpose "fix it" company for appliances, but the softness of Fumiko's tone stopped her. Her stomach tightened. Perhaps I should go, Ann thought. I could bring some fresh milk and bread over.

"Mom," Sam interrupted her thoughts, "are the popovers ready?"

"Yes," she answered quickly and took a deep breath. "Fumiko, call me if those appliance people don't work out."

"Of course, thank you for all your trouble. Thank you," Fumiko whispered.

Fumiko did not call, and by Monday morning Ann had put the incident out of her mind. However, the day was particularly cold and by three o'clock Ann was again concerned. She remembered Fumiko's hesitant tone and decided to call. Fumiko again apologized for bothering Ann. The refrigerator was fixed, and her son was better. The landlord agreed to have the rugs cleaned. Satisfied with the news, Ann ended the conversation. However, twenty minutes later she felt uneasy once more. Although Fumiko had apologized profusely for bothering Ann, her choice of words made the conversation formal. The slightly distant tone nagged at Ann. Ann understood Fumiko's desire to be cared for. Ann had demanded the same nurturing relationship from friends when she'd first come to America. She'd asked for their advice on finding an apartment, and even on purchasing a car. Americans had been bewildered.

Ann dialed her favorite florist, and ordered flowers for Fumiko and her family, dictating a note of concern for their well-being. Then Ann sighed with relief and pushed Fumiko and her troubles out of her mind.

The next morning the phone rang early. "Ann-san, oh, Ann-san, the flowers are so beautiful," Fumiko gushed. "So wonderful. Thank you. Thank you. I feel obligated to you. Very obligated."

"No obligation," Ann interrupted. "I sent the flowers from feeling."

Fumiko was silent for several seconds. "I understand, I understand," she replied softly.

Soon thereafter, Ann invited Fumiko and two other Japanese women to work with her on a pamphlet describing the university to Japanese visitors. Over the next months they had many long meetings; often after discussing the project, the women relaxed and spoke about their lives, delighting where there was a similarity of experience, hopes, or dreams. As the weeks went by, the conversations became more intimate: for instance, one woman spoke of her frequent drinking, rationalizing her binges as normal; another woman felt trapped by her children. Fumiko herself wanted to work professionally, either in America or back in Japan.

The openness of these discussions put Ann at ease. She spoke of the frustrations of working and being a mother to small children. The women listened. After one long meeting where Ann had spoken in some detail about her life, Fumiko nodded sympathetically, patted Ann's arms, and said, "You're our big sister, Ann. We listen to you. We learn from you." One night Fumiko asked Ann to take the alcoholic to a clinic for a checkup, explaining that the woman was ill that morning, and Ann would be a good translator. Ann did all she was asked, conscious that her increasing involvement with the Japanese women's lives in America would create further obligations on all sides.

Late that spring Ann prepared for a business trip to Japan. Her secretary called the women and let them know that the meetings scheduled for the next two weeks were canceled. The day before Ann was to leave, Fumiko dropped by the office. She was flushed and spoke quickly. "My parents live in Tokyo," she explained. "Please call them with any problems. My father knows many people. He will help you. Please call." She handed Ann the address.

Ann bowed her thanks, but already her mind was whirling. She knew Fumiko wanted her to call. Fumiko had probably already told her mother. It would be awkward if Ann ignored the address. However, she'd be in Tokyo for only ten days, and the rare times she was free were too precious to waste. There were a few old friends left in Tokyo whom she looked forward to catching up with and a few old haunts she wanted to visit. Perhaps if she called toward the end of her trip, Fumiko's family would be busy. Yes, that was the solution.

As planned, Ann called Fumiko's parents three days before she was to leave Japan. Fumiko's mother sounded pleased, as though she'd been expecting the call. They tried to set up a date, but Fumiko's brother was graduating that weekend and Ann's schedule was full. They ended the conversation with a phrase or two about the difficulty of life in Tokyo and a promise from Fumiko's mother to consult with the family and call Ann that evening. The evening came and went with no messages from Fumiko's mother. Ann was pleased. She decided she would call Fumiko's mother just before leaving Japan.

The next morning she was paged at breakfast. She left her table and walked over to the house phone.

"Hello."

"Hello, Fumiko here," a faint voice answered.

"Fumiko! Where are you?" Ann asked in a stunned voice.

"America, of course," Fumiko laughed. "Thank you for calling my parents."

"Quite all right," Ann answered, suddenly ashamed that she'd left the call until the last minute.

"My mother would like to meet you," Fumiko continued. "She has heard so much about you. About your kindness to me in America, about the beautiful flowers, about your helping me with American life. So kind, so very kind."

"It was nothing," Ann said quickly, using the Japanese polite form. She felt cornered and pressed her head against the wall. Why? Why? A call from America. The expense and the trouble were obvious. Fumiko's role as a go-between suggested the apparent delicacy of the situation. Suddenly she realized how many long-distance calls had gone into this moment. They had her—yes, no doubt about it. Mentally she said good-bye to her weekend plans with old friends. She could not move to the right or left without someone losing face.

"Let's see if we can find a time for you to meet my parents," Fumiko coaxed.

"Oh yes, let's," Ann made her voice bright.

For the next several minutes, Ann and Fumiko played with schedules. Fumiko again patiently explained her parents' obligations with her brother's graduation. Ann replied with her review of the various business appointments she had during the week and on through the weekend. Finally they agreed, a meeting was impossible. Ann assured Fumiko that in the future before coming to Japan, she would let everyone know her schedule. Fumiko's farewell was warm, excusing herself again and again for the intrusion on Ann's busy schedule. Ann replied in kind, emphasizing her work schedule in Tokyo. By the time the phone call ended Ann was exhausted. She sat staring at her soft-boiled egg. Well, she had tried, she rationalized. The worst thing was that during part of their conversation, she wanted to see Fumiko's family. The game was over, she thought, and sighed with relief.

During the next two days Ann forgot about Fumiko and her family. On her last day, she had seven appointments back to back. By the time Ann returned to the hotel, she was both exhausted and pleased. Business in Tokyo had gone well—the Japanese companies had been cooperative. Most of the negotiations had been conducted in Japanese. Life in Tokyo was life in the fast lane, she thought wearily as she nodded to the hotel clerk. It was time to go home.

"You have a package," the clerk said, handing her a box wrapped in beautiful rice paper. Involuntarily, Ann took a step backward.

Fumiko's mother: she might have known. Overwhelmed, she slumped into a comfortable chair in the lobby and closed her eyes. As her fingers touched the uneven paper surface she tried to think.

Ann had been sure she'd come out ahead on this one. Only the day before, she'd felt smug about Fumiko, completely satisfied with the way she'd handled the situation. The years she'd lived in Japan as a girl had paid off. She knew the obligation game and had prided herself on being a good player. What a joke! Where had she gone wrong?

She slowly unwrapped the package. She knew that the rice paper was expensive and that the wrapping had been chosen carefully for its light pink color and texture. Inside was a box with Christian Dior written in gold letters in the right-hand corner. She removed the lid. The tissue paper was also light pink, and she saw that the purse was pink as well. It was a small round purse with a long strap, the kind of purse a mother would buy for a young girl to match her first pair of heels. Ann ran her hands along the soft leather. It must have cost an arm and a leg. She felt defeated—then angry—then finally ridiculous. She thought she'd won. What arrogance! Hundreds of years of training in creating a web of obligations that tied people together. Of course she'd been outwitted. The bag was inappropriate but the effort and the expense were obvious.

Ann slowly opened the card. "Dear Miss Ann," the card read. "The purse is for your daughter. I hope she enjoys it. Thank you for taking care of Fumiko in America. Fumiko has told me of your many kindnesses."

Ann started to laugh. Of course, she thought. The laughter made her throat hurt; it even made her stomach ache. Of course, daughter for daughter: how right, how perfect. She stopped laughing. It was hopeless. She couldn't even break even. The thought depressed her, and she put the purse back in the box.

Suddenly she had an idea. A wonderful circus that Ann had seen before was due in town soon. It was a small, European-style circus with elegant acts, incredible costumes, and real charm. Fumiko, her husband, and her little boy would love it. She'd invite them for a short lunch and then both families would go to the circus. Contented, she leaned back in her chair and thought of Fumiko's bright eyes, and how they would glow when she saw the trapeze lady. The memory of Fumiko's face made her happy. After all, Ann was Fumiko's big sister. She did like Fumiko very much, she decided.

Analysis:

Relationships are often initiated in Japan by a request made from one party to another in the "know me" phase. This request might be irrational and demanding. The underlying assumption is that the relationship will be intimate and intrusive. Ann has spent enough time in Japan to understand that Fumiko is asking for unlimited support. Fumiko wants to enter into intimacy (amae) with Ann. Fumiko is not necessarily asking for a practical solution to her difficulties. Rather, Fumiko wants an empathic relationship, where Ann will not only be a mentor but also take on the emotional burden of Fumiko's plight as if it were her own. Ann's solution—providing the names of plumbers and doctors—does not address Fumiko's needs (Fumiko's cold voice and formal language the next day prove that). Fumiko has chosen Ann purposely, and Ann must acknowledge the situation.

Ann feels some obligation toward Fumiko, which she discharges by sending Fumiko and her family flowers. Fumiko's face has been saved. Her warm response indicates to Ann that Fumiko feels she has picked the right benefactor. However, to be on the safe side and for the sake of formality, Fumiko lets Ann know she is worried about the obligation incurred as a result of the flowers. Ann immediately understands Fumiko's concern, which she dismisses with the phrase "I sent the flowers from feeling."

Kimochi, or feeling, is the loophole out of the obligation system. Once openly expressed, an individual has the freedom to act as the heart dictates without consideration of the consequences, and the recipient is also put at ease. All this is especially important in the "know me" stage of a relationship, before trust has been established. The hierarchy of obligations is so onerous that Japanese themselves avoid the entrapment of the system with the excuse of kimochi. Feeling releases both the giver and the receiver to act in concert with their emotions, implying a return to a more childlike and innocent relationship, one where knowledge of the difficulties inherent in society are not relevant. Ann's excuse of giving the gift on the basis of kimochi rather than obligation allows Fumiko to feel vindicated in her decision to select Ann as a mentor. The relief in Fumiko's voice confirms Ann's hunch that Fumiko is looking for an intimate, nurturing relationship.

Japanese are educated to accept the strict control of an obligation system. Some obligations (on)—*those owed to parents, teachers, or the emperor—can never be repaid. In order to preserve one's name and keep a sense of shame at bay, a Japanese must constantly keep this indebtedness in mind. In business and in friendship, obligations* (giri) *have to be repaid in kind. Japanese carefully calculate the worth of a favor in terms of the spirit in which it was delivered and the apparent sensitivity to the situation. Thus, communication through gesture is common in Japan.*

Ann's relationship with Fumiko is now firmly established. The relationship deepens during the months of working on the pamphlet. Ann forms an intimate working group with Fumiko and two other Japanese women. Although they don't go drinking at night (as would be common in a comparable men's work group), the meetings end on an intimate note. In groups of this sort in Japan, problems are aired without expectation of advice. This is especially true in a group setting, where singling out and labeling of a problem in public might mean loss of face. In this setting talk seems to strengthen intimacy.

It should also be noted that, in Japan, alcohol is traditionally thought of as a boon to life rather than a problem. The women accept the alcoholic's admission of drinking, both because drink is an accepted part of Japanese culture and public acknowledgment of a weakness is inadmissible. While the idea of group therapy itself is not an accepted part of the Japanese culture, group discussion often attempts to normalize problems through sharing confidences. However, in private Fumiko is concerned. She calls Ann and asks her to take the woman in question for a checkup. Fumiko's request that Ann assume a mentor role in this delicate situation underscores her desire to have Ann involved in her life.

On the basis of the bonds that have been formed, Fumiko takes another step toward intimacy by giving Ann her parents' address and phone number. Ann realizes that Fumiko expects her to call even though Fumiko, covering all bases, saves face by implying she is giving Ann the number in case Ann is in trouble. Ann recognizes the real situation (honne), *but attempts to avoid contact by calling Fumiko's parents shortly before she has to return to America. As Ann suspects, spring is a busy time for Japanese families. In this case Fumiko's brother's graduation has created a full schedule for the family. Ann is secretly delighted. However, Fumiko's call from America reveals the complexity of the situation. Fumiko is used by the family as a go-between. Go-betweens in Japan are commonly employed when the parties involved are afraid that direct communication will result in loss of face. In this case Fumiko's mother feels awkward about her inability to see Ann, especially because she feels beholden to Ann for taking care of Fumiko. Thus, Fumiko's mother and Fumiko herself feel that her call from America is appropriate.*

Go-betweens are crucial in a society where awkward face-to-face situations are to be avoided at all costs. It is vital in such a society to build a coterie of people who can serve this function. Go-betweens in Japan not only provide connections but are crucial in determining what is really happening in a given situation. These people must be continually cultivated. They are an important asset both in business and in the business of life, and this is especially true in the early phases of a relationship. Neither Fumiko nor her parents feel comfortable enough to be perfectly blunt with Ann. Fumiko is not only providing a buffer in a potentially awkward situation; she is also testing Ann's true feelings. By this point Ann is more engaged in the relationship; finally, she is sincerely trying to accommodate Fumiko's family to her schedule.

After the conversation with Fumiko, Ann feels the slate is clean. However, the gift of the purse reveals the considerable obligation that Fumiko's mother feels toward Ann. The fact that it's a present for Ann's daughter underscores Ann's role as a mentor and protector of her own daughter, Fumiko.

Ann deepens the relationship by deciding to invite Fumiko and her family to a circus. By this time Ann realizes Fumiko's investment in the relationship and is committed to making it work. She wants to please Fumiko and her family and also realizes the invitation will give the relationship appropriate weight.

Ann's decision creates a win/win situation for herself and Fumiko. For example, Fumiko may plan to send her child to an American summer camp someday, after her return to Japan. In this case, Ann will be expected to act as the child's guardian in America. Ann has the right to call on Fumiko for a similar favor. The relationship will continue to mature, and with appropriate attention, they will continue to be "human capital" in each other's lives.

PETER: Being Taken Seriously

Peter West, president of National Consulting Group (NCG), shook his head as he replaced the receiver. Americans like to talk, he thought, Japanese like to listen. Peter took a deep breath. He'd learned how to listen from the Japanese. He'd learned that showing that you knew it all was just not that important. He'd learned just to give enough to make the Japanese come back for more. He'd learned that the Japanese respected his withholding. He'd learned distance. He'd learned to be a better businessman.

This call from Tamba, vice president of TONI, a leading Japanese electronics firm, was a good example. In his third call in less than a week, Tamba claimed that TONI was interested in signing a contract with NCG. Tamba needed to gather the key people at a meeting. Would Peter provide information about the service NCG would provide? As soon as the key people at TONI had this information, Tamba assured Peter, TONI would sign.

Peter grinned. TONI was the sixth and latest Japanese company interested in a contract with NCG. Each company was at a different stage of negotiation, and had followed roughly the same pattern of research and meetings. One contract would be signed next week, another after a few more questions had been answered. Based on his experience, Peter estimated the mean time for signing this new contract was at least a year. Although Tamba insisted TONI would sign immediately after the meeting, Peter knew better. It took a long time to develop trust with Japanese. The situation was tricky. It was too easy to give away the shop—then nothing happened. Peter leaned back in his chair. He remembered Kansei Denki, the first Japanese company that had approached him. He'd been such a greenhorn—so eager, so American over a year ago.

The first inquiry from Kansei Denki came in September from Richard Brown, president of Kansei Denki USA. Brown had heard of NCG's service and wanted to know more about what NCG offered.

Brown asked Peter some questions forwarded by Matsumoto, vice president of Kansei Maintenance, Japan; Peter answered them patiently. Two days later, Peter received another phone call from Brown with more questions. By the time Peter received his third phone call, he was fed up. However, this time Brown was enthusiastic, and wanted Peter to meet Matsumoto. Could Peter fly to Japan that week? Excited by the response, Peter immediately made an appointment with Matsumoto.

Armed with charts and figures, Peter spent two hours illustrating to Matsumoto and two other Kansei Denki Japan executives how the introduction of NCG's process-control software would reduce Kansei Denki's maintenance budget. Matsumoto and his colleagues were enthusiastic. After the meeting, Matsumoto and his colleagues took Peter to an expensive French restaurant for a wonderful meal. Peter returned to America confident that NCG had a real opportunity to make a deal.

Four days after returning to America, Peter received a call from Howard Williams, the Kansei Denki USA executive in charge of maintenance. Matsumoto felt that Williams would be interested in NCG's services. Could they meet? Again Peter was delighted. He scheduled the meeting for the next day.

A half hour into his presentation, Williams held up his hand. "Enough. I agree with Matsumoto," he stated. "Kansei Denki and NCG must do business." For the next hour Williams sold Kansei Denki: it was a large entrepreneurial firm that could accept and utilize new technology; it had a lot of influence in Japan, as well as multiple subsidiaries in the United States; and so on.

After the meeting, Peter rushed to his office in a fever of excitement. Normally calm and self-assured, Peter prided himself on making the "right" contacts, surrounding himself with the "right" people, and developing the "right" business plan. But this was different, Peter reasoned, this was Japan. No matter that the exact type of partnership wasn't discussed. NCG was on its way. Pacific Rim, watch out! In a frenzy Peter composed a letter to Kansei Denki defining and pricing NCG's services. He structured Kansei Denki's commitment so that over time a partnership could evolve from the arm's-length contracts.

A week later Peter made an appointment to see Williams. When the day came, Williams was ill, but Sato, top man from Kansei Denki Japan who happened to be in the States, arranged to meet with him. Peter used the opportunity to educate Sato about re-engineering and set up another meeting with Williams.

Two days later Peter received a fax from Sato, who was back in Japan. Sato wanted him to come give a seminar on re-engineering for Kansei Denki's top executives and engineers. Peter felt satisfied. Before his second trip to Japan, he met with Williams and Tom White, Williams's second in command. Both White and Williams assured Peter that Kansei Denki USA's massive system would be perfect for re-engineering. White requested that Peter send in a team to price the system and make a specific proposal. Peter agreed. White told Peter confidentially that Williams was still a little uneasy. Could Peter do this system for free just to gain Williams's confidence? Peter emphatically turned down White's proposal.

Peter's presentation in Japan was scheduled for the morning. Kansei Denki provided an excellent technical translator and the room was packed. Peter described re-engineering step-by-step in minute detail, on the assumption that this meeting was the next step to building trust and providing documentation necessary for Kansei Denki to reach an internal consensus on the contract with NCG. Although Peter outlined the necessary steps involved in re-engineering, he withheld the names of the "tool" companies. If Kansei Denki knew which firms provided the necessary process software for the re-engineering system, Peter thought it might try to do its own re-engineering in-house. Kansei Denki certainly had the capability to do so; Peter was impressed with the quality of the Japanese engineers.

The Kansei Denki executives arranged a fabulous fifteen-course lunch of Japanese delicacies after the meeting. There were many toasts to Kansei Denki and NCG's future.

Two days later Peter received a message at his hotel from Matsumoto, who asked that Peter call him immediately at home. Peter smiled. The deal was done, he thought as he dialed.

"Matsumoto-san, hello."

"West-san, thank you for calling me at home. I'm sorry to cause so much trouble."

"No problem," Peter answered. There was a silence. Peter waited.

Matsumoto coughed. "West-san, I have a few questions."

"Yes," Peter answered quickly. A few questions, he thought uneasily. A three-hour presentation *and* a two-hour lunch and Kansei Denki still had a few questions?

"How big is your company?"

"Thirty employees," Peter replied.

"When was it started?"

Peter ground his teeth. "Four years ago."

"Kansei Denki might need another meeting," Matsumoto finished. "I will call you."

The next day Peter received another call from Matsumoto. Matsumoto asked more questions. Peter inquired about the deal with Williams and Kansei Denki USA. Kansei Denki USA makes its own decisions, Matsumoto said. You must talk to Williams separately. Peter nodded. He was still a little uneasy, but overall he thought he'd made two deals.

Upon Peter's return to the United States, he sent a follow-up letter to Matsumoto giving a price for the job on the Japanese system. He also tried to reach Williams, but he was out of town for two weeks. Two weeks later Williams hadn't returned the call, and Peter also hadn't heard from Japan. Frustrated, Peter called Tokyo. Matsumoto told Peter that Kansei Denki Japan needed more information on how Kansei Denki Japan and NCG would work together. He also implied that a list of the "tool" companies would help facilitate the process.

Two more weeks passed. Peter again called Japan. Matsumoto promised to send a proposal. Two months later Peter met with Matsumoto and Sato in Tokyo. The meeting was inconclusive. Kansei Denki Japan was still studying the proposal.

Now Peter shook his head, dialed the extension of Ethan, his top engineer, and thought of how many hours of hard work it had taken to develop an effective strategy for the Japanese market. First, Peter decided to open an office in Tokyo. He balanced the expense against the opportunity to meet potential customers through networking. After his experience with Kansei Denki, Peter decided that knowledge of customers and their needs could be achieved only by completely orchestrated meetings; this knowledge was vital to the suc-

cess of NCG. With the help of consultants he analyzed what preparation and trust meant to a Japanese company. Finally he formulated
a plan that would involve the Japanese on a paying basis without
anyone losing face.

"Ethan," Peter said urgently, "I need your help!"

"I'll be right there," Ethan replied.

By the time Ethan entered the room, Peter had a file labeled
"general presentation" on his desk.

"Another general presentation?" Ethan asked.

"That's right," Peter answered. "TONI, one of the biggest."

"Great!"

"Keep it very sketchy, Ethan. Just enough so they will come back
for more. No prices, understand. We will also make them pay for this
briefing like the others."

"Good," Ethan replied. "Business will start right away."

"Yes," Peter agreed. "Then no one is milked. When people pay,
everyone is serious. After all, as I told TONI, NCG is a busy company. An engineer's time is money. We have to serve our paying
clients first. Our reputation depends on quick, dependable service.
We can't help that. Just the facts of life. Of course, there will be no
charge if TONI wants to wait for a presentation."

"They never want to wait, Peter."

"Right, but best to leave an opening. A choice sets a better overall
tone to the interaction."

"By the way," Ethan said, handing Peter a piece of paper, "I
drafted the promised letter to Kobe SS."

Peter smiled. "Everything but the prices. Let them—"

"Come back and ask for more," Ethan finished softly.

Analysis:

*This case reveals the fine line in business between building trust and
simply providing information to a potential competitor like Kansei
Denki who has deep pockets, excellent engineers, and a tradition of
development in-house. Many American companies feel they do not get
beyond the "know me" phase of a relationship with a Japanese company. They are bitter about "giving away too much" without any
return. Japanese companies, they claim, soak up information. Peter's
problem with Kansei Denki is typical of a high-technology service*

company where the issue is not new technology but a mastery and systematized use of the "tools"—in this case process software necessary for re-engineering.

In fact, the Japanese have a tradition of gathering and codifying information. As far back as four thousand years ago (Jomon and Yayoi periods) Japanese returned from visits to China with useful minerals and tools. This tradition intensified around A.D. 600 (Nara period) under the guidance of Prince Shōtoku, who imported Buddhism, Confucianism, Chinese script, and other Chinese artistic and philosophical traditions. The twelfth century (Kamakura period) brought Zen Buddhism and Zen arts from China into the mainstream of Japanese thought and culture. Finally, from the time of the opening of Japan in the late nineteenth century (Meiji period) to the present day, Japanese have systematically borrowed ideas, systems of education and government, and technological know-how from the West.

This history shows how information gathering has become one of the most important occupations in Japan. The Japanese right to know and then to use that knowledge to develop a technological edge is a time-honored tradition. Original ideas are not considered sacred in Japan. Many patents filed there, for instance, are simply modifications on an idea, rather than an original idea as in America. Not only are these Japanese patents considered acceptable, but the careers of those engineers who file them are enhanced, especially because companies routinely exchange patents instead of money in cross-licensing agreements.

In addition, Japanese companies do much of their education in-house, and they expect engineering problems to be solved in the company. For instance, it is common for Japanese engineers to take their master's and Ph.D. degrees in the company, with advice from a professor at the university. Companies also provide up to two years' college education for their employees. This vertical organization also means that whenever possible a Japanese company will shy away from consultants and want to provide its own services.

Peter West is enticed by Kansei Denki's immediate interest in his project. Because this is NCG's first interaction with a Japanese company, Peter does not have the necessary go-betweens to draw on for information about Kansei Denki's intentions. Peter knows little about Kansei Denki except by reputation. Involvement of appropriate go-

betweens would ensure advice on strategy and better treatment from Kansei Denki in the "know me" stage of the relationship. NCG would then be part of a system and Kansei Denki would be accountable. The involvement of go-betweens is a crucial part of preparation in the "know me" stage and is designed to protect as well as to inform the outsider. Peter and NCG are considered outsiders, and as such are to be used to Kansei Denki's best advantage.

At this point, Kansei Denki is also unclear about its actual intent. According to Peter, re-engineering will save Kansei Denki millions of dollars. As part of their responsibility to Kansei Denki, Matsumoto and Sato, among others, need to educate Kansei Denki about re-engineering. Peter seems only too eager to provide Kansei Denki with the necessary information. Since he has not prepared for his encounter in the "know me" stage of the relationship, they are under no obligation to give him any consideration. Since he is not part of any system, he will be used.

By the time Williams of Kansei Denki USA implies that NCG and Kansei Denki will do extensive business, Peter is clearly out of his depth. His fantasies are fueled by Williams's reference to Kansei Denki's deep pockets and many subsidiaries in America. In addition, Peter has read articles about the billions of surplus yen in Japanese companies like Kansei Denki. Since Japanese companies are governed by consensus and are therefore slow to move, and building trust is the key issue in doing business with the Japanese, it seems logical to Peter that the Japanese would demand many information meetings, both in America and in Japan. Without realizing it, Peter has stopped using his common business sense.

In Japan, Peter is exposed to the hospitality of a Japanese company that has something to learn. It is important to note that the Japanese, as his hosts, will anticipate and cater to Peter's every need. His schedule is worked out ahead of time. He is entertained at expensive restaurants and his talks are well attended. For Peter this treatment means the deal is done; however, for the Japanese, elaborate hosting means, beyond their honor as hosts, that they have something to learn.

Peter refuses to acknowledge that information meetings only lead to more information meetings and more questions. The situation finally becomes obvious when Peter cannot reach either Williams or Matsumoto. Two months later Kansei Denki Japan is still "studying the proposal." *Kansei Denki's passive response to Peter is typical of Japanese behavior. It is difficult for Japanese to say no. Therefore, Japanese either use language like "difficult" or they are unavailable. This is especially true at the "know me" stage of a relationship, where intimate contacts have not been established. Americans who expect clear answers are confused and angered by this behavior.*

Peter's solution to his problems with Kansei Denki and any other Japanese companies seeking business with NCG is elegant. Instead of using a situation-by-situation approach, Peter constructs a system that protects NCG. He thus protects his own "house," and the Japanese comprehend that the situation is not personal, but necessary for NCG's survival. Peter makes it clear to the Japanese that NCG is a busy company. What Peter tells Japanese companies is: "NCG would like to provide an information meeting; however, NCG's schedule is tight. NCG has to service clients first." If, on the other hand, the Japanese company is a paying client, NCG will provide education and services. Peter's solution to his problem takes into account the Japanese idea of face. He merely states a position based on his financial need and his obligation to provide timely service to his clients. If the Japanese company is serious, it has an option to buy in.

In addition, Peter's system takes NCG out of the category of information provider. By actually doing business, NCG will build personal networks necessary to establish trust, and gradually the contracts will expand. To this end, Peter also opens an office in Tokyo. He recognizes NCG's need for go-betweens and for involvement on a daily basis in the Japanese business community.

With Peter's strategy in place, NCG is taken seriously from the start. NCG's position is stated without rancor, and a harmonious tone prevails.

TRUST ME

The "trust me" stage is the series of interactions at the beginning of a working relationship with the Japanese when foreigners are expected to demonstrate an appreciation of obligation and commitment. Acceptance is hard-earned for non-Japanese. Foreigners must be aware of the subtle tests inherent in this stage. Japanese feel a strong connection between effort and commitment. The "trust me" phase tests commitment to the project and the ability to understand the situation from the other's perspective.

Trust is a matter of reliability, commitment, and sincerity. It is determined by the willingness to systematically identify with the goals of the group. This stage of a working relationship can be particularly hard on most foreigners. Japanese pay careful attention to attitude and motivation. In an office situation, a worker is expected to be willing to sacrifice for the sake of the project. Both in negotiation between companies and when a foreigner works with Japanese, this period can be frustrating, because Japanese still consider the foreign firm or employee to be on the outside, and feedback is minimal. Bob understands this, and soon after his arrival in Japan demonstrates his commitment to the group by diligently performing the lowest job in the laboratory as proof that he knows his duty and is part of the group. Bob slowly builds the backbone of relationships through work and granting favors, thus incurring obligation, before being accepted into the group. George and Sarah also repeatedly demonstrate their commitment to their groups by building networks throughout an extended period before a working relationship begins. Fred does not subordinate his individual needs to a situation and as a result is not accepted by the group.

In addition to noting motivation and spirit, Japanese respect those who understand the politics of the workplace. The importance of choosing a well-respected mentor (in addition to one's assigned mentor) and of identifying oneself with the "right" group cannot be underestimated. These social skills and the ability to facilitate a situation and ease tensions within the group, as well as make a contribution to the group, are highly valued skills in Japan. Bob is careful in this respect and eventually his intuitive political sense allows him to become a full working member of the group.

Jose's situation is more complicated. He realizes that, because he lacks a mentor in his group and is "on loan" from a Japanese university, he will never be accepted into the group. Therefore, he works as effectively as possible as an outsider. Many foreigners will find themselves in Jose's situation and will have to define their goals clearly if the experience is to be a success.

The interactions in the "trust me" phase are still formal. In the workplace, successful outsiders are self-effacing and quick to participate in even the most menial aspects of work. Complaints are not tolerated and endurance is tested. Japanese expect the newcomer to work long hours and pay attention to the most minute details of an assignment.

In this section, the cases concentrate on understanding the treatment of the newcomer in the workplace. The cases reveal much about coping with various tests of motivation and attitude toward work in the "trust me" phase of the relationship.

BOB: Integration into the Group

You've come a long way, buddy, Bob thought, as he climbed into Toa Company's official black limousine. Kobayashi, his *kacho* (section chief), gave quick orders to the driver. "Now you will meet Oda-*sensei*, my professor," Kobayashi said, patting Bob's knee.

"I'm honored," Bob replied.

"Oda-*sensei* read your papers," Kobayashi said. "He liked them very much. We had a good talk about the contents. Oda-*sensei* sits on many government committees. This is an important paper."

Bob lowered his eyes and said nothing.

"You will be the first foreigner to give a seminar to his group."

Bob was silent.

"You are the first person from our house in three years."

Bob flushed and looked out the window. It had taken months of hard work and careful observation to graduate from the position of a foreign guest (a polite expression for "intern") to a working member of Kobayashi's laboratory and the house of Toa. He'd almost left Japan after the first week. Thank God for Kobayashi, thank God for his language and cultural training, thank God for good old Yankee horse sense, he thought. As the driver weaved his way through the small streets of Tokyo, Bob thought back to Shibata, his appointed mentor, and his first impressions of Japan.

Shibata met him at Narita Airport. He stood next to the bus ticket counter holding a TOA sign. Bob was relieved. This was the Japan of his dreams, efficient and hospitable, he thought as he greeted Shibata.

Shibata had already bought the bus tickets to Tokyo. He was quiet as they boarded the bus. Bob closed his eyes as soon as they were seated, waves of fatigue rolling over him. The twenty-hour plane trip was beginning to take its toll. Shibata sat quietly.

"Do you have a girlfriend?"

Bob opened his eyes. "Do I what?"

"A girlfriend?" Shibata repeated.

"Yes."

"You must miss her."

"Yes."

"Do you go to bed with her?"

Bob winced and glanced at Shibata. His expression was intent, and he sat very straight in his seat as if anticipating the next question. What a jerk, Bob thought. "I miss her," Bob repeated softly.

"In Japan we are conservative," Shibata continued. "But maybe you can get a girlfriend in Japan. Is your girlfriend Japanese?"

Bob blushed. In a minute he would punch Shibata in the jaw. He turned instead and stared stonily at the Japanese Disney World to the left of the highway. The familiar buildings and domes depressed him. Maybe Japan was a mistake, he thought. Several minutes passed.

"Why do you want to work at Toa?" Shibata asked in the same flat tone.

"It has a good reputation." Bob glanced at Shibata uneasily. Could Japanese read minds?

"We work hard in Japan. Americans don't work so hard."

Bob clenched his fists.

The bus slowed. The driver announced the terminal was just ahead. Shibata began making dinner plans for sushi. Bob said nothing. He felt like throwing up, and using his return ticket to the States. The rest of the evening passed in a blur. Shibata continued pounding him with questions, this time about his work. Bob answered some questions and not others. The answers didn't seem to matter to Shibata. He ended the evening with a lecture on American sloppiness. Americans must stop pushing Japanese around, Shibata said.

By the time the taxi arrived at the dorm, Bob was grateful. He bowed his thanks to Shibata. Shibata waited. Bob smiled and bowed again. Finally Shibata left.

Two young Japanese men approached him. They both wore jeans and their hair was cropped short in the latest style.

"Onuma desu." The taller man bowed.

"Ogawa desu," the other man said.

Following their example, Bob introduced himself.

Onuma took charge. He showed Bob his room. Together they laid Bob's quilt on the tatami floor. Then Onuma took Bob through the lobby to the bath. As they passed through the lobby, a group of twenty Japanese men also dressed in jeans were talking and drinking beer. Bob smiled, expecting to be introduced. However, Onuma did not stop. The group fell silent as they passed. Bob fingered his tie, again hit by fatigue. He tried to concentrate on what Onuma was saying, but it was no use. On the way back from the bath, Onuma was silent. He delivered Bob back to his room and Bob was asleep as soon as his head hit the pillow.

The next day Onuma walked with him to the laboratory and invited him for lunch. At the laboratory, Kobayashi showed him around. Bob bowed and smiled. While his Japanese-language training allowed him to understand what was being said, speaking was more difficult. Everyone was friendly. Even Shibata smiled and bowed as though they'd just met. Although Kobayashi did not discuss his project specifically, Bob was glad Kobayashi and the members of the laboratory were friendly, and he was glad to have a desk.

By late afternoon, however, Bob was edgy. When he politely asked Yamamoto, his bench partner, about his work project, Yamamoto was evasive. Bob wandered around the laboratory. Everyone was polite. He spoke with Tim, an American intern from Cutler University. Tim described his project. Bob was not impressed, and, although they spoke in English, he had the distinct feeling everyone was listening. At five Kobayashi suggested that Bob leave. "You are tired from the trip," he said kindly. Bob nodded and walked with Tim back to the dormitory.

Tim rushed off to an appointment in town. That night Bob ate dinner alone. He stayed in his room and wrote letters. Then he worried about where to get stamps. By eleven o'clock he was restless and went to the lobby. It was full of engineers. He recognized Yamamoto and several engineers from his laboratory. As he approached, the group fell silent. He stood grinning stupidly for several seconds before excusing himself and stumbling back to his room. Did they hate him? Did they just not accept newcomers? Was there something wrong with the way he spoke?

At four in the morning he was awake. His hands were clammy and he felt short of breath. He stood uncertainly, squatted, and put his head between his legs. Why am I here? he asked himself again and again. What did I do this for? They hate me. I can't even mail a letter. He covered his face and rocked back and forth. The motion of his body gradually calmed him. He stayed up the rest of the night writing in his diary. By morning he was calm.

Bob spent the morning reading papers in his field. By noon he was tired. Yamamoto invited him to lunch. As they entered the cafeteria, Tim yelled, "Hey, Bob, over here." He motioned to a table with three other foreigners. Bob pretended he hadn't heard and followed Yamamoto to the group table. Shibata also nodded at him. When Bob mentioned that Shibata had picked him up at the airport, the table fell silent.

At five o'clock Kobayashi nodded to Bob. "It's five," he said. "You may leave now."

Tim stood waiting for him by the door.

Bob said, "Thanks, I think I'll stay a bit more."

As the days passed Bob became more familiar with the laboratory and made friends in his group. Yamamoto, Onuma, and even Kobayashi were supportive. He learned that Shibata was considered an idiot by most people in the group and his opinions were ignored. However, although the laboratory was pleasant, Bob still did not have work. After the first month, Bob mentioned to Yamamoto in desperation that he'd done a good deal of research in America. Yamamoto nodded but did not make any suggestions.

Bob began to look at the running of the laboratory more carefully. He noticed that each Monday at nine, everybody below the rank of *kacho* would do chores; he also saw that the mop was not in use at that time. The following Monday he awoke at seven, dressed, ate breakfast, and ran to the laboratory. By nine o'clock he had mopped the floors. Bob also took over the daily task of emptying the trash bucket. He laughingly explained to his amazed colleagues that trash was the responsibility of the youngest in the group. Bob found other ways to be useful the rest of the week: when Onuma spilled a bucket of water, Bob mopped the floor. He helped Yamamoto with his English, and he lent Ogawa his Japanese-English dictionary. In addition, he kept chips and beer in his room for the occasional visitor.

The following Monday after he mopped the floor, Bob saw Tim

pick up Scientific American and settle down for a good read. Tim had been at Toa a year but still had no real project, Bob remembered. Bob granted that Tim was desperate. He was reading articles on computer chips in hopes that with his up-to-date knowledge, he would be called on by Kobayashi *kacho* to do important work.

"Tim," Kobayashi said, approaching his desk.

"Yes," Tim's face brightened.

"Would you go over the English in these papers? I have to present them for the laboratory at a meeting in New York."

Tim's face paled. He stared at his desk. "I don't correct English. I am an engineer. In fact, I was the best engineer in my Cutler class." Tim pointed to a professional journal. "I published in this one as a junior in college. I am not an English teacher."

Kobayashi paled. He cleared his throat. His smile was bright. "Of course, of course," he said quickly. "My mistake, my mistake." He backed away from the desk.

Tim sat down and picked up the journal. He was breathing heavily. Slowly, the conversation in the room resumed. Kobayashi *kacho* called a group meeting.

Bob watched Kobayashi for the rest of the day. Like Tim, Bob was aware that a series of new experiments in his field would begin shortly. The staff would be assigned into sections in the next two weeks. For the past two days, in preparation for the experiments, data had been read from a monitor every two hours. That morning Bob watched Kobayashi turn on the wall switch to activate the monitor. Later that day, Bob glanced at his watch: four o'clock—it was time. Quickly he ran across the room and flipped the switch. The TV screen crowded with figures. Kobayashi smiled.

From that point on, at least four times a day, Bob ran across the room to turn on the monitor. Kobayashi smiled each time, but did not mention the forthcoming experiments. In fact the next day, Kobayashi appointed Onuma and Ogawa and several others to the experimental team. Tim cursed when he heard about the makeup of the team, muttering that he would leave Japan as soon as possible. Bob nodded. He stared at his desk. Six weeks and still no project. He began to read a journal and sketch some ideas in his notebook. At five o'clock, Tim grabbed his coat and stormed out. At five-thirty, Bob watched Onuma, Ogawa, and Kobayashi meet in the far corner of the laboratory.

Kobayashi approached him at six-thirty. "Aren't you going to dinner?"

"Not yet," Bob replied. "In a little while."

"All the work for today has been finished," Kobayashi replied. "We are just about to run a session."

Bob nodded. He was aware the experiments were run in shifts. He was also aware that Kobayashi was watching him. "I'd like to help," he said softly.

"Not necessary. You must be tired. We have everybody we need."

Bob was silent. The next thirty seconds were the longest Bob had ever spent. They seemed like hours. "I'll stay awhile," Bob finally muttered.

Kobayashi turned away. During the next hour Bob watched Kobayashi and his team complete the preparations for the experiment. He stood next to Onuma while Kobayashi gave the final instructions. "Someone will have to take the late shift," Kobayashi stated.

"I can," Bob replied quickly.

"All right," Kobayashi answered briskly. "I'll stay also."

Bob stared at the floor. He was afraid that if he looked up, Kobayashi would notice his tears. They stung his eyes, and he coughed to hide his condition. So much time, effort, and thought had gone into building networks and trust to get to this point. He had a project. He was part of the team. Kobayashi and he would do the experiment together.

During the next month Bob worked as part of the team, always with Kobayashi or Onuma. One day, six weeks after Bob had begun work, Kobayashi wanted to use the monitor. Bob ran over to the switch, but, turning around, he saw that the monitor was already on. Kobayashi's hand was on a switch above the machine. Bob walked back slowly. All this time the switch had been right next to the machine. Why hadn't someone told him? He'd been running across the room like a monkey four times a day for weeks. He stared at the switch with a questioning expression. Kobayashi ignored the look and asked Bob to take notes while he read the figures off the machine.

In the weeks that followed, Kobayashi gave Bob more responsibility. Bob was pleased with his work and felt satisfied for the first time since arriving in Japan. However, he was aware that in subtle ways his position as an outsider hadn't changed. Most obviously, Bob didn't have the combination to the inner safe in which the crystals vital to the experiments were kept. This meant he had to ask a regular employee to open the inner safe each time he needed a crystal. One night he couldn't find anyone. He was about to abandon the experiment when Onuma appeared and gave him the crystals from the inner safe. "You are working hard," Onuma said.

"Yes," Bob nodded.

"Perhaps we should have some tea," Onuma said.

Onuma heaped the bright green powder of traditional tea into large earthen mugs. His hand moved gracefully and Bob wondered whether Onuma had studied tea ceremony. Suddenly he realized that he didn't know Onuma at all. The thought discouraged him, and he pressed his hand briefly against his eyes. "I didn't realize it was so late," Bob said.

"You are often here this late," Onuma laughed.

For the next half hour, Onuma asked Bob about his home in America and about baseball. Onuma was a great fan of American baseball. "It was lucky I came along," Onuma said, nodding at the crystal.

Bob frowned. "Yes," he said in a tired voice.

"Have a good night," Onuma said cheerfully as he left the laboratory.

The next day, when Bob unlocked the outer safe, he saw eighty crystals lined up—enough for more than a year's work. This was as much as Onuma could do, Bob thought, as he ran his hands over the crystals. Step-by-step, he had become part of the group. Starting with sweeping the laboratory and taking out the trash, then creating networks in the laboratory, and finally showing his willingness to work.

The driver pulled into the large red gates of the University of Tokyo. Bob felt his heart quicken. Kobayashi leaned toward him. "Bob-kun," he said softly, using the informal familiar ending. "Let's do it in the style of the house of Toa." Kobayashi pointed to the characters on the building that read ELECTRICAL ENGINEERING.

Analysis:

The idea of human beings as a resource (humanware) permeates Japanese life. Children attend afterschool classes (juku) designed to prepare students for the college exam; by junior high school, 80 percent of children are enrolled in them. Ninety percent of Japanese children graduate from high school, and each year more than eight hundred thousand students compete for five hundred thousand spaces at the universities around the country. Acceptance to the right university determines much of a person's professional future. For example, approximately 80 percent of the staff of the Ministry of International Trade and Industry (MITI) has graduated from the University of Tokyo. In the case of the steel industry, more than one third of company presidents have graduated from the University of Tokyo.

Success often depends on being accepted into the group, but that acceptance does not occur automatically. People are watched and tested at various points in their careers. They must exhibit both the correct amount of loyalty and spirit if they are to succeed. New recruits in a Japanese company typically go through a training period of two years. During this time they rotate jobs through the company and attend training retreats where the history of the company is discussed. On these retreats many companies test their employees' spiritual depth and physical stamina by demanding arduous physical feats of their new employees. All this means the company devotes considerable time, effort, and thought to conditioning and nurturing new recruits. In addition, these recruits are all hired in the late spring, and new hires form a strong bond with one another.

As a foreign researcher, Bob does not have the benefit of the two-year training period. In addition, even though he comes from a university and was introduced to Toa by a professor who has strong links with the company, Bob is on his own. Not only must he understand the politics of the work situation, but he must also gain the trust and support of his colleagues. All this must take place in a short period of time, because he is on assignment in Japan for just one year and new recruits are tested at the beginning of their tenure.

It is vital for Bob to handle the "trust me" phase correctly if he is going to be incorporated into the working life of a Japanese company.

He must demonstrate his willingness to work for the sake of the group, and he must demonstrate his ability without showing up his colleagues.

Bob understands that in order to penetrate the group, he must ally himself with insiders in his laboratory. He intuits through body language, observes seating arrangements, and is careful to associate with Yamamoto and his friends. He learns that Shibata is considered an outsider and observes that Tim has not made much headway in the group. Bob makes his alliances clear by avoiding Tim's invitation to lunch.

In addition, Bob also senses the importance of working after hours. Although encouraged by Kobayashi kacho and others to leave at five, Bob stays late, separating himself further from employees such as Tim. All this is never addressed directly. Bob merely acts intuitively given the situation.

Loyalty in a professional context in Japan is a calculated act. This means that bonding must occur with the right professor in order to enter the right company. Once accepted into that company, bonding with the right group inside the company is vital. These calculations are important for maintaining harmony and the status quo in the Japanese system. The trade-offs are explicit in the Japanese system in terms of lifelong employment and the protection an extended network affords.

Bob notices that members of the laboratory under the rank of kacho are assigned chores. Again, Bob does not address the situation directly but enthusiastically contributes time and effort to group chores. He sees that the mop is idle and undertakes to rectify that situation by arriving early on "chore" day to mop the floors, and he empties the wastebasket. All this further demonstrates his commitment to the group.

Communication through gesture is vital in a culture that places enormous value on face. Bob never addresses the situation directly but insinuates himself into the working group. By assuming responsibility for a certain chore as the youngest member of the group, Bob claims no job is beneath him. Kobayashi kacho and other colleagues in the laboratory accept his premise and by doing so de facto accept Bob. Bob understands that belonging to the group in Japan is more important than where you fit on the hierarchy. Once he is accepted into the group, the group has an interest in protecting and, if Bob is talented, promoting Bob.

Tim, however, has no understanding of the concept of loyalty or the group. He explicitly expresses his anger about lacking a project and considers work such as editing the English on his kacho's paper beneath him. In this situation the kacho smiles and excuses himself while really relegating Tim to the outside (thus illustrating the difference between tatemae and honne). Kobayashi's lack of directness saves everyone's face. Saving face means that unacceptable attitudes must not be publicly revealed. This is important not only to the person with questionable behavior but is also of equal importance to the integrity of a person who is made uncomfortable by the behavior. Here, with Tim, a Japanese must play the role of the host and maintain a surface harmony. Kobayashi kacho's acceptance of this responsibility means the real situation of Tim's lack of work will never be addressed.

Bob also sees the value of doing favors for individuals. He lends one colleague a book, he mops up a spill for another, he helps a third with his English. His colleagues incur a certain obligation (giri) to Bob, thus expanding his networks. Again, carefully orchestrated obligation in a vertically organized society is important in maintaining the status quo. Japanese do not move from one company to another. Therefore, relationships are calculated and attended to carefully, and obligations often structure the strong bonds that exist in Japanese companies. Small favors are a sign of trust. Bob is slowly building his network in the laboratory by gaining the personal trust of his colleagues. Bob cements these relationships by stocking up on beer and crackers for the occasional guest to his dormitory room.

Although Bob is accepted as a member of the laboratory through his established network, he is not yet assigned a project. Bob does not address even this problem directly, instead insinuating himself in Kobayashi kacho's project by running across the room to turn on the monitor. While Kobayashi kacho accepts Bob's efforts with a smile, he still does not assign him to the project. Nevertheless, Bob diligently continues to run across the room to switch on the monitor. Bob does not address this situation directly either, but displays his determination to participate on the project by volunteering for a late shift. When Kobayashi kacho turns on the monitor by flipping a switch directly next to it, Bob realizes that Kobayashi kacho *allowed him to turn on the switch earlier because this was initially Bob's only way of participating. Kobayashi* kacho *is protecting Bob's face (*kao*) by not revealing that this effort is unnecessary.*

Although Bob works successfully on the team as a visiting researcher, he does not have full access to the equipment. When Onuma makes sure Bob has access to the crystals outside the inner safe, Onuma obeys the letter of the law while showing his trust in Bob. As a foreign intern, Bob cannot be part of the innermost group in a Japanese company. Both he and Onuma understand this. However, Onuma feels justified in circumventing the rules because Bob has proven himself to be a trusted member of Toa. Bob's year at Toa culminates with his delivery of a paper to Kobayashi kacho's *teacher at the University of Tokyo. Kobayashi* kacho *realizes the importance also, and by using the affectionate ending "kun," incorporates Bob into the house of Toa.*

GEORGE: Establishing Trust

George sat in the twelve tatami-mat room, which opened onto a small Japanese garden with a fish pond. The family—*his* family—was gathered around the table. Mrs. Otani asked if he wanted a second bowl of rice. He handed his rice bowl to Kyoshi, his younger brother, and the family laughed.

"I remember when you first came," Mr. Otani said. "You didn't eat for days, Mother was worried. She made American hamburgers and spaghetti. I never ate so many hamburgers and so much spaghetti."

George smiled as he received the rice and eyed his birthday cake in the corner of the room. For the past three years he'd celebrated his birthday with the Otanis. It was the second time he'd been invited back to Japan after his initial stay with a Japanese company. He would always belong to the Otani house, he thought, just as he would always be connected to that company.

George belongs to a program that places American scientists and engineers in companies in Japan after an orientation training program that now includes two years of Japanese language. (George, who was one of the first interns, took only one year of Japanese.) George was placed for a year in Niki, a leading Japanese electronics firm. Niki had arranged for George to stay at first with Otani, a leading executive in the company who has since retired to head a subsidiary. Otani lived with his wife and two children in a comfortable suburb of Tokyo about twenty minutes from work, and George stayed with the Otanis for three months, after which he moved to the Niki dormitory.

As the Otani family sang "Happy Birthday" in Japanese, George was filled with pride. His mind flashed back to those first bewildering weeks when he'd relied for his survival on his Wisconsin "good sense" and watched and waited. There had been times when he'd been so tired that he'd thought only of finishing dinner quickly and going to bed, so he wouldn't have to speak any more Japanese or answer any more questions. On those days his smile felt frozen. However, patience had yielded rewards beyond his imagination: unbelievable access to research, these short returns to Niki, and finally a feeling of community that held the implication of future benefits no matter where he worked.

It had still been hot in Tokyo when George arrived at Narita Airport in early September. Otani met him at the airport, bowed, and presented himself as Niki's Otani. George also bowed and, trying to remember the appropriate greeting from his first-year Japanese class, finally stammered, "George *desu*." Otani smiled and took his bag. George followed, worrying whether he should let Otani carry his luggage. By the time they'd reached the car, George had a headache and had forgotten most of his Japanese. Otani was silent as they hit the main highway to Tokyo. "It's hot," George said.

Otani grunted.

"It's hotter than America."

Again Otani grunted.

George closed his eyes and dreamed of a milk shake.

That night the Otanis had steak for dinner. George felt groggy and only nibbled. When Mrs. Otani announced the bath was ready, Mr. Otani rose from the table. Mrs. Otani smiled and suggested that George go to bed.

The next morning George rose early and made his way to the bathroom. It was a traditional Japanese bath with a deep tub, a slatted wooden floor, and a shower in the corner. Used to a morning shower, he quickly used the shower hose, dressed, and went in for breakfast. Otani looked at his wet hair but said nothing. They ate quickly and although Otani usually took the train, he insisted on taking George to the laboratory by taxi.

Soon after Otani introduced George to his group, George realized that Otani was the boss of Kayugi, his group leader. Kayugi introduced him as "George, who is now living with Otani-san." The members of the group smiled, but George was aware of their formality and obvious deference to his living arrangements. Although he was assigned an independent project in his field and everyone was kind, he left the laboratory feeling depressed.

That night after dinner, when Mrs. Otani again announced the

bath was ready, Otani immediately left the table. George continued
talking about his day as Mrs. Otani cleared the table. He was tired
and relieved to go to bed. The next morning he again took a shower.

This pattern continued for the first week. Finally, one night after
Mrs. Otani's announcement, Otani rose slowly and looked at George
for a moment. The glance was intense and George flushed and stared
at the ground. "The bath is hot at night," Otani said. George took a
bath after Otani that night and skipped his morning shower the next
day.

During the next weeks George worked hard at the laboratory.
Kayugi was an invaluable help, ordering equipment for him, walking
him to the station at night after a company party to make sure he
would return to the Otani house by a reasonable hour, showing him
how to go through the lunch line, and even showing him how to use
the men's room, where the flush toilets had no seat. At first George
hated the hovering and constant assumptions that Kayugi made
about his lack of knowledge and need for care, and would often leave
the office outraged by what he considered an infantilization. After a
long walk, George would return to the office calmed down. George
said nothing about his feelings because he watched Kayugi play a
similar role with other people in the office, badgering them about
their work habits, marriage plans, etc.

Although Otani worked at another location, he periodically came
to the office. Once he was standing with Kayugi discussing a matter
of mutual concern. When George and two other group members
joined them, the discussion became general. One group member
insisted that with overtime work they would be able to complete the
project. Everyone agreed. Suddenly, they looked at George, who did
not usually stay past six. He flushed and looked at Kayugi for help.
Kayugi, who usually guided him, stared past him. He then looked at
Otani, who stepped back, folded his hands, and stared at the floor.

"Perhaps because George is from America, he isn't used to overtime," one co-worker said. "They have a lot of money there."

George took a deep breath. He wanted to tell them that he didn't
get overtime like the two Japanese engineers, but he knew they
understood this. He also wanted to say that in America people don't
work without being paid. He knew they knew this too. "I'm a student
from Vernon Technical Institute," he said as a way of defining
himself. "I'm just a student, but if I can help in any way . . ."

Kayugi smiled. Otani's face brightened and he folded his hands. "George-kun," Kayugi said, using the informal affectionate ending for the first time, "that's good."

After that George worked many nights without pay. Kayugi continued to call him George-kun and occasionally referred to his coming from the great university Vernon Technical Institute. He now invited George to weekly group meetings. George's relationship with the Otani family continued to grow; for instance, even though he was exhausted at night he often helped Kyoshi with his English homework.

Six weeks after he arrived in Japan, he came home at ten after a long day at the office. Mrs. Otani was waiting for him with tea and cookies. They sat at the dining room table talking about the weather. Finally, Mrs. Otani leaned toward him and patted his arm. "You're tired," she said.

"No," he answered. "I'm okay."

He remained silent.

"Here," she said and pushed a house key across the table. "I want you to have this."

George stared at the house key.

"You belong to this house," she said softly.

Analysis:

In an inside/outside culture like Japan, tests are a normal part of rites of passage. This is true for the Japanese as well as the foreigner. To become part of the system an individual must prove himself worthy in terms of both attitude and ability. Japanese frequently mention confidence associated with a task (jishin) in assessing a person's desire to become part of the mainstream. Ability, coupled with this confidence, will determine an individual's success or failure in Japanese society.

Although testing occurs at all stages of relationships with the Japanese, it is more frequent in the "trust me" phase of a relationship. Tests are designed both to establish a degree of commitment to a given group or project and to assess the individual's understanding of the situation. The fact that these tests must be passed underscores the idea of the group as an elite—those who pass the tests and enter the group feel a corresponding loyalty to the elite.

These testing situations are further complicated because, as a result of culture and language, Japanese communicate indirectly. Language is a special issue in the "trust me" phase of the relationship. The more someone is on the outside, the more formal and polite forms of language will be used. Japanese are most formally "gracious" in the "know me" and "trust me" stages of the relationship, using formal language that is deliberately vague and suggestive. This brand of indirect communication can be a major frustration for foreigners. The construction of the Japanese language lends itself to accommodating a situation rather than engaging in debate. In addition, Japanese culture encourages indirect communication that saves face for those involved. In a highly charged atmosphere where an individual is tested, the ability to decipher nuance is vital.

George begins his stay in the Otani household with no understanding of Japanese life and customs. The importance of the bathing order after dinner, an integral part of Japanese family life, escapes him. The Japanese bath is important not only for cleanliness; the bathing order also reveals the hierarchy within the family, and the common tub underscores the value of frugality in Japanese life. George's morning shower upsets the routine of the household, increases the gas bill, and saps the hot water supply.

Although Otani is concerned, he can't acknowledge the situation head-on because of this mode of indirect communication. Otani is inhibited further because of George's status as a guest. In Japan, hospitality demands an awareness of the needs of guests, and guests fall into a dependent relationship (amae) with hosts. This means that both sides are constrained—the host in fulfilling his obligation as caretaker, and the guest in being a sensitive recipient of the host's generosity. Direct comment from either side would point out the inability of the host or guest to play their role adequately and would mean loss of face.

Otani communicates his displeasure in the morning by staring at George's wet hair. When George proves immune to Otani's hints, Otani comments after supper that "the bath is hot at night." Through body language and suggestive comments, George finally understands that Otani would prefer that he bathe at night and in a certain order. The family relaxes and George passes the first rite of initiation.

At the start of a relationship, Japanese feel directly responsible for people under their care. Their integrity is bound up with the person's success in a new situation. To this end, a boss or mentor may orches-

trate every aspect of an individual's life. Kayugi, George's immediate boss, assumes responsibility and is protective of him, but George often experiences Kayugi's concern as interference. Kayugi walks him to the subway, and shows him the cafeteria line. This constant nurturing can be baffling, even irritating, but an overly paternalistic attitude is especially important to the Japanese in the "trust me" stage of the relationship. As the relationship matures, Kayugi's attitude will become more casual.

To some extent this paternalistic attitude is common in all stages of Japanese work life. People are not expected to solve problems on their own, nor is the notion of privacy valued. Kayugi's involvement with and understanding of his staff and workers is part of his job. It is entirely appropriate that Kayugi reveal his concern and empathy toward his subordinates through gesture. This dependent superior-to-inferior (sempai/kohai) *relationship recurs in all facets of Japanese society.*

Although George settles into a routine with the Otani family and with the laboratory, he still is definitely an outsider. When Otani and Kayugi discuss the completion of a project with a small group of engineers, including George, he is confused. What seems to be happening in the situation (tatemae) *is that an open discussion is taking place between members of the group regarding work schedules and overtime. However, what actually is happening* (honne) *is that George's commitment to the group is being tested.*

George is right in not bringing up the issue of unpaid overtime. Whether it is fair is irrelevant to the Japanese, especially because George is not part of the system and therefore has no voice in this situation. Consensus exists only for members of the group who have passed into the "believe me" phase of the relationship. George must integrate into the group by revealing his understanding and willingness to help the situation. His declaration of loyalty by agreeing to work overtime is a well-calculated decision. George expects that eventually, as part of the system, he will be rewarded. George has been in Japan long enough to understand the importance of passage into the group. His humble response ("I'm just a student, but . . .) reveals his understanding that the situation is more important than his personal needs and that he is ready to become part of the team. Kayugi immediately responds by adding the familiar suffix "kun" to George's name, thus assuring George that he has passed the test and now belongs to the group.

The situation at the Otani household parallels the one at work. Unsolicited, George helps the Otani's child with his English homework and is generally sensitive to the needs of the household, manifesting his commitment to the group through gesture. Mrs. Otani rewards George with trust and the household key. Her reference to George as belonging to this house reveals both the feudal nature of the Japanese household and the implications of that system for those who are on the inside. George might be tested in the future, but the tests will be few and far between, and they will focus more on assessing the strength of the current relationship.

SARAH: Establishing a Tone

The economy trip to Tokyo had made many stops and had taken forty-eight hours, and Sarah felt quite ill by the time the plane landed at Narita Airport. John barely spoke as they went through customs. As Sarah looked at John's pale young face in the fluorescent light of the customs room, she felt uneasy about her role in encouraging John to take a job for two years with TNN Corporation. It will be an adventure, she'd insisted. TNN is one of the largest electronics firms in Japan. Tanaka's laboratory was doing some of the best work in Japan in John's field. Besides, he'd worked with Tanaka at the university and Sarah was fond of Tanaka and his wife. Both John's quiet nature and his belief in the work ethic would serve him well in Japan.

Tanaka was waiting just outside customs. Sarah checked her impulse to embrace him as she had as a matter of course in America—Tanaka stood too straight and his expression was too serious. Tanaka bowed formally; she returned his bow. The laboratory was two hours from Tokyo and the married dormitories were located ten minutes from the laboratory, Tanaka explained. His wife had prepared a meal. As they drove, John and Tanaka discussed the latest published work in their field. Sarah dozed.

Sarah felt ill again by the time they arrived at Tanaka's house. Yukiko, Tanaka's wife, ushered them into a Japanese-style room with a beautifully set table. Tanaka seated John with his back to an alcove that was opposite the door. The alcove housed a scroll with a black-and-white ink painting of persimmons. Yukiko explained persimmons ripen in the fall.

Sarah was seated next to John. The food—course after course of small delicacies—was all delicious. Sarah tried to speak, but her Japanese was too elementary. Yukiko, who appeared to have forgotten her English, served. Sarah tried to follow John and Tanaka's conversation, but her head hurt. Sarah noticed Yukiko's eyes widen when Sarah asked for more sushi. The soy sauce made her thirsty, and she held her glass for more beer. Tanaka's face reddened as he poured the beer. Sarah wondered if Japanese women didn't drink— Yukiko herself was hardly eating or drinking. She sat near the door with her hands folded on her lap. By the time dinner was over and Tanaka showed them their apartment, Sarah's cheeks hurt from smiling.

The next few weeks were exhausting. Through a foreign information service, Sarah found a job at a school for autistic children in Tokyo. Glad that she was able to continue working in a professional capacity, Sarah accepted the two-hour commute to Tokyo. John was also relieved that Sarah had found work and applied for housing closer to Sarah's job. Tanaka told him the transfer would take place in a few months.

However, Sarah soon realized that any position of responsibility would be difficult to attain at this school. The teaching was interesting, but as a part-time teacher she wasn't invited to faculty meetings and she was never consulted about her students. Sarah asked if she could become full-time, because she expected to be living closer to Tokyo in a matter of months. Ishihara, the prim, gray-haired principal, noted Sarah's request with a smile.

Frustrated, Sarah began using her spare time to teach English at another school in Tokyo. While the work was lucrative, she still felt isolated and would return exhausted to the apartment. Japanese smiles meant nothing, she decided. The constant small gifts of fruit and other sundries from neighbors and casual acquaintances bewildered her. Several times she'd seen wives peering into shopping bags that a woman had left at the bottom of the apartment stairs while she carried her children up to her apartment. There was no privacy. She didn't trust anybody—they were all busybodies. A stranger in a strange land, she thought one day, blinking away the tears on the long ride from Tokyo back to the apartment.

In desperation, Sarah joined a women's cultural association in Tokyo that arranged visits to Japanese homes and signed up for a neighborhood cooking class. Although the women in both groups were friendly, they described Americans as aggressive, uncaring, and materialistic. At night John and she compared notes and discussed their own values. In one cooking class after a particularly strong declaration about America from Emiko, a plump woman with a wide smile, Sarah lost her temper. "I believe in family. John and I feel family values are very important. I am also Jewish," Sarah declared, having recently realized that many Japanese bookstores carried anti-Semitic literature. "Jews believe in education."

The women were silent. Emiko vigorously chopped an onion. "That's similar to Japanese," said Hatsuko, a bright-eyed woman who lived in the same apartment building and periodically had left John and Sarah packages of fruit.

The silence in the room lengthened. Sarah scraped chopped onion into a bowl. She wondered if she'd been too outspoken. The women avoided eye contact. Hatsuko also scraped onion into her bowl. "You and John seem very close," Hatsuko said softly. The other women moved nearer.

"We are fortunate," Sarah replied.

Eriko, a tiny woman with a wide, good-humored face, laughed and picked up a paper bag. "See this," she said. "I call my husband 'garbage bag.'"

"Eriko's right," Emiko said. "Husbands are only good on pay-days."

The women laughed and the class ended in good humor. Sarah noted that although Hatsuko covered her mouth and laughed with the others, she'd seen Hatsuko and her husband holding hands on numerous occasions. On the way back to the apartment, Hatsuko walked next to Sarah. "Many women here would like to learn English," she said.

"I'd be glad to teach them."

"You're not too busy?"

"No."

"I'll arrange it," Hatsuko replied.

Two days later, Hatsuko phoned Sarah with a class schedule. The lessons were to be in the afternoons at different homes. Because the pay was comparable to the school where she taught English, Sarah quit that job. Each afternoon, five woman gathered in a small apartment. Whenever the lessons were interrupted by children's demands, Sarah was amazed by the patience of the mothers. In particular, Emiko would run to her children in the middle of a recitation.

In one instance, Takao-chan, Emiko's child, burst into the room and began hitting his mother. Emiko knelt by Takao-chan and listened to his story, which, with interruptions for crying and pulling Emiko's hair, took at least fifteen minutes. The other women poured ice tea and chatted amiably throughout the tantrum. When the lesson finally resumed, Sarah was exhausted. Although Sarah tried to establish some ground rules during the lessons, children's needs continued to dominate. More women asked Hatsuko to arrange lessons and within two weeks Sarah was teaching several groups.

On the two-month anniversary of Sarah and John's arrival in Japan, the petition for transfer to a company apartment in Tokyo was granted. Sarah and John talked late into the night. Japan was still difficult for Sarah, John said. An apartment in Tokyo would mean access to other foreigners. Sarah agreed, but acknowledged that being in the country with these women had made her think about her values. John hesitated—both of them knew it would be easier for him if they stayed. He often worked late and his diligence had started to pay off. Both he and Tanaka were excited.

As she described her English classes to John, Sarah remembered her relationship with Hatsuko. After the last lesson, Hatsuko said, "We are friends now. I want to be your friend." Sarah responded by putting her arm around Hatsuko's slender waist, and they walked home that way. In the end, Sarah thought of neither John nor her own new self-awareness, but recalled Hatsuko's excited voice, in making the decision to stay.

The lessons lasted at least ninety minutes. Typically the women would work for the first half of the class, then the books were put away and tea was served. Slowly the women told their stories, the funny parts in Japanese, the parts they felt more deeply in English. Sarah took her direction from Hatsuko and did not comment upon or judge their remarks.

As their intimacy developed, Sarah found herself involved with the women's lives. She took a dinner to Emiko's family when Emiko was ill. She baby-sat for Takao-chan the next day. The women often did small favors for her in return.

At Hatsuko's suggestion, the women invited Sarah to a formal dinner and a kimono dressing party. Sarah was flattered but was also intimidated by the event. Hatsuko, who had just received several kimonos from a deceased relative, was to host the dinner. The invitation was issued in solemn language and Sarah's answer was also formal. Up to this point the women had always met in the afternoon on an informal basis. But this was different, this was serious. What if they had nothing to say to one another? What if everyone solemnly sipped green tea? After consultation with John, she decided to wear a wool suit and bring traditional bean cakes.

Hatsuko's apartment was at the rear of the building, overlooking a small playground. In corner apartments like hers, the rooms were larger by several mats. Since Hatsuko was still childless and her husband was often away on company business, the rooms were uncluttered.

When Sarah arrived on time and saw the women lined up at the entrance, her heart sank. As she suspected, they were dressed in their best, and their expressions were formal. She bowed, they returned her bow; they smiled, she returned their smiles. Emiko usually greeted her with a joke about her height. Hatsuko inevitably patted her arm. When she opened her English textbook, Yasuko, who drank, always suggested that the lesson begin with a glass of wine. Now Sarah cleared her throat. She had the feeling this was some sort of test. But what sort? She was aware of her height: she nearly reached the ceiling beam. She was a head taller than everybody in the room. Her size, her shape, made her an impostor. Her cheeks flushed. She sat down, but the women lifted her to a standing position.

Hatsuko smiled. "The kimono," she said, pointing to a beautiful silk kimono hanging in the corner of the room. Slowly Sarah pulled off her jacket and her blouse. The women watched. Then she dropped her skirt. The cool air gave her goose bumps. Why had she agreed to this? The women bound her breasts in a material that chafed. It was hard to breathe. Again she felt too large for the room and too large for the kimono. Suddenly she began to giggle. The women stepped back. Their mouths opened. Sarah caught Hatsuko's eyes. "I'm too large," she said, putting her hands under her breasts.

Hatsuko stepped close and stuck out *her* chest. "Not me." she laughed.

The other women came forward, touching their own breasts, touching each other, laughing, and removing their clothes. Sarah sank to the floor again and watched Hatsuko and Emiko slip into kimonos. Emiko pushed the nape of the kimono back in the manner of a geisha and the other women followed suit. Finally when the women were dressed, Hatsuko brought out powder, rouge, and lipstick. She powdered Sarah's face before the others. The women exclaimed on the transformations. When they were all costumed and made up, Hatsuko took pictures, as did the other women. The evening ended with beer and sushi. The women roared as Emiko hiked up her kimono to perform a north-country folk dance, the dance of the bear.

Over the course of the next year, the remaining barriers slowly dissolved. Although Sarah kept her job in Tokyo, she spent an increasing amount of time with Hatsuko and her friends. They took trips to Tokyo on the pretext of going to Kabuki theater or attending a tea ceremony class. But in reality it was a chance for the women to escape the monotony of their lives and a chance for Sarah to participate in Japanese culture with Japanese.

It was time to leave. Sarah scanned her apartment. She'd come to love the six-tatami-mat rooms, the tiny kitchen, and the even smaller bath that made up the company married dormitory housing. She and John had become best friends in these rooms. Japan had brought them closer than she ever imagined possible. It had changed her—it had changed them both, she thought, picking up two large Japanese tea cups. The cups had first caught her eye when Tanaka, John's boss, had slid open the door to the apartment two years ago. "From my wife," Tanaka had muttered, noting her look of appreciation. Now she picked up the cups and turned them slowly. A Japanese saying inscribed in blue ran the length of the cup. Tanaka had explained the poem was about fall and the change of weather. "It's almost fall," he'd said as he'd handed her the cups. Holding the cups, Sarah sat down in front of the low table. It is almost fall again, she thought. John entered the room, took her hand, and pulled her against him. "Time now," he said gently.

The women were lined up in front of two cars. Emiko, Hatsuko, Yasuko, and the others. As Sarah passed, each woman clasped her hands, promising to write and to continue studying English. "Sarah-san," Eriko said, "you have made our life bright. I'll never forget you."

Hatsuko led the way to her husband's car. Sarah was to ride with her in the back seat, she explained to bewildered John. "Tanaka will take you," she told John. "It's more comfortable for Sarah this way," she explained.

Hatsuko's husband drove slowly out of the compound. Sarah turned to wave. The women bowed, waved, and bowed again. Sarah felt Hatsuko's small fingers close on her own.

"You are my sister," Hatsuko said softly.

Analysis:

Foreigners are often confused by the dichotomy of women's roles in Japanese society. On the surface, women seem completely dominated and live to serve men. On closer inspection, Japanese women have a powerful role in both their households and society at large. Women are responsible for the education and nurturing of Japan's most valuable resource, its children.

Sarah's survival in a company dormitory located two hours from Tokyo depends on successful entry into a woman's world. Sarah's story covers all four stages of communication with the Japanese, but it underlines the critical importance of the "trust me" stage.

Sarah's entry into Japanese society is accompanied by social customs that leave Sarah confused. Intuitive by nature, Sarah does not hug Tanaka at the airport as was their customary greeting in America. Tanaka "holds himself too stiff" and consequently she follows Tanaka's lead and bows. In Japan public greetings, no matter how intimate, are expressed formally. The setting is not right to reveal intimate feelings. Tanaka feels that the lack of appropriateness would cause loss of face for all concerned.

Thus, Sarah is introduced to the compartmentalized world of Japan. Though newcomers, Sarah and John are in the "trust me" stage of the relationship because they have established a friendship with the Tanakas in the United States. Extreme caution and formality are the rule at this stage, especially in public. Japanese feel that emotions should be expressed in accordance with the stage of the relationship and with the setting. It is totally inappropriate to carry over an emotion from another time or place. This situation-dependent approach is confusing to Westerners, who take a more integrated approach to relationships.

Tanaka takes Sarah and John to his house for dinner. Although the couples have been friendly in America, Tanaka considers the dinner a formal introduction to Japan. Formal meals are often a way of establishing a trust relationship in Japanese culture. Tanaka seats John with his back to the alcove. Because it is the position farthest from the door and was long considered the least vulnerable position to attack, it is now the traditional seat of honor in Japan. Yukiko sits next to the door in the most vulnerable position. Although John and Sarah are unaware of the subtleties of the seating arrangement, they are sensible enough to wait to be seated.

However, their patience does not endure when it comes to the dinner. Sarah lets the Tanakas know that she would like more sushi and asks for more beer. In each case, Sarah is confused by Yukiko's reaction. By stating her needs, Sarah is making explicit the shortcoming of the hosts, which is a cause for loss of face. (Despite the time they spent in the United States, the Tanakas have reverted to a Japanese mode of operations and values upon their return to Japan.)

A dependent relationship (amae) is encouraged when Japanese entertain. Every wish of the guest is to be anticipated. Guests are seated according to rank. They are not offered choices during dinner, nor are they expected to make demands. Japanese never fill their own glass—a neighbor plays host by filling the glass. (There is a small ritual attached to this service in which the server indicates his interest in pouring the beer by holding out the beer bottle and the recipient accepts the gesture by raising his glass; then the roles are reversed and the recipient becomes the server.) All this etiquette sets the tone for the evening and for the ensuing relationship.

Although Sarah easily obtains work in the following months, she generally feels the same alienation she felt at the Tanaka's welcome dinner. The smiles, the presents, and her exclusion from meetings at the autistic school make Sarah fundamentally uneasy. She joins a cooking group in the neighborhood, which ties her closer to the women's world of Japan. The women test her by describing Americans as materialistic, uncaring, and aggressive. Finally she defends and further defines herself by mentioning her Jewish heritage. Hatsuko, a housewife in the group, immediately identifies "Jewish" characteristics with Japanese values. The women begin to warm to Sarah. In introductions and conversations there is often an effort to "connect" by emphasizing common characteristics such as location (i.e., place of birth, type of university, using the same train line). Here Hatsuko links Japanese and Jewish characteristics.

Hatsuko further befriends Sarah by arranging English classes. Here Hatsuko is acting in the traditional mentoring role that characterizes the beginnings of many relationships in Japan. Hatsuko is acting as Sarah's window (madoguchi) to the world. Sarah understands this and accepts Hatsuko's kindness.

Instinctively, Sarah observes Hatsuko's behavior in group situations, especially Hatsuko's lack of public comment on what the other women say about their lives. Sarah is learning an important lesson about face (kao) and how it operates in Japanese culture. Most conversations are brought to closure through a genuine search for commonality of purpose. What can be agreed upon is emphasized rather than the opposite. To this end, analysis of remarks are considered crude and too revealing to give the conversation a face-saving tone (wa). The Japanese women use the English lessons as a way of bonding and as a way of airing grievances. Again because of face, the complaints are distanced by the use of English.

During these English classes, Sarah also learns a great deal about the importance of the relationship between a Japanese mother and her child. The child's tantrums are tolerated even in the middle of the lesson. The mother's first priority is always the child and its incorporation into the group. She will be responsible for the child's performance at school and ultimately in life. This role of kyoiku Mama, *"dutiful mother," has the respect of the whole society. Women understand and accept the amount of energy required to nurture a child properly. They have separate lives from the men and within their world a woman's authority and values are absolute.*

However, the same tolerance for children does not hold for husbands. Traditionally Japanese women complain about men and about their marriages. For instance, Eriko openly talks of her husband as fit only to bring home paychecks. Women feel secure in their households no matter how difficult the marital relationship. Husbands turn over their pay to their wives, who then allocate an allowance to the man. Sarah observes that although Hatsuko's marriage is happy, she does not destroy the harmony of the group by defending husbands in general.

Hatsuko then intensifies the relationship by inviting Sarah to a formal dinner and kimono dressing party. Sarah understands by the seriousness of the invitation and the elaborate preparation that the event is a test. Sarah is again exposed to the compartmentalized world of Japan. As she suspects, despite the friendship among the women, the party is grotesquely formal. She feels large and awkward, incapable of breaking any barriers. Nevertheless, in this strained situation, Sarah resorts to instinct and creates a commonality through the concern and humor women the world over share about the size and shape of their breasts. This instinctual response is respected by the Japanese women, and with Hatsuko's help, the strained atmosphere dissolves at once. Sarah is more completely integrated into the group.

For the remainder of Sarah's stay in Japan, Hatsuko continues to act as guide and mentor, and the relationship between the two women deepens. Hatsuko and the other Japanese women used Sarah as a catalyst to make their lives more interesting, and Sarah used the Japanese women to understand and become part of Japan. As so often is the case, the relationship equalized over time, as illustrated by Hatsuko's parting remark to Sarah: "You are my sister."

JOSE: Working Effectively as an Outsider

Jose sat with his hands folded on his lap and nodded at the six Yamato Corporation executives across the table. He had been answering questions about the research and the people in his section at Yamato Corporation for two hours and his head hurt. From the beginning of the meeting it had been clear from the remarks of the Yamato Corporation executives such as "We enjoyed having you" that this was a traditional Japanese cross-check meeting. The questions appeared senseless, especially since these senior executives seemed to know the people and the research in his section as well as he. It is the Japanese way, he thought, patiently answering the next question about a co-worker. "He is a very imaginative researcher and is sincere in all ways . . ."

"Yes, we agree, we intend to promote him," a vice president of Yamato Corporation said while his colleagues nodded and smiled.

Jose also nodded. He was proud of his patience both during this predictable meeting and during his tenure at Yamato Corporation. He now possessed the vital information he needed to complete his thesis on robotics at the University of Tokyo.

For the past four months he'd been living in a science-fiction movie and seen things that he never dreamed possible: robots programmed to operate advanced nuclear reactors, elegant robotic arms that could manipulate flimsy materials, robots with sensing devices that could check for leaks, robots that climbed stairs. Japan had a technological hold on the twenty-first century, and he was part of it. He had endured a great deal to gather this information. But equally important to his project, Jose felt exposure to Yamato Corporation had heightened his awareness of the possibilities in robotic research. That was inspiring. He smiled as he remembered his first exhausting day at Yamato Corporation.

. . .

He had already passed his oral exams at the University of Tokyo. Jose began working for Yamato Corporation with the understanding that he was on loan from the university for six months. Jose had proposed the stay at Yamato Corporation to his professor, as he felt that the university did not have either the sophisticated equipment or available experts to help him with his thesis. His Japanese professor agreed with Jose and made the arrangements through a former student, who was now a section chief at Yamato Corporation, to have him work at the company.

The first day on the job was tiring. Jose had to leave his apartment at six-thirty for the two-hour commute to Yamato Corporation. Upon his arrival he was escorted through the big building to his section. It was immediately clear that, except for the section chief, the seven people in the group did not have engineering degrees. They were mostly technicians who had been trained at Yamato Corporation's own in-house college. Ito, his section chief, introduced Jose, mentioning his background, and explained Jose's status as a trainee and Jose's project. Very conscious of the others' hostility, Jose gave a low bow.

Over the next few days, Jose learned the ropes of the laboratory. He worked at an "island desk" facing a co-worker named Kato and was aware that his phone calls as well as his conduct were being closely watched.

Among others, Kato questioned him incessantly about his life. As always, Kato would start a conversation by talking about the weather, shift to the problems of commuting to Yamato Corporation, and then, after about twenty minutes, abruptly switch to personal questions.

"Do you have a girlfriend?" he asked.

Jose was proud of Annette, his girlfriend, a very successful French businesswoman. However, looking at Kato's frayed shirt collar, he hesitated. He knew Kato's room in the Yamato dormitory still did not have heat, and he knew that Kato worked until ten each night and was in the laboratory by nine on Saturdays. Kato didn't have a girlfriend and it looked unlikely that he ever would. "No," Jose said quietly.

"Did you have one in Argentina?"

"No," he answered again quietly.

"You must have had a fancy apartment in Argentina," Kato said in a soft tone. "Do you have a picture?"

Kato was smiling openly. Feeling momentarily lonely and in need of recognition, Jose reached into his wallet for a picture of his Argentinean girlfriend wearing a bikini standing outside his newly purchased condo in Buenos Aires. But when Kato sighed and said, "Foreigners are so rich," Jose jerked his head up and flushed. He pulled out a picture of his parents standing in a park. "My parents," he said. Kato nodded.

Jose decided to take advantage of this brief exchange. "Kato-san, I need to work on the mainframe computer. How do I get it started?"

"That might be difficult," Kato answered.

"I need the computer for my work," Jose insisted. He suspected Kato was worried about Yamato Corporation secrets and access to the computer data base. (Just that morning Kato had snapped at him for looking at diagrams of robotic arms; when Jose's questions revealed his knowledge of the field, Kato had become pale and turned away.) Although the computer was vital to his work, Jose decided not to press the matter.

The next day Jose read papers and worked on formulas. Kato was in a good mood because his experiment had gone well and he proudly showed Jose his new robot. "It's better than anything in America," Kato said, pointing to the charts.

Jose agreed, not only to appease Kato but also because he thought there was a chance it might be true. Jose did not bring up the use of the computer, nor did he go to their superior, Ito, about the problem. This situation persisted, and by Friday Jose had developed a flicker in one eye. As he was leaving to catch the six o'clock train, Kato stopped him at the door. He was holding a stack of computer cards in his hands. "You can use the computer with these cards. Punch in the commands."

Jose looked at the stack of cards. Having used similar cards in the early seventies, he knew how time-consuming working with them was. Jose also knew any protest would just add friction.

For the next month, Jose used the computer cards and tried to be agreeable. While his colleagues were helpful, they were still selective about giving him information such as where components for the robots were made. He, in turn, was careful to behave like a "proper student" from the University of Tokyo who was at Yamato Corporation to use the up-to-date equipment.

One Monday he woke up late with a headache. Annette suggested he drive her red Mercedes to work. He did so and managed to arrive early. By the time he parked the car near the rear of the huge parking lot he felt much better. He had been in the office only twenty minutes when a member of his group asked about the Mercedes in the parking lot. Jose was silent. All morning, co-workers continued to speculate about the car. Finally he admitted driving it to work.

Ito nodded. "Good, I'd like to see it. I've never been in a Mercedes. Do you mind showing us? I didn't know you liked sports cars."

"It's not mine," Jose said carefully. "I borrowed it from a friend."

As he and Ito walked out the door, Jose noticed that his entire group was following.

"Foreigner?" Ito asked casually.

"No," Jose answered. "Japanese. Actually, it is not even his. He borrowed it from his older brother."

"Then it belongs to the older brother."

"I'm not really sure," Jose answered.

When they reached the Mercedes, Jose got in first and slipped the registration into a hiding place. One by one every man in his section drove the Mercedes around the parking lot. When the last man got out of the Mercedes, Jose was sweating.

"Nice car," Kato said. "The person who owns it is lucky. Usually it is the foreigners who are rich enough to own a car like this. It's not Japanese style. Japanese don't like to show off."

"Yes, you're right, not really Japanese style," Jose shrugged, indicating, like Kato, that Jose had no idea who that might be.

Jose was careful to take a roundabout route to Tokyo that night, and he never drove the Mercedes to work again.

After the Mercedes incident Kato continued to make remarks against foreigners; he also criticized Jose for not following the Yamato Corporation policy of using both sides of the paper for computer printouts and for not keeping a record of the number of pencils he took from Supplies. In addition Jose frequently was not allowed to use the computer because it was "broken." In spite of these and other problems, he found his work interesting and was learning a great deal and was making real progress.

One day Kato took him aside. "I want to show you something," he said. Jose followed Kato to the section chief's desk. Ito was not there and the desk had been cleared. "He lost power," Kato said, pulling open an emptied drawer. Jose nodded; he understood his days were numbered and he began to work more hours per day to finish his thesis.

Finally the meeting with Yamato's corporate people was ending, and the six Yamato executives smiled broadly as Jose bowed low over the desk. "It has been a rare privilege working at Yamato Corporation," he said. "You have a wonderful company and a sincere staff. Thank you so much for allowing me the honor." The Yamato Corporation executives smiled and Jose lowered his eyes. He would have gone on, but sensed he had said enough. Yamato Corporation had opened a future for him that he never dreamed possible, and the technical skills he had acquired had solidified his position in his department at the University of Tokyo.

The top executive stood, smiled, and after a short bow left the room. The others followed and soon the secretary who had served tea came to escort him out of the building. Just before he turned the corner of the building, he looked up. Six faces observed him from the window. The department chief waved. Jose bowed and waved in return, relieved that he hadn't taken Annette up on her offer to pick him up in her Mercedes.

Analysis:

In some cases, integration into a Japanese working group is impossible. Regardless of the reason—the person in question wasn't properly introduced, his alliances to other groups are suspect, his group is not well respected, involvement with the individual in question is of no perceived benefit to the group—the group doesn't feel any responsibility to the individual and is often suspicious of the individual's motives. Consequently, Japanese are often perceived as harsh and withholding. Even though the person will always remain on the "outside," when handled appropriately these situations can still yield good results for an individual who has well-defined, achievable goals.

Through the introduction of his professor, Jose has been able to join Yamato Corporation, a high-technology company. Though his profes-

sor has good contacts elsewhere in the company, in his immediate situation Jose feels "at sea." No one in Jose's laboratory has a deep connection to Jose's University of Tokyo professor either as a colleague or as a former student. Jose's professor's connections to other people in Yamato Corporation facilitated his placement, but Jose does not have the benefit of a "connection" in the laboratory, someone who would discharge an obligation by taking care of him; nor does he come to the group as part of a larger network. His colleagues are technicians trained to perform complex tasks. Yamato Corporation has provided them with the equivalent of two years of college education through a company college (this is a common practice in Japan).

Jose is further alienated from the group by the fact that he hasn't been assigned a mentor. A mentor is extremely important in the "trust me" stage of a relationship. He acts as a go-between to the group and mediates apparent differences or misunderstandings. As the person is incorporated into the group, the mentor becomes less important. Jose's stay at Yamato Corporation is too brief to warrant his inclusion in the mentoring system most Japanese companies foster. He thus has no "window" (madoguchi) to enter the group.

At the office Jose sits at an island desk across from Kato. Kato considers it appropriate not only to observe Jose, but also to ask him questions.

The attitude toward privacy is different in Japan. In a traditional Japanese house the concept of a "private" life does not exist in the same way it does in the West. In the workplace, everyone works in the same open space. People are expected and indeed make it their business to know a great deal about each other's lives, the rationale being that this information provides insight into character and will help a supervisor or colleague assess various situations.

Jose quickly deflects Kato's personal questions and merges with the group. By showing Kato pictures of his parents, he creates a commonality with Kato and avoids a potentially awkward situation where he might be perceived as a "playboy" and where Kato might feel competitive.

Nevertheless, because his stay at Yamato Corporation is a short one, Jose will always be an outsider to Kato and will never pass to the "believe me" stage of the relationship. From the group's point of view Kato's job is to make it clear to Jose that he is an outsider and also to protect the group from Jose if necessary.

For instance, when Jose mentions his need for the computer to Kato, Jose exhibits understanding of his position as an outsider. He is also patient (nintai) with Kato's passive-aggressive response of forcing Jose to use cumbersome and outdated computer cards. With this move, Kato solves the problem of his lack of authority. As an outsider, any complaints of Jose's would not be taken seriously and would destroy any goodwill with Kato. Jose accepts his exclusion and continues to work toward the completion of his project on the robotic arm.

The Mercedes incident reinforces Jose's determination to make his situation workable. Jose deflects his co-workers' questions by stating that the car belongs to a Japanese friend who has, in turn, borrowed it from an "older brother." He does not challenge Kato's statements about Japanese modesty, thus working to develop a feeling of consensus and harmony.

At the "trust me" phase it is important to define realistic professional objectives. Acceptance into the group is not part of Jose's agenda, and since he knows he will never pass into the "believe me" phase of the relationship he must concentrate on achieving what he wants to at Yamato Corporation.

As Jose makes progress with his project, Kato becomes increasingly rigid and engineers more impediments to Jose's progress. Finally when Kato shows him the empty desk of a co-worker, Jose understands it is time to leave. Kato expresses Yamato Corporation's intentions indirectly so as to prepare Jose for his termination notice. Avoidance of surprise saves face by laying the groundwork for a smooth transition. When Jose's project is near completion, he leaves Yamato Corporation satisfied that he has handled the situation well.

However, Yamato Corporation still has an agenda for Jose. In a final meeting with the executives Jose is grilled on the working group. This cross-checking is institutionalized in Japanese culture. The management of Yamato Corporation want observations verified, even by someone on the "outside." Jose understands this and handles the long meeting with patience. Dispatching this duty with care is part of Jose's obligation to be of service to the company and to his professor for providing him with this opportunity. Jose is not even put out by Yamato Corporation's last scrutiny of him from their corporate offices; instead, he is simply grateful not to have revealed too much of himself by allowing Annette to pick him up in her car.

FRED: Cover-ups and Indiscretion

Fred looked at the eight Japanese gentlemen around the table. Yanegawa and two others from Personnel, Nagai and a co-worker from his laboratory, and the rest he'd assumed to be Senko Corporation general administrators. They'd been discussing his insurance now for the last two hours. Yanegawa, the head of Personnel, had been vigilant about outlining the history and Senko's lack of apparent responsibility. "Except for the goodness of Senko's heart," Yanegawa intoned, "this meeting would not be held. Senko is a family. When you are part of Senko, you are part of that family." Yanegawa stared at Fred as if waiting for an affirmative nod.

Fred lowered his gaze. They were waiting. The air was thick with tension. He counted slowly to himself. He would not apologize, he would never apologize. He'd learned about silence in Japan. Oddly, Yanegawa had been his greatest teacher in matters of silence. There had been dozens of meetings on his insurance issue, dozens of lectures on the idea of the family. Yanegawa would fight to the bitter end to protect the lack of competence of his colleagues in the powerful Personnel Department. No one would ever know who in Personnel had not explained the need for Fred to sign the overseas insurance forms. Perhaps it was the great man Yanegawa himself, perhaps it was a subordinate. Now *that* was family, Fred thought bitterly. Stick together and cover each other. No one could afford to be honest.

Would he get the insurance in the end? Nagai, his boss, had reassured him it was a matter of time. A matter of time, Fred thought in disgust. How much time was necessary for one simple promised document? Nagai knew more than he let on. As sympathetic as he was to Fred, in the end he was a Senko man first and Fred was an outsider. Nagai would support Yanegawa. The Japanese were talking among themselves as if he weren't in the room. He closed his eyes. Why couldn't he walk out? How had all this started?

· · ·

It had been a year ago in September when Fred had arrived at Senko, a large company with a leading market share in electronic goods, to complete an internship and what he hoped would be the best adventure of his life. The letters from Nagai had been warm and full of exciting technical information. Fred had been overwhelmed by Senko's generosity the night of his arrival—Nagai himself had hosted a beautiful banquet at an exclusive restaurant near the laboratory.

The next week Fred had gone to Nagai and asked to be switched from intern status to regular employee. At that time Japan seemed so marvelous and the Japanese so polite that Fred dismissed the fact that it was a 1½-hour train ride from his dorm to the laboratory. After all, many Japanese also commuted 1½ hours each way to work. Besides, Fred was young and he enjoyed the view. His work was exciting and Nagai was wonderful.

He was delighted when several months later Nagai informed him he was now a regular employee with life-long work benefits plus health insurance, a twice-yearly bonus, and a paid vacation. Fred continued working on his language skills, preparing for the presentation of his material in Japanese at a laboratory group meeting in four months. He would work hard at Senko and even squeeze in a two-week vacation before his presentation.

Fred didn't mind the long hours at Senko. After all, he reasoned, to be the best was not easy, and he was a perfectionist. He was lucky to be in the right place at the right time. Everything was happening in Japan.

Fred made plans to meet his sister, who was doing a medical internship in Nairobi. As Fred packed his bags he thought of the presents he would bring back for Nagai and his other co-workers in Tokyo.

The accident happened at two thirty-three on a sunny Saturday at an intersection about an hour out of Nairobi. Fred had the right-of-way when he was hit broadside. The oncoming vehicle swerved across the road. Its driver died immediately on impact, the others were seriously injured. According to police reports, the passengers in the oncoming car had been drinking. By the time the police arrived, Fred and his sister were unconscious. They were rushed to a nearby hospital for immediate transfusions.

Senko reacted immediately. Mr. Shiroaki, the Senko representative in Nairobi, visited Fred twice at the hospital, once when he was unconscious and once before he was transported back to America. Senko was reassured, Mr. Shiroaki said, by Fred's speedy recovery. Fred was not to worry. He must take all his energy to get well. Nagai had been beside himself in Japan.

In the tortuous weeks that followed, people from Senko called Fred repeatedly both at the hospital and later at home. Nagai and the laboratory sent his Japanese-language books. They were concerned that he would forget his Japanese, and they were concerned that he would become depressed. Nagai wrote that he was planning to visit Fred on a forthcoming trip to the States. Would Fred be well enough to receive him? Fred's answer was an emphatic yes. By this time, two months had elapsed since the accident and Fred was bored and slightly irritable. He had broached the question of insurance several times with Nagai, who'd checked with Yanegawa in Personnel. Nagai's reports were inconclusive. Fred had not taken travel insurance.

"I never heard of it."

"All employees must have travel insurance when they go abroad."

"Why didn't someone tell me?"

"Personnel . . ."

"Personnel didn't," Fred interrupted. "Yanegawa-san never mentioned it."

Personnel is a powerful department in any Japanese company. But at Senko, Personnel seemed particularly strong. From the beginning Nagai had checked all decisions regarding Fred with Personnel. For instance, Fred was sure Nagai had tried to put him in a better dormitory, one closer to the laboratory. He had even overheard a phone conversation between Yanegawa and Nagai about his housing situation. Yet, in the end Nagai had always bowed to Yanegawa's wishes and had defended the Personnel Department on several occasions with other foreigners.

There was a long pause.

At any rate, they would discuss all these matters on Nagai's forthcoming trip. Yanegawa would also be present. Could they come for tea? By all means, Fred answered, thinking that Charleston was rather out of their way just for tea. His mother gestured from across the room. "What about insurance?" she asked. Fred felt uneasy. His parents had to prepay the hospital bill of $30,000. He hoped the planned tea with Nagai and Yanegawa would settle the matter.

On the last Saturday in September. Nagai and Yanegawa, accompanied by three other Japanese, arrived at Fred's house for tea. Fred and his sister met them in wheelchairs. Fred felt ridiculous, overtures of the children's rhyme, *Jack and Jill*, he thought—but one look at Yanegawa's serious expression made him realize the importance of the meeting, and how far out of their way the Japanese had come.

Yanegawa began the conversation by politely asking after Fred's health, and that of his sister, and stating Senko's delight in their speedy recovery. There was a long pause. Fred tried to read the expression on Nagai's face, which was curiously blank. His mother passed the cookies; his father coughed. Fred was reminded that $30,000 was a great deal for his parents. The pause lengthened. Nagai coughed.

"Senko will be happy to pay insurance money," Yanegawa said, "if you come back to Japan."

"He is in a wheelchair," Fred's father began. "We understood that when Fred signed the contract, health insurance was covered. We understood this kind of misfortune would be taken care of. It's in the contract." His father's face reddened.

Yanegawa looked at the floor. He shook his head.

"Dad, it's okay," Fred interrupted. "I didn't sign the overseas insurance."

"That's because you didn't know about the overseas insurance."

Yanegawa flushed and continued looking at the floor. Nagai's smile seemed plastered on his face. For a moment Fred had second thoughts. Why didn't Nagai speak up? Nagai knew he had never received an overseas insurance form. Nagai must have an explanation, Fred thought. Overall, Japanese companies operate like families.

"For how long must he work?" his father asked.

"One year."

"Then all insurance will be paid?" his father asked. His expression was one of disbelief.

"Yes," Yanegawa answered.

Fred sipped his tea. The idea rather excited him. He couldn't leave for a few weeks until he got out of the blasted wheelchair. It would be good to speak Japanese again, it would be good to finish what he started. He remembered the speech. Perhaps he could still give it this year? "Yes," he answered suddenly.

"Are you sure about this, Freddie?" his mother was at his side.

"Yes," his answer was certain. "It will be good for me professionally. Nagai and I do good work together." He smiled at Nagai, who returned his smile. The Japanese were absolutely delighted. They smiled, shook Fred's hand again and again. By the time they left, it was nearly seven and Fred's mother, carried away by the excitement, fretted that she should have invited Nagai and the others for supper. In this pleasant atmosphere, no one thought to ask for a document. The fact that there was nothing on paper occurred to Fred only when he was on the plane, and for a moment he saw the worried face of his mother. He promised himself he would settle the insurance matter as soon as he returned to Senko.

Yanegawa met with Fred almost immediately. However, nothing was resolved. Yanegawa met with him again two weeks later. Fred read his contract carefully. It was impossible: Senko wanted back rent on the dormitory and back taxes on that rent. "Yanegawa," Fred began carefully, "when I returned to Japan, Senko agreed to increase my pay by thirty-five thousand yen per month. What are these costs?"

"Just routine," Yanegawa answered.

Fred thought for a moment. The accumulated sum of back rent and taxes also came to ¥35,000. Was it an accident? Yanegawa's face was noncommittal. "I am concerned about my insurance," Fred continued. "It is important that I be paid quickly. My parents must be reimbursed and I filled out the forms over two months ago."

"The insurance takes time."

"How much time?"

Yanegawa smiled. "Time," he answered again.

Fred put his hand on his bad knee. The knee trembled. How stupid, how naive. To come back on the promise of a smile without a contract. Then Fred remembered Jim's anger. He had been hired as an engineer the year before Fred arrived. The details of his contract had not been worked out before his arrival in Japan. As a result the document Jim signed in Japan did not provide for any bonus or leave.

Yanegawa and the Personnel Department stood behind that document. Despite Jim's protests that he had been promised the bonus and the leave, he lost the battle after a few months. Initially Jim's boss had been sympathetic but helpless, and in the end, the boss had defended Personnel's decision.

Fred took a deep breath. He should have listened to Jim. He was at their mercy. Even Nagai didn't care about being fair or being right. It was obvious that he would support the Personnel Department. He rubbed the knee, hoping to ease the trembling. The dorm was just too far away, he thought, and it was located on a hill. Because he was still on crutches, it took more than two hours to get to the laboratory. "Yanegawa," he began slowly. "I need to take the bus to the station. My knee is not strong and the dormitory is on a hill. I have to stand in the train. The bus costs one hundred thirty-seven yen each way."

Yanegawa jotted a note. "Senko will look into it."

"I have been to see a doctor, Doctor Nomura, who has many Senko patients."

Yanegawa's eyes hardened. "Yes?"

"He says the leg is being damaged from the constant standing. I need bus fare, and more important, I need a closer place to live."

"Senko will . . ."

"Yanegawa-san, this is the sixth meeting. These issues were brought up at the first meeting."

"Excuse me," Yanegawa rose. "I'll return in a minute."

Fred tapped his fingers on the desk. He could barely control his trembling. Then a folder caught his eye. FOREIGN EMPLOYEES. Without a moment's hesitation, he opened the folder. His fingers ran down the names. "¥35,000 foreign compensation" was noted by each name. Even foreigners who were permanent hires were aware that they were a special group—even in the company dorms, no foreigner was assigned a Japanese roommate. Fred sat back. He laughed and closed the folder. He'd heard foreign researchers complain about the Japanese giving preferential treatment to some of them over others. Senko had given him what other foreign employees had been getting all along, and then they'd tried to take it back. He couldn't believe it. His forehead broke out into a cold sweat. At first Nagai had been kind and listened carefully to all Fred's complaints. Recently however, each time he'd asked Nagai to inquire, his fingers had been rapped. He wasn't doing things in the Japanese way, Nagai said. Nagai was concerned. All Fred could think about was the insurance. Last week Fred had been too angry to continue working on his project. He sat at his desk and stared out the window. If Senko wasn't going to keep their end of the bargain, he wasn't going to keep his. Nagai had asked him if his leg hurt, but Fred had shook his head and continued staring at the street below.

"Okay," Yanegawa's voice was behind him. "Senko will give you an apartment close to the laboratory, and you may pay the difference with money you will earn by working overtime."

Fred gulped. Were they all crazy? He should hit Yanegawa over the head with the folder. Senko was diabolical. He was being ruined. Nothing was fair. He should receive the same base pay as other foreign employees, he should receive the insurance money, his housing situation should be fixed. It was unfair—unfair—unfair. His head pounded. "I'll think about it," he said in a wheezy voice.

After October Fred stopped working completely. He reasoned if Senko was going to be "unfair" then he would not perform. Meeting after meeting was scheduled with the Personnel Department, but the insurance seemed no closer to being paid. With each week Fred's depression worsened. Finally in late November Yanegawa, Nagai, and other officials of Senko met with Fred. Senko produced a document saying they would pay 90 percent of Fred's $30,000 hospital bill now and 10 percent in a month. Fred's hands shook as he looked over the contract. Everything seemed to be in order.

"Fine," Fred said, "but . . . I would also like a written apology."

There was dead silence in the room. The grins seemed plastered to the Japanese faces as if they'd been born smiling. Nagai's eyes bulged from his head. Yanegawa took a note, the rest of the gentlemen were frozen.

"An apology," Yanegawa repeated.

"Yes," Fred repeated. "An apology."

There was a long pause. Nagai looked at the table. Yanegawa's face reddened.

"What for?" Yanegawa asked.

"Your being unfair."

"Unfair?" Yanegawa's voice was quiet. "You did not sign the

overseas insurance form. Unfair. You are paid thirty thousand dollars—unfair?"

"I want an apology."

"We will think this over," Yanegawa replied and adjourned the meeting.

That was over a month ago, Fred thought, looking around the room at the eight Japanese men.

"We are a family," Yanegawa continued. "Fred, you will be paid in full, this month, for your insurance." There was a long pause.

Fred knew he should dismiss himself, thank Senko, thank his colleagues, apologize for causing so much trouble, thank them for their time, their effort. Yanegawa was waiting. Nagai was waiting. But Fred did nothing. He read the contract carefully—taking his time, seeing if it was genuine. His leg ached a lot less now, and as he read, he forgot about his uncertainty, instead concentrating on the legal language while the Japanese waited.

That night Fred walked slowly from the bus stop back to the dorm. He had decided to leave Senko that month for America. That thought curiously gave him little joy. He fingered the contract as he walked into the large front hall. By the time he reached his room he felt numb. Slowly he lay out his quilt. The cotton felt soft against his skin. He lay motionless. The pillow was wet. Only then he realized he'd been crying.

Analysis:

Japanese regard their company as a family and refer to it as a house (uchi). *Each house has a different identity, history, and attitude toward work and employees. Typically, new hires are rotated through many jobs over a two-year training period. Recruits are encouraged to become members of the company "house" and are expected to subordinate their personal point of view to the good of that house. In addition, most training includes attending company retreats, where company history and policy are explained and where recruits are put through bonding exercises that emphasize spiritual training* (seishin).

Fred, like many Americans, is initially charmed by the hospitality of his Japanese hosts. He wants to become part of the Senko uchi *without concrete knowledge of the testing and training that occurs in the "know me"* and *"trust me"* phases of a relationship in Japan. Because Senko is considered a desirable company, it is able to recruit top-notch candidates from elite universities. Recruits are highly recommended by a professor, must pass a test, and be interviewed: even their families are interviewed and investigated. Senko offers these recruits lifetime employment (shu-shin koyo). All this means prospective employees are deeply invested in the company by the time they are hired. Their feelings of commitment are reinforced by the two-year training period.

In his state of enchantment, Fred applies for and is granted full employee status. Hiring foreigners such as Fred as employees is part of an effort on the part of many Japanese companies to effect a policy of internationalization. Japanese are aware that these foreigners have not been exposed to the *"know me"* and *"trust me"* phases of the relationship and consequently often have difficulty with the degree of commitment and loyalty expected from a Japanese employee.

Fred is largely unaware of training in company morality (shikomu). Concepts such as negation of self (jubun ga nai) in favor of the group also elude him. Finally, Fred is unaware of the compartmentalized structure (bu) of a Japanese company, which can lead to power struggles and communication problems. Although Nagai, Fred's boss, is sympathetic to Fred's dilemma about his insurance payments and understands that the Personnel Department was remiss in not providing the required insurance forms for overseas travel, he can do little to help Fred because of the power of Personnel, because Fred is an outsider, and most importantly because Fred does not accept subordinating himself to the system.

After the accident, Fred's enthusiasm for Senko is sustained by Senko's genuine concern. Senko's visit to Charleston reveals the extent to which the paternalistic attitude (onjo shugi) toward employees pervades Japanese companies. It is not unusual for companies to help arrange marriages for their employees, and to attend marriage ceremonies and funerals.

In his gratitude for Senko's concern, Fred is not as careful with Senko as he would have been with an American company, and does not ask for documentation. A critical part of Japanese business practice, documentation removes responsibility from the individual. In Fred's case, a mutually agreed-upon contract, signed before Fred *returns to Japan, would be processed by Senko without comment. The issue of the contract should have been brought up during the Charleston visit, as it would place the blame for his insistence on a document on an acceptable reason, such as his parents' concern. However, because no such contract exists, Fred becomes a pawn in the hands of the Personnel Department.*

Upon his return to Japan, Fred considers his treatment unfair, is furious, and stops working, which causes the situation to deteriorate. Fred is considered a working memeber of the company, yet he refuses to understand that he must be determined and address the situation by being cheerful and working hard. At this point Fred has unwittingly taken on Yanegawa and Personnel by publicly questioning the Personnel Department's competence. Personnel is a powerful section of most Japanese companies and is responsible for recruiting employees as well as for decisions involving their promotion.

Yanegawa's auger (giseisha) stems from his desire to protect his department and deflect the responsibility (sekinin) for Fred's lack of knowledge about overseas insurance. Taking revenge will remove the onus of Fred's public accusation of Personnel's incompetence.

Fred's demand for an apology reveals his lack of understanding of Japanese ethics, the Japanese company (uchi), and the notion of etiquette (saho), which is closely aligned with virtue. According to Japanese standards, publicly forcing Personnel to admit to wrongful behavior demeans both Fred and Senko. Fred has won the insurance money, and wants Yanegawa to admit his mistake. With this demand, Fred is not prudent (jicho) about protecting himself from public criticism. Everyone in the room is aware that Yanegawa and the Personnel Department made a mistake. Everyone is also aware that Yanegawa has punished Fred by having repeated meetings on the subject of his insurance and that his living situation is untenable. Japanese make it their business to know all aspects of a situation and it must be assumed that Fred's problems have been thoroughly discussed. To point out the obvious is counterproductive.

In this case, Senko is giving Fred a chance to clear his slate through an apology to the group. Irrespective of right or wrong, like all workers, Fred must honor and protect the system. Fred's apology would restore the harmony (wa) at Senko and would acknowledge that his problems have caused internal strife at Senko. Apologies (moshiwake gozaimasen) *in Japan are used to ease situations and protect the system. If the transgression is great, the apology must be made in person and show sincerity. Japanese give great weight to the notion of apology and are apt to forgive the mistake. Fred does not understand that his responsibility to preserve a sense of well-being is a crucial aspect of being part of the Senko family.*

At the final meeting Fred raises the traditional American lament of "unfair," a complaint that is bewildering to the Japanese. Yanegawa leaves Fred with the impression that the mistake was on both sides and there is no right or wrong. Again, this is a traditional Japanese approach to a problem. It is important that each participant of any conflict leave the arena with his face (kao) intact. Also, there is a real antipathy to closing doors that might be useful in the future. Fred looks at this situation from the standpoint of a victim and is closing doors instead of creating opportunities.

BELIEVE ME

The "believe me" phase includes active participation in Japanese business practice and Japanese society. This stage is characterized by a bonding in work relationships when your company has a credible history with another institution: knowledge of the assignment, the institutions and people involved, cultivation of dependable networks, and comfort on the part of all parties with the level of commitment of the participants. The degree of your preparation and involvement in the "know me" and "trust me" phase affects the tone of the interaction in the "believe me" phase. If your relationship is solid at this stage, participants will believe that mutually acceptable solutions to problems are achievable goals. Every effort must be made by you or your company to extend networks in this phase, even in the competitive situation of negotiating a deal. The cases of Mary, Dave, Roy, Craig, Jean, and Ken illustrate this point. In each case, extending contacts becomes an important goal.

Investing your time and energy in understanding a company or situation often results in mutual appreciation of each institution's point of view and engenders respect for the rules and mores that characterize them. Historically, Japanese tend to leave an institution intact, even though the power base within the organization has changed entirely, so that the rules governing business methods will not be challenged. Relationships at this stage can be characterized as an effort not to confront but to bend or find loopholes in the rules to realize a common goal. Mary and Dr. Edwards, Matt, Jean, and Craig work behind the scenes, conscious that the surface situation has to be maintained to achieve their goals. Ken works around the unity of the *keiretsu* system and at the same time extends his contacts within that system. Tony, however, betrays the confidence of the go-between and nearly ruins his negotiation.

These cases illustrate the tremendous maneuvering behind the scenes in the "believe me" stage. Off-the-record meetings in bars and restaurants are important in developing resolutions to problems. Go-betweens—mediators who have a good working relationship with all parties—are sought regularly for their counsel. Silence is used instead of confrontation to express displeasure. In these ways, possible business scenarios are explored, and each side increases its understanding of the other without setting up an explicit win/lose environment. Optimally, discussions, crucial in smoothing over differences, are an effort to ensure that all parties become associates working toward a common goal.

The tone of the interaction in this phase is confidential and warm. Gift giving is personalized, designed to acknowledge the individual, and other thoughtful gestures such as extending invitations to exclusive resorts and restaurants are used to incur obligation. The resulting friendships have a pragmatic value, which can be confusing to Westerners who feel seduced by the constant attention. Because the interactions at this phase are founded on trust, any wrongdoing is immediately addressed and apologized for in person. Taking responsibility shows sincerity and reveals character. Tony is directed by his mentor to apologize for his transgression. Ken uses an apology to ease difficult situations and to extend his contacts.

Negotiation through the use of documentation is important in doing business with the Japanese at all stages. However, in a working relationship, documentation serves the purpose of avoiding direct confrontation and shows diligent preparation that allows situations to speak for themselves and encourages more cordiality in negotiations. Craig, Matt, and Ken use documentation in their negotiations to help seal personal relationships between negotiators. The documents must be well presented, and it is advisable to have a technical expert on hand to answer questions as they arise.

The stories in this section illuminate the way Japanese operate and work together in their own companies and in negotiations during the "believe me" phase where some trust has already been established. This working phase of the relationships deepens the obligations and extends networks for all involved. At this stage, the issue is not whether the parties can work together, but rather how they will accomplish the goal of a successful interaction.

MARY: How to Say No

Mary sat in the office of Yamada, her boss for 2 ½ years, and lifted her Limoges teacup. She knew Yamada was aware of the purpose of the meeting, an advance in pay and also an extension of her vacation time so she could visit her mother in the States, who had just had a stroke. Mary had prepared Yamada for her visit by casually mentioning both concerns to a Japanese colleague.

Mary smiled. She'd learned a great deal in the 2 ½ years she'd been working as a writer and editor for a Japanese government agency located in Paris. Agency employees served the Japanese foreign ministry, as well as economic and political analysts also employed there. Her job was to edit in English, and in many cases write original speeches in English for the Japanese. Although the work itself was difficult enough, working in a Japanese environment was often much more taxing than she'd anticipated. She had worked hard to understand the Japanese, she thought, as she watched Yamada sip his tea. There were so many incidents she had handled correctly by trusting her instincts.

She'd been working at the job only a week when Yamada called her on a Saturday morning at her home. His voice had a frantic edge and she listened attentively, fearing she'd made some terrible mistake at the office. "I am worried about my window," he said.

"Your window," she answered.

"Yes, it won't open."

"Your window won't open," she repeated, dumbfounded, wondering if this was some Japanese code for a terrible mishap.

Yamada continued. He sounded almost in tears. "It was so hot last night I couldn't sleep. Our baby has a rash and cried all night. There was no air."

"Did you call your landlady?" Mary asked weakly.

There was a pause. She repeated the question. There was another pause. Finally she said, "I'll call your landlady."

She sensed that on the other end of the line Yamada was smiling.

In the following weeks there were more requests. Yamada's dishwasher broke, and Mary spent the better part of a week locating the broken part. The daughter of Yamada's assistant needed help with her French homework. The only time she had available was on Saturday morning. Mary agreed to tutor her.

When Yamada's boss in Tokyo lost his expensive gloves, Mary spent several days questioning hotels and restaurants before the gloves turned up; Mary sent them to Tokyo with a note signed by Yamada. Other staff members who worked for the Japanese at the agency chided her about her search for the gloves, saying Mary was being used. Two weeks after she sent the gloves to Tokyo, a top member of the foreign ministry knocked on her door, bowed, and handed her a beautifully wrapped present. "Thank you for helping," he said, backing out of the room.

Mary's desire to do well was also evident in her perfectionist approach to her work. She'd read a great deal on economics and liked to discuss current economic issues. Six months after she was hired, she was asked to correct an article by Watanabe, a senior economist, which was to be published in a prominent newspaper. Mary had an unusually good rapport with Watanabe and in the past had spent many enjoyable hours discussing issues such as culture shock with him. Watanabe also had a good sense of humor, and Mary looked forward to their collaboration on the article.

Since Mary knew a great deal about economics and enjoyed writing, she spent hours on the article, sending it back repeatedly to Watanabe with extensive corrections. By the fifth draft, Watanabe was clearly irritated, but Mary was still not satisfied. On the Friday before the article was due, Mary stayed late and brought the corrected version to Watanabe in person. He was talking to Yamada, her boss, when she entered the room. As she handed Watanabe the article and asked for another change, Watanabe made a derogatory remark in Japanese to Yamada. They both laughed.

Mary flushed, looked at the ground, and bit her lip. Now was the time, she thought, to calmly point out the accuracy of her corrections; she would make her point and leave. However, when she looked up at Yamada, his face was bright red and his eyes evaded both hers and Watanabe's. She took a deep breath, realizing at once that

Yamada understood the situation and that although she'd lost face, a direct confrontation would only exacerbate the problem. She remained in the office until Watanabe had made the necessary emendation and then left.

The article received excellent reviews and Watanabe took her to lunch with other senior staffers to celebrate. Mary continued to be pleasant at the office but avoided any unnecessary meetings. On several occasions Watanabe tried to engage her in conversation, but she always made an excuse and left the room. Mary never referred to the article and when Yamada told her Watanabe deeply appreciated her help, she answered, "I guess I just must have driven him nuts." The subject was never mentioned again.

Six months after the article appeared, Adachi, a new senior manager, arrived from Tokyo. He sent a memo to all five non-Japanese female personnel asking for their "help" in making visitors more comfortable by serving tea. The implication of the memo was that those serving tea would also be responsible for washing up. The memo caused a great deal of consternation among the female staff members, and three refused to comply. The Japanese in turn were upset by the women's anger. Adachi invested in expensive Limoges teacups to emphasize the importance of tea service. The tension lasted for several weeks.

One Monday morning Alice, a British secretary, ran into Mary's office. "The teacups are dirty!" she exclaimed. "They're in the kitchen just waiting to be washed. The staff must have had a meeting over the weekend. Who do they think we are anyway? I'm going straight to Adachi, and tell him that we're not his bloody servants. I'm going . . ."

"Wait," Mary interrupted gently, "wait, don't do anything."

"You don't expect me to wash their dirty dishes! These cups are not being used by visitors. It was an internal meeting. Let them do it themselves," she fumed. "Their memo said they needed our help with visitors. They have to realize we are professionals, not their mothers. I just won't do it. I'm going to tell him off."

"I know what the memo said," Mary replied. "Don't wash the cup, don't confront Adachi-san. Don't do anything. Those cups will be washed."

"They aren't going to wash them themselves," Alice replied. "I think we should explain to Adachi the principle of the thing. It's the principle."

"They know the principle," Mary replied. "Just wait. Talk to the other women. Don't do anything."

Alice left the office upset. Every morning that week, the other four female office workers noted the dirty cups in the kitchen, but at Mary's insistence they neither mentioned the cups nor washed them. Visitors were served tea from the old cups. On the following Monday morning Alice bounded into Mary's office. "They're washed!" she announced. Mary smiled.

Now Yamada leaned back in his chair. "Take as much time as you want. A mother's illness is important. I'll arrange for you to have all the money you need. If you require anything else, please just ask, Mary."

Mary smiled and picked up a teacup, turning it so the pink flower faced her. Yamada also lifted his cup. "The tea is good," he said.

"Yes," Mary answered simply, "the tea is good."

Analysis:

The implicit nature of Japanese language affects behavior and compounds the issues of face. When possible, Japanese will avoid explicit statements even in the "believe me" stage of the relationship. This is especially true in the day-to-day situations that evolve in a working group where maintaining harmony is a priority. Situations will be hinted at, but often real dilemmas will be solved through gesture or use of a go-between. Westerners, who believe unfair or problematic situations must be addressed directly to redress a wrong or at the very least to "clear the air," are often bewildered and even angered by the lack of forthrightness in Japan.

Although Mary has no knowledge of Japanese culture, she understands that Yamada's desperate phone call about something as easily solvable as a stuck window is really a request for solidarity. She correctly senses that Japanese culture "expects" commitment from its employees beyond those most Westerners regard as acceptable. Small personal favors incur obligation on both sides. There is a correlation between the amount of trust invested in an employee and that employee's willingness to go beyond the letter of his or her contract.

Meticulous attention to detail is noted as is the spirit (gishin) with which these requests are carried out, particularly the sincerity of commitment. In order to be accepted into the "believe me" and "marry me" phases of the relationship, employees are expected to invest themselves totally in their jobs. Although it appears that Yamada is helpless and asking for a dependent relationship (amae), both Mary and Yamada understand that Yamada's personal requests are made in the context of a professional situation. Mary might never be close to Yamada, but through her actions she can impart the feeling that she is committed to him as part of her work. Although Mary is ridiculed by her European colleagues for spending the better part of a week locating the gloves, she is rewarded with a gift presented by a traveling top Japanese official, evidence that Mary is gaining a reputation.

When Mary feels her professional integrity is at stake, she concentrates on making Watanabe's article perfect. Watanabe's remark is an insult to Mary, but he has been shown up in front of a colleague. By putting her personal desires for perfection above the situation, Mary has not paid attention to Watanabe's shame (haji). Mary should have pulled back and acted selflessly (jibun ga nai) in favor of the situation or well-being of the group, by approaching Watanabe in private. By being too invested in her determination to be right, Mary has lost sight of her goal to gain trust, which she had so carefully pursued in the glove incident.

Although Watanabe's comments make her angry, Mary is wise enough to show her displeasure through a skillful retreat rather than through complaints. Even when Yamada proves he is an adept manager by acting on his own accord as a go-between, saying how much Watanabe appreciated her help, Mary closes the conversation by taking the blame on herself, saying she "must have driven him nuts." Mary has learned to reveal displeasure and anger without addressing the problem directly, and without disturbing the group. In addition, she has learned the role of apology (moshiwake gozaimasen) by assuming responsibility for any upset. Mary clears past wrongs in the "believe me" stage of the relationship where everyone is committed to working with each other.

Mary puts these lessons to work when confronted with the unwashed teacups. Like her colleague Alice, Mary is taken aback by

Adachi's memo implying that the female staff must not only serve tea to guests but wash and dry the cups as well. Upset by the staff's hostility, Adachi buys Limoges teacups to emphasize the importance of complying with his request.

In this situation, Mary deals with Adachi by simply not complying with Adachi's directive. Visitors were served from old cups while the Limoges remained unwashed. Mary understands from her observations that in a direct confrontation even if a Japanese becomes confused and gives in, the instigator will be relegated to the "outer world"; thus, even if she wins the battle she loses the war. Her advice to take a passive-aggressive stance brings home the staff's point of view and reveals their potential power as a working group.

The attitude of "losing to win" and turning an opponent's aggressive behavior against himself is common in the "believe me" stage of the relationship. Everybody has an investment in keeping the harmony of the group. The Japanese in authority are reluctant to dictate in this case because they realize the situation has progressed so far that they will lose eventually even if they win in the short run.

Yamada's trust in Mary does not stem from her compliance and subservient behavior, but rather from her understanding of situations and her appreciation of the need for harmony in the Japanese working group. For instance, with the teacups Mary has neither documented the incident nor involved outside authority. She has solved the problem internally.

Yamada appreciates Mary's care. For instance, she has taken the trouble through go-betweens to warn him about the nature of her request before the meeting. Yamada understands that Mary knows her limits as an employee, and he is comfortable with her because of this knowledge. As part of Yamada's group, Mary finds that her individual needs and her wishes are respected.

DAVE: Reneging on a Contract While Expanding Relationships

Dave Ritter ran his index finger down the column of figures for the third time. Ultra Beam Electronics was losing at least a million dollars a month to develop a component that they would sell to Yamashoji for $200 apiece. Ultra Beam wouldn't even get credit because the product was destined for incorporation into the Yamashoji system. What kind of naiveté had allowed Ultra Beam to sign such a one-sided contract? The Yamashoji contract must have slipped through the cracks in the last year while Ultra Beam was reorganizing all its departments. Lack of research was the real problem, Dave decided, as he picked up the phone and dialed Bud Stone, Ultra Beam's president.

"Bud, Dave here."

"Yes, Dave." Bud's tone was friendly. Dave had known Bud for over twenty years. It was at Bud's recommendation that Dave had gone to Japan as Ultra Beam's representative. Bud had even supported Dave's request to study Japanese at an intensive language program first. Dave spent four productive years in Japan before returning to Ultra Beam's U.S. headquarters two years ago.

"It's about the Yamashoji contract."

"I've seen the figures," Bud said. "I don't think it's a good bet for Ultra Beam."

"No, it's not."

"I can't understand how this happened," Bud continued. "We have to cut bait. You worked in Japan for four years. There must be a way of getting out of a bad deal. The legal fees will be enormous."

"Let's try and keep the lawyers out of this."

Bud was silent.

"It's important to remain on good terms," Dave said. Even though he could almost hear Bud's opposition, Dave couldn't explain the importance of that statement to Bud or to any American. When he had tried to do so in the past, Bud had always told him that he lived in a dream world and that Ultra Beam's lawyers were usually successful in handling business problems.

However, Dave had learned the hard way that creating an enemy in Japan was to be avoided at all costs. The Japanese had long memories. Ultra Beam's executives wanted the considerable business the firm had done over the years with Yamashoji to continue if not expand. At least in that, Dave thought, Ultra Beam's long-term strategy was in accord with Japan.

Bud's voice was nervous. "Dave, you still there?"

"Yes, let's call the others. I want the Board to be involved in this as well."

"We're behind you, Dave."

During the next few days Ultra Beam held several meetings at its home office involving various levels of management, including the development group. The American engineers and management agreed that the costs were prohibitive and the Yamashoji contract must be terminated. Upper management, including the Board, was convinced that, with his Japan experience, Dave was the only one to handle the job. Dave was reluctant about accepting the assignment until Ultra Beam agreed to give him the necessary time, independence, and financial support.

Dave quickly set up a meeting with Nada, senior vice president of Yamashoji Electronics, in Yamashoji's corporate offices in downtown Tokyo. Dave opened the meeting with a clear statement of the impossibility of the situation for Ultra Beam.

"We are looking at one million dollars per month for development of a two-hundred-dollar item that will be sold as part of Yamashoji's system. It doesn't make financial sense. Development is proceeding slowly. We are just at the beginning stages. Now is the time to stop. It is not too late."

Nada bowed his head. He remained in this position for several seconds. "You have made a commitment," he said. "This is serious. You had time to study the proposal before you signed. Plenty of time. Yamashoji Electronics has made commitments to its customers.

That is also serious. Frankly speaking, you must keep your commitments." Nada wiped his brow.

The room was silent. Dave glanced at the clock. He was used to the silences at meetings in Japan. As he'd foreseen, it would be a long road to an amicable solution.

During the next few weeks, several letters were exchanged between Nada and Dave. Dave politely and patiently repeated his case: the situation was unrealistic from Ultra Beam's point of view. Nada responded in the same tone, reiterating again the importance of commitment in Japan.

Two months later, another meeting was held, this time at Yamashoji's American headquarters in Detroit. Each side restated its position and there seemed to be no solution. Dave remained firm in his stance; this time he also said that although some components had been completed, there would be no shipment until the terms of termination of the contract had been worked out. "You should understand that we cannot make these shipments if we don't know the future. The future will determine all business arrangements."

Nada stared at the table.

Dave's voice became gentle. "Our financial planning office is very strict."

Nada looked up and nodded.

Another battery of letters followed. Nada involved a middle manager, Kobayashi. Dave noted that the tone of Kobayashi's letters was not as rigid. He asked other Yamashoji managers about Kobayashi's background and found that Kobayashi, who had never worked with Nada before, had a reputation for technical excellence and for fair play. When Kobayashi suggested a meeting midway, they agreed on Alaska. Dave was pleased the meeting would not be in another Yamashoji office building.

It rained in Anchorage on the morning of the meeting, but by afternoon the sun was out, and Dave's spirits were buoyed by the crisp air. Kobayashi and two engineers represented Yamashoji. Dave brought two engineers from the development division at Ultra Beam who had been working with the Yamashoji engineers on developing the component that would be sold as part of the Yamashoji system. Dave's engineers had prepared data relevant to expense and projected time of development.

Dave began the meeting with a discussion of the history of the situation. Although he did not shrink from Ultra Beam's responsibility, he also pointed out that the development of the project was at an early stage. Even though any tampering with a commitment was a severe offense, he restated that the expense of continuing the project was prohibitive considering the product cost only $200, and was destined to be part of a Yamashoji system.

Kobayashi listened patiently. "I understand," he said briefly, "but you must also understand Yamashoji's position. We keep our customers for years. We can do this because our customers believe that Yamashoji will keep its commitments, no matter how small or how large. Ultra Beam and Yamashoji have done business for years. Yamashoji trusted your commitment enough to make promises to our customers. In Japan that is important."

The room was silent. Dave shifted his position in his chair slightly and hung his head. He concentrated on imitating the pained expression he'd witnessed in Japanese counterparts when they were presented with situations of unresolvable conflict, sudden change of plans, or an inability to right a wrong. Now, with his head lowered, his brow creased, and his legs pressed against the side of the chair, Dave revealed through his posture Ultra Beam's acceptance of its responsibility for the problem.

Kobayashi cleared his throat. "Yamashoji will take two thousand components that meet regulation standards. When Yamashoji has received the two thousand, all R and D will cease and Ultra Beam will have no further obligations."

Dave slowly straightened his back. It was the first breakthrough in the case. Yamashoji had agreed in essence to terminate the contract early. Whether the figure would be two thousand or less would be agreed on later. It was the principle—an early termination—that was important. He sighed with relief.

Problems like the quality of the components could be addressed later. Like most other Japanese companies, Yamashoji had rigorous standards of quality. For the American engineers at Ultra Beam a working component was a good component; for Yamashoji engineers the component had to comply with certain specifications at each stage of its development.

Kobayashi's face was remarkably open. Dave decided to use

Kobayashi's obvious goodwill to address a different issue. He flicked a slide on the screen and began to explain the problem of the delivery timetable of another product.

Kobayashi's voice was loud. "Turn that machine off. If you continue to show those slides there will be no more meetings."

Dave pushed the off button. He sat back and decided that he liked Kobayashi and his straightforward manner.

The next week Dave arranged for another meeting to be held in a month in the continental United States. Kobayashi and the same two engineers came from the Yamashoji side. Dave brought only one engineer. The discussion centered around lowering the number of components Ultra Beam was obligated to produce before Ultra Beam's R&D efforts on components would cease. Kobayashi was adamant about sticking with the two thousand. Dave left the meeting determined to acquire more data.

In the following weeks Dave reviewed all Ultra Beam's business with Yamashoji. He also interviewed both the Japanese and Americans who were working on the joint R&D project. Dave's analysis found that in addition to the problem of differences in quality control, there were personnel problems.

He checked the Japanese engineers carefully. Many problems stemmed from Kanda, a Yamashoji senior engineer, who refused to cooperate because certain specifications had not been met. Because the components worked after repeated testing, Ultra Beam's own engineers were satisfied and refused to consider Kanda's objections. Dave had casually asked several managers at Yamashoji about Kanda and they reported that Kanda might be difficult.

During this period Dave continued to correspond with Kobayashi. His letters were warm, and he often followed a fax with a phone call. Kobayashi agreed to meet in a month's time in Tokyo.

Kobayashi's brief introduction at that meeting was friendly. He expressly gave Dave greetings from Nada. Dave noted the two engineers also appeared relaxed. Dave responded in kind and entered into the spirit of the meeting by describing Ultra Beam's long history with Yamashoji.

Kobayashi spoke slowly. "Yamashoji needs more parts for the teaching machine."

Dave nodded. He knew Yamashoji was low on these other parts

that Ultra Beam routinely supplied. He also knew that Yamashoji could not get these other parts easily from another vendor and was prepared to use this fact in the negotiation. "It will be delicate to ship any parts until this situation is resolved. In fact it will be impossible." Dave said as he flipped through some overhead view graphs describing the expense of the current project and the lack of ultimate financial incentives for Ultra Beam. Dave knew Kobayashi was aware of the figures and the fact that it would take at least four months for Ultra Beam to manufacture the much-needed teaching-machine component. The graphs merely underscored the seriousness of the situation.

Dave continued. "Ultra Beam feels that two thousand components is an unreasonable number. Also the price per component of two hundred dollars is too low."

For the next three hours Kobayashi and Dave argued over the figures. Kobayashi dug in his heels. Dave took a deep breath. He only had one ace left—Kanda. Given the man's reputation for unpleasantness, it had been an act of bad faith on the part of Yamashoji to include Kanda in such a delicate joint venture. However, Dave also knew that creating an enemy in a Japanese company was dangerous and that company people, no matter what the situation, were likely to support one another. Dave took a deep breath, deciding to take a chance. "Kanda has been giving Ultra Beam's engineers a lot of trouble," he said.

Dave waited. The room was silent. Kobayashi twiddled his pencil. The other engineers stared at the floor.

"Okay," Kobayashi said suddenly. "If Ultra Beam produces five hundred components by July 1, the price for each component will be fifteen hundred dollars. This will end Ultra Beam's obligations and will be the conclusion of a successful project."

Dave controlled his smile and nodded seriously to everything Kobayashi said. The deal was done, he thought. Two years and seven months and nearly thirty million dollars later, Ultra Beam had terminated the project.

Kobayashi and the Yamashoji engineers were also smiling. They would supply some of their contracted customers and report that the development of a workable component meant the project had been a success. Other customers could be steered elsewhere. Business with Ultra Beam would continue and perhaps even expand. After all, Kobayashi and Dave knew each other well now and a certain trust had developed. The engineers had even tacitly supported Dave's criticism of Kanda. Although everything was now in order, Dave wondered whether perhaps he should even have mentioned Kanda. The Yamashoji engineers were too quiet on the subject and though the mention of Kanda's unprofessional behavior had yielded short-term results, the long-term effect of an enemy at Yamashoji could be a real liability.

Dave brushed away his dark thoughts and looked at the satisfied faces around the room. Kobayashi and the other Yamashoji engineers were talking amiably with the Ultra Beam engineers. There were no lawyers in the room. Kobayashi was a new friend at Yamashoji for Ultra Beam. Yes, the project was certainly a success, Dave decided. And yet the thought of Kanda still nagged at him. Perhaps he should have let that one alone, after all.

Analysis:

The Confucian system of settling disputes out of court underscores Japanese awareness that, as members of a small island nation, all Japanese are part of one system, and it is to everyone's advantage to keep that system functioning smoothly. Japanese routinely make efforts to avoid use of the courts in the settlement of disputes at every stage. Despite the facts that many Japanese receive legal training and every company has a legal department, litigation is the last recourse in solving differences. Westerners often find confusing the importance placed on extending the relationship in terms of trust and commitment during a time of disagreement and hard negotiation.

The president of Ultra Beam, who realizes he must cut off the Yamashoji deal, wants lawyers to start negotiations to break the contract. In spite of misgivings, Ultra Beam wisely commits to Dave's plan to negotiate the conditions of the termination. The American home office of any firm doing extensive business with the Japanese has to appreciate the importance of maintaining its networks as components of trust. In Japanese business practice hard-earned trust remains crucial. Japanese will make every effort to maintain a relationship that is in the "believe me" phase (they are not as committed in the earlier "know me" and "trust me" stages).

Dave's straightforward strategy for negotiation is common where there has been trust developed by working together in the "believe me" phase of interactions with Japanese. He accepts blame for signing the contract. This admission of guilt (moshiwake gozaimasen) *is important in Japan and is used to maintain order in the Japanese system. While apology is crucial at all phases of relationships, it is particularly effective in terms of correcting difficulties in the "believe me" phase. In the "know me" and "trust me" stages, the bonding is superficial and therefore the apology carries less weight.*

At the same time Dave stands firm that the R&D is too costly given the retail price of the final product. Thus, Dave provides a framework for discussing the problem. He does not surprise the Japanese or try to outwit them. This is important in a society where decisions are made by a group (ringi) *and proposals are systematically circulated horizontally and then vertically for approval* (ringi seido) *(in this system, employees are given a voice that depends on accuracy of information and precludes surprises).*

In the succeeding meeting in Detroit both sides repeat the same arguments. Dave's threats of non-delivery of components are logical. He also defuses the situation by mentioning pressure from the financial planning division of Ultra Beam. Using internal pressure as a basis for negotiation avoids more personalized attacks.

Dave's claims at the Anchorage meeting are backed by research into finance and personalities. Dave understands the role of silence and body language, using both effectively to reveal his discomfort with the situation. Finally, he has prepared his strategy carefully and links the current impasse in negotiation with other longstanding business deals by making it clear that for Ultra Beam and Yamashoji to continue in business, this situation must be resolved. Only once does Dave show his lack of reverence for the seriousness of a particular negotiation by introducing a wholly new topic: the delivery timetable for a different product. This sudden and seemingly arbitrary switch of agenda shows poor planning and is therefore a breach of Japanese etiquette (saho), *values that are equated with virtue in Japan.*

Only in the final negotiation does Dave use information that enters into the personal arena. In a tense moment Dave refers to Kanda's troublesome behavior. At this point Dave feels comfortable about his comments because his research has revealed Kanda's "difficult" repu-

tation, and that by sending such a person to the joint venture Yamashoji is reneging on its obligation (on) to the project. Dave understands that according to Japanese tradition, Yamashoji's preparation should have involved research on the character of the Japanese engineers destined for the joint project. From interviews with Japanese engineers, Dave appreciates that the Japanese regret assigning Kanda to the project. Preparation means commitment in Japan, and Dave decides to use this information about the Japanese lack of preparation to gain advantage. However, Dave also understands that there are no secrets in Japan. Kanda will harbor a grudge against Ultra Beam, and at some point may take revenge. This scenario is especially true when people who are involved in the same organization have certain expectations of dependence.

The final agreement satisfies Yamashoji, and the R&D project is declared a success, proven by the delivery of the promised components. Patience (nintai) has proven invaluable in maintaining harmony between the two companies. Business will undoubtedly expand through the guidance of Dave and Kobayashi. The two men have learned to trust each other, as have the Japanese and American engineers who have worked on the joint venture. However, Dave is still uneasy. In hindsight he realizes that Ultra Beam's short-term gains in questioning Yamashoji's choice of Kanda for the project might not be worth the long-term liability of Kanda's hatred.

TONY: Confidentiality

Tony lifted the receiver. The joint venture between TV Associates and SNK was a year old now and had gone more smoothly than he dared imagine. Hori, the go-between, who had done business with both SNK and TV Associates for years, had been crucial. In fact Hori had introduced Tony to Murata, SNK's president, at an exclusive golf club in Tokyo just after Tony's arrival in Japan.

It was when Tony decided to negotiate with SNK for the early return of Sato, a key negotiator and engineer, that Tony knew Hori was the right choice as go-between. Sato had been "lent" to the joint venture with SNK for four years. However, TV Associates was developing a new technology with another Japanese company and needed Sato to facilitate the deal because he understood that technology so well. Hori agreed immediately to help Tony negotiate with SNK.

Tony grinned, thinking how business in Japan was not so difficult once you understood the principles. Even the contract between TV Associates and SNK was based on trust—Japanese style. Just like the books said, he thought. That trust and Hori's counsel had permitted Sato to return early to TV Associates from TV Associates' joint venture with SNK. Everyone said you couldn't change the terms of a contract in Japan, but the early return of Sato to TV Associates had proven the naysayers wrong. Now he would tell Hori about the previous night's dinner with SNK.

"Hori-san," Tony's voice was warm.

"Ah, Holm-san," Hori replied.

"I called to let you know about last night's dinner."

Hori was silent.

"It went very well," Tony continued. "SNK seems happy with the joint venture. Even President Murata of SNK was there. We had many toasts to TV Associates and SNK's future."

Hori was again silent.

Tony spoke more rapidly. "I thanked Murata for returning Sato to

TV Associates. Getting Sato back two years early is wonderful. I want to thank you also for all the behind-the-scenes work."

Silence.

Tony was running out of things to say. He cleared his throat and tried to think. Because Hori's talkativeness often irritated him, Tony wondered if Hori was ill.

Hori cleared his throat. "May I speak frankly if I can, Holm-san? You made a bad mistake. You must apologize to SNK, today."

"Apologize? What for?"

"For bad behavior. You must take a gift to Murata's office and bow many times. You must go today."

"But . . ."

The phone clicked.

Tony leaned back in his chair. What had gone wrong? Apologize for what? It was a perfect meeting: the food, the sake, the comradery. He'd waited until the end of the dinner when everyone was mellow to thank Murata. Hori had told him just the night before that everything had been fixed: the SNK board had voted that Sato be allowed to return to TV Associates early.

Tony had been so careful, so Japanese. All the details had been well thought out.

With Hori's help, the negotiations for Sato's early return to TV Associates had begun nearly a year ago. Tony first broached the subject casually at a quarterly meeting review with Miyasu, the joint venture man from SNK, by making a general statement that people lent to the joint venture might be rotated back to their companies sooner. He did not mention any names. Miyasu agreed and said he would discuss it with SNK.

At a luncheon meeting with Miyasu about a month later, Tony brought up the subject of Sato's early return to TV Associates and mentioned that Sato could be replaced by another capable man from TV Associates. Then he talked a great deal about the good qualities of Omura, who would take Sato's place at the joint venture. Aware that Miyasu would check his information, Tony had gone to some length to do homework on Omura. During successive meetings over the next four months, Tony brought up the issue of rotation. Miyasu was noncommittal but did not seem to oppose the idea.

By the time almost ten months had passed since TV Associates had started negotiations for Sato's early return, Tony was getting pressure from his Board to begin preparing for the negotiation of the new contract where he needed Sato's help. With Hori's help, Tony formalized the situation by sending a memo on January 10 to SNK asking that June be set as a compromise date for the rotation of Sato back into TV Associates. On the same day, Tony promoted Sato to vice president within TV Associates to be sure Sato was recognized as valuable to TV Associates.

SNK responded on January 15. They were very optimistic about the rotation because of the credentials of the new man, Omura.

On January 30 Hori called to say that SNK had voted for the rotation of Sato back to TV Associates. Hori whispered that SNK's agreement was mainly due to TV Associates' recognition of Sato through his new title.

"Why?" Tony asked. Hori smiled a knowing smile, as if Tony was just playing dumb.

Tony was confounded when he heard that Sato's promotion was the reason SNK agreed to his return, because that decision had had nothing to do with the present negotiations with SNK. He mentioned this again to Hori, who looked bewildered and changed the subject.

A dinner meeting with SNK was held in a private room at a small Japanese restaurant, with three people from SNK and three people from TV Associates in attendance. The mood was light and Tony learned that Murata liked to climb mountains in Nepal. Since Tony also liked to climb, they made a tentative date to look at slides of various climbs. When dinner drew to a close Tony was flushed with triumph at his ability in handling the complexities of the negotiation. All his suggestions and planting the seeds had worked out better than he expected. Every American instinct to just lay it all out on the table had been buried. He was becoming an expert on Japan, he decided. He filled Murata's sake cup.

"Thank you for allowing Sato's early return to TV Associates. I know it was trouble."

Murata became grave. "Don't mention it . . . nothing . . . nothing," Murata said hurriedly. He waved his hand in front of his face, paid the bill, and stood. The other Japanese followed.

·   ·   ·

At the time Tony hadn't given this hurried departure much thought. Now he was really confused. It was clear that Hori had given him the correct information. Should he have mentioned it to Murata only in private? But why? Sato's return would soon be public knowledge.

Under the circumstances, perhaps giving Murata a book on Nepal was too personal. Tony decided on a book on Philadelphia, the hometown of TV Associates. He stood and practiced bowing his head almost to his waist. Halfway through the bow, Tony felt ridiculous. He straightened quickly and dialed SNK's number.

"Holm from TV Associates. I would like an appointment with Murata-san today."

The secretary hesitated. "Just a moment." Tony began to perspire. The telephone, on hold, played Bing Crosby singing "White Christmas." What if Murata was too angry to see him? He'd heard that business relationships could be that way: one minute, friends; the next, cut out of everything. The music stopped when the secretary came back on the line.

Tony thanked her for a two o'clock appointment. He put down the telephone and thought for a moment. Hori was waiting. He dialed Hori's number, knowing that he had to call but almost certain that Hori already knew of his appointment with Murata.

At two Tony was seated in a conference room in Murata's office. Murata talked pleasantly about the joint venture and joked about the weather. By two-thirty, Tony felt exhausted. He stood and bowed low. "Please excuse last night," he said briefly and handed Murata the book on Philadelphia.

Murata put the gift to one side. For a moment the room was still. Murata was still seated. Finally Murata said in a soft voice. "Sit down, Holm-san. I understand. Sit down."

Tony was about to apologize again, but Murata was talking about future business plans. His voice was even, and gradually Tony also joined the discussion.

Analysis:

Much of Japanese business is settled behind the scenes through a combination of the use of go-betweens and informal discussions. Although these off-the-record negotiations are routine and expected, they require tact, subtle acknowledgment of complexities, and atten-

tion to the sensitivities of those involved. While this holds true for all stages of negotiation it is especially true during the "believe me" stage, where there is an assumption of trust.

At the start of the case, Hori acts out his role as a go-between by telling Tony to call SNK and apologize. As a liaison between TV Associates and SNK, Hori has been in touch with President Murata of SNK after the dinner and relates to Tony that Murata is angry with Tony's behavior. Hori insists that Tony apologize to Murata that day. Face-to-face apologies in Japanese culture are important. Taking responsibility for mistakes is crucial to establishing personal integrity, goes a long way to clearing one's name, and makes it possible to forgive the offender.

Hori is not only responsible for the off-the-record conversations between the two parties but is also responsible for smoothing over any misunderstandings that have occurred. The go-between's reputation depends on his ability to have all sides consider the negotiation a win/win situation. Thus, a go-between such as Hori who has considerable reputation in business and is at the "believe me" stage of the relationship with all parties is best suited for the role.

Tony feels he has acted in good faith and has done the things Japanese culture requires. Not only has he done considerable nemawashi (advance documentation and consultation) and prepared for the subject of Sato's return, but he also used Hori as his adviser to lay the groundwork. Tony is counting on Miyasu's appreciation of his extensive research on Omura's credentials as Sato's replacement for the job. Preparation of this sort means commitment and is valued by Japanese.

Nemawashi plays an important role in Japanese business practice. Even in the "believe me" or "marry me" stage, formal meetings only function to give an official stamp to what has already been decided through informal discussions. In order for these informal discussions to be effective, the "right" people have to be approached with the proposal. This determination of the correct group or person in a society so conscious of the linkage between group and rank (kata-gaki) is often in the hands of the go-between. The go-between must know both groups well in order to succeed.

When Tony simultaneously promotes Sato to define his position at TV Associates, the promotion is seen by SNK not as a personal reward for Sato, but as part of TV Associates' strategy to assure SNK of Sato's importance. Tony is surprised at Hori's acknowledgment of Sato's promotion, because he had not considered the status conscious-ness of the Japanese in his strategy. However, SNK considers all TV Associates' actions as related to the situation, not to an individual.

Before the dinner with SNK, Tony is delighted to learn from Hori that SNK's board has agreed to let Sato return to TV Associates early. The dinner with TV Associates is full of the usual good-hu-mored small talk. Toward the end of the evening Tony feels comfort-able enough to thank SNK for their decision.

Tony's comment reveals his use of Hori as a go-between and makes it clear that he has gained his knowledge of the decision of SNK's Board through a circuitous route. This public admission puts Murata of SNK, Hori (as the go-between), and Tony himself (as the orchestra-tor of a manipulation) in a compromising position. Tony should have waited for the official announcement, thus avoiding any admission of the off-the-record information sources. Although go-betweens and off-the-record meetings are used routinely in Japan, they are not referred to in public.

Murata's response is to leave the restaurant quickly. He cannot express his rage directly to Tony, because that would constitute public self-incrimination. Murata's only recourse is to call Hori. Hori in turn is justifiably angry because, as go-between, he is responsible for the behavior of all the parties involved. His reputation as an astute busi-nessman and as a go-between rests on his ability to settle disputes without disturbing the harmony by exposing the truth of a situation. (Later, Tony will pay amends to Hori by taking him out to dinner where they will discuss the situation.)

Tony must first apologize to Murata for his indiscretion. This must be done face-to-face with a gift. Tony's quick response tells Murata that the apology is sincere. Apologies in Japan are taken seriously as a way of restoring a serene surface to a given situation, especially in the "believe me" phase of a relationship where there has been involve-ment and commitment. They are also an obvious investment in a system. In addition, Tony's compliance with the system underscores Hori's role as a go-between and as a manager of the situation. Har-mony is restored through Tony's gesture because it reassures every-one that the system works.

HENRY: Gaining Authority on the Job

It'd been a long voyage to the corporate office at Yadi Electronics. He must remember to thank Ota, his boss, for arranging this unexpected honor. "Excuse me," said a young girl dressed in a black skirt and white blouse. She bowed, and served green tea. Henry muttered his thanks in Japanese. Brad, also a researcher from America, thanked the girl in English. After a year in Japan, Brad still didn't speak Japanese.

"Gentlemen," Suzuki, a corporate division section chief began, "Yadi Electronics was pleased to have you with us this year." He paused.

Henry bowed. "We were pleased to be here." Four Japanese including Suzuki smiled and nodded briefly. They exchanged pleasantries about the lateness of the rainy season. The clear skies meant it would be very bad in June, Suzuki insisted. The other men nodded and murmured their assent.

Brad cleared his throat. "Suzuki-san," Brad said, "I've been meaning to ask Yadi Electronics . . ."

Suzuki's face froze. The other Japanese shifted in their seats. Their polite laughter put Henry on edge. He wanted to reach out and pinch Brad's arm. What was he doing? Hadn't he learned anything? Inappropriate! Absurd!

"I've a friend, John North, who is interested in the business aspects of Japanese companies."

Suzuki tapped his pencil on the table. "How nice."

"He's a talented person," Brad continued without pause.

"How nice."

Henry groaned as Brad launched into John's background. The Japanese nodded sympathetically. Heartened by the smiles, Brad went into even more detail, describing John's college as "one of the best in the States." It was too late for Brad, Henry thought—Brad would never understand and Henry would never be able to explain.

It had taken him more than a year to learn what he knew now: over a year of feeling alone and often despondent, of wondering if he was saying the right thing, of pondering each decision, of smothering questions that automatically popped into his head. He recalled vividly his first bewildering days at the laboratory.

From the start Henry was grateful for the authority that his boss Ota allowed him. On the first day Ota had given Henry his own project.

"You know this area," Ota said briefly after ushering him to his desk. "Yukizaki-san will help you." He indicated the man sitting across from him, who immediately stood and bowed.

"Thank you," Henry answered, bowing to both Ota and Yukizaki.

The next day, eager to start work, Henry walked with Yukizaki from the dormitory to the laboratory. Yukizaki seemed amiable and when Henry asked him where the necessary equipment was kept, Yukizaki quickly showed him. As the day wore on, Henry needed more help and Yukizaki always obliged.

After six weeks, Henry felt comfortable in the laboratory. He knew where most of the equipment was located, and he also was beginning to produce some results. He noted that Ota's group was the largest in the laboratory. Henry smiled at his bench mate and asked, "Yukizaki-san, why is our group the largest in this section?"

"It's the largest, that's all," Yukizaki replied curtly.

"Oh, but . . ." Henry began to phrase another question, but Yukizaki had turned away.

"Does Onuma-san's group down the hall work on a similar area?" Henry asked in a smug tone. He was proud of his ability to observe situations.

Yukizaki gave him a hard look. "Why do you want to know? Do you want to join Onuma-san's group?"

Henry flushed at Yukizaki's harsh tone. Minutes later he made an excuse and left the room. His heart was still pounding as he went down the hall. What had he done wrong? Did Yukizaki really hate him? Was his friend Brad right about Japanese hating all foreigners? In the bathroom he splashed water on his face and tried to collect himself.

The following day Yukizaki's attitude had returned to normal. He smiled when Henry entered the room and offered him a cup of tea.

Henry relaxed: Yukizaki must have had a bad day yesterday, which could happen to anyone. "Yukizaki-san," Henry said, "what kind of work does Sugai-san do? It looks interesting."

Yukizaki's face froze. He put down his teacup and stared at the desk. "Are you a spy?" he asked unpleasantly.

Shaken, Henry blinked and also put his cup on the table. The tea leaves had settled to the bottom of the cup. He ran his fingers over the rim and tried to think.

In the weeks that followed Henry felt estranged. He no longer walked with Yukizaki from the dormitory to the laboratory each morning. At lunch he sat with Brad or alone at the back of the cafeteria. Although his work continued to go well, he felt more and more uncertain. In his imagination, he likened the laboratory to a jail. There were too many rules: books were not allowed to be stacked on desks above a certain level; all cups had to be thrown in the trash can, which was a five-minute walk from the laboratory; both sides of the computer paper had to be used, as was true of memo pads; certain entrances were reserved for employees above a certain rank. The dormitories even had a curfew.

The women's dorm was especially strict—the women were punished for lateness with telephone duty and other chores. He'd found that out during a chat with the caretaker of the women's dormitory, whom he'd met at a small bar on his way home from the laboratory. After several beers, the caretaker had produced a book of photos of women in his dormitory. "Do you like any?" the caretaker had asked, slyly flipping through the pages. Henry was so offended, he made an abrupt excuse and left.

All this put Henry in a terrible mood. The day after the episode with the dorm caretaker Henry was especially sensitive. He lowered his eyes whenever Yukizaki tried to start a conversation. It seemed that everybody in the laboratory was looking at him. He imagined the co-workers were talking about him when he passed. His heart fluttered when he walked across the room, and he was hyperventilating and sweating.

After taking a walk around the building to calm himself, he felt more in control. He smiled at Yukizaki. Yukizaki smiled cheerfully in return and showed him the latest results. As he leaned over Yukizaki's shoulder, he noticed a memo from Ota announcing a meeting about the work Henry had done. Next to the memo was a packet of information about the work.

"This looks like a nice packet."

"Yes," Yukizaki replied. "Very useful."

"I haven't received mine yet. I wonder if they have run out?"

Yukizaki was silent.

Henry let the pause stand for some moments. "May I see the packet?"

"Of course, I'll give it to you after I've read it."

As Henry went to his desk, he noticed that several desks had the same packet of information.

He waited all afternoon for his packet to arrive. By four o'clock he was feeling edgy. The meeting was scheduled for the next day. Yukizaki's packet had disappeared. In fact most of the packets on his colleagues' desks were gone. Taking a deep breath, he walked slowly over to Ota. "Excuse me," Henry said.

"Ah, Brown-san. How are you?"

"Fine, just fine," he answered in a low voice, using formal Japanese.

There was a long pause.

"Ota-san," Henry finally uttered. "I have not received a copy of the information for tomorrow's meeting."

Ota's face was blank. He toyed with his pencil. "Oh," he finally said. "Yes, of course."

Henry waited several more seconds but Ota did not finish the sentence. Feeling desperate, Henry returned to his desk. A few minutes later, Ota motioned to Yukizaki and they left the room together. Henry's heart pounded. He glanced at the door—nothing. When Yukizaki returned to his desk soon thereafter, Henry could not read his expression.

"It's almost five," Henry said. "May I have the papers?"

"I don't have them here."

Henry gritted his teeth. "Why not?"

"I lent them to a friend."

Henry was silent. Ota was chairing a small meeting at the other side of the office. Henry was sure it was about the larger meeting tomorrow. All the key players except for Yukizaki were there. It was his work, Henry thought bitterly. They were having a meeting on his baby. Hadn't he made the big advances in this project? Hadn't he made things happen?

The next morning Henry arrived at the laboratory early. The meeting was scheduled for eleven-thirty. He was determined to speak to Ota before the meeting. By ten Ota hadn't arrived. Yukizaki and some scientists working on the project were reviewing some data. When Henry sauntered over, the group fell silent. He stood grinning stupidly for several moments before making an excuse and returning to his seat. At ten forty-five Ota appeared.

"Ota-san," Henry began slowly, "good morning."

"Good morning, Brown-san," Ota replied.

Henry mopped his forehead. He was perspiring heavily. Involuntarily he glanced at Yukizaki and the others and cleared his throat. Ota continued to smile pleasantly. "I'd like to attend the meeting," he blurted.

"Oh, yes, the meeting," Ota repeated.

"Yes, it's on my work."

Ota made a noise in back of his throat. The room was silent. It seemed everyone had stopped talking. Henry felt Yukizaki's eyes boring through him. "I have to ask," Ota finally said.

Henry stood for several minutes before returning to his seat. It was now five minutes after eleven. He picked up a magazine and began reading the table of contents. Minutes went by. At eleven-fifteen, Ota walked to Henry's desk and drew up a chair. "Brown-san," he said softly, "it's about the meeting. I should tell you this meeting is about marketing. Price issues will be discussed. It's a sensitive area. I'm afraid it's not a good idea for you to attend that meeting."

"Of course," Henry said quickly, without looking up. "I understand. Marketing issues, of course." He heard Ota's retreat. Marketing *was* a sensitive area, Henry thought; he'd never felt like such a fool. The magazine in front of him blurred. He waited several minutes until the room cleared for the meeting, then he slowly walked out of the building. At the small *soba* shop around the corner he quaffed several beers.

During the next weeks Henry worked hard on the project. He read memos and weekly reports by the group and asked few questions. Yukizaki and Ota continued to be friendly. Stirred by the rumor that

MITI was funding a new project, Ota was busy researching the feasibility of a project. Since the project was in Henry's field, Ota frequently consulted him and Yukizaki. Yukizaki was in favor of a demo project, but privately Henry thought that a demo was a bad idea.

Instead, Henry believed that Yadi Electronic should initiate a full research project on the topic. He pressed for a meeting for which he prepared extensively. After several requests Ota scheduled the meeting. Ota started the meeting by explaining the project in detail. Henry saw that Yukizaki took notes, although he knew the information. Then Ota asked for opinions. Seizing his chance, Henry launched into a detailed plan for immediate research. He handed out data to support his idea. Ota nodded as Henry explained how his research tied in with the new project. Henry was proud of the background material he'd collected and frequently pointed to various charts to prove his points. Ota murmured as he pored over the data. Then there was silence in the room.

When Ota raised his head, he said with consideration, "Very interesting. You have done a great deal of work. Very good idea. We will start with a demo." Ota nodded at Yukizaki.

Henry sat back, not believing his ears. He'd prepared so carefully. What more could he have done? His color-coded charts were up to date. He had worked for hours on their presentation and bought the supplies himself. It was obvious from the data he presented that a demo was a waste of time and money. Ota bowed his customary dismissal. Henry left the room.

In the days that followed, Henry continued to work hard. He attended weekly meetings on the demo and asked questions only when he thought it might contribute to the direction of the discussion.

He also worked with Ota on a paper that was to be submitted that spring to a professional journal. Henry was pleased with the results. In late April he realized that he hadn't seen the last draft of the paper in some weeks. He asked Ota if he might review a copy. Ota demurred for several days.

Finally early one morning Henry found a copy on his desk. The paper was in order but the cover page stated that a patent would be filed on the work. Henry hadn't heard of a patent. He immediately went to Ota's office.

"The paper looks good," Henry said quietly.

"Yes." Ota smiled.

"The patent should be interesting."

Ota was silent. He looked at the paper and then out his window. Henry was also silent. Ota sipped his tea. The large clock in Ota's office counted the seconds. Ota had not moved. At one minute, Henry was still counting.

"The patent is in rough form," Ota finally said.

Henry cleared his throat. There was another long pause.

"You can see the patent in a couple of days."

Henry cleared his throat again.

Henry let three days pass before approaching Ota again. "Ota-san." Henry smiled, handing his boss the latest work. "The experiments came out well."

"Good, good."

Henry stood next to Ota's desk. He felt like a fool one minute and relaxed the next. Ota toyed with his pencil. Henry waited.

Ota was silent.

Henry continued to stand quietly. He took a deep breath. Several more seconds passed. Ota still did not respond. Henry maintained his stance. Ota reached in his drawer and took out several sheets of paper.

"Here," he said, handing them to Henry.

Henry read the cover page carefully. His name was not there. He studied the page. Finally he said softly, "I am interested in the patent."

"Don't worry about your name, you only get one hundred dollars for a patent," Ota said, laughing. "The pay is nothing. Don't bother about a patent."

"That's fine," Henry answered quickly. "I'm not that interested in money. It is not an issue of money. One hundred dollars is fine. I want my name on the patent."

"Good," Ota replied, taking back the patent. "You will have to sign for that." Ota's voice was warm. "You have worked hard. I know that. Long hours. Long hard hours."

Henry nodded and signed the paper.

"Sometimes it's difficult, Henry-kun," Ota said kindly. Henry remained silent. Ota had never spoken to him in this tone of voice, and he had never used the affectionate ending "kun." But several times in the last week Ota had paused in front of Henry's desk late at night and mentioned that Henry looked tired and should get some rest. The day before Ota had presented him with two tickets to a baseball game.

Henry smiled and quickly left the room. To the astonishment of his colleagues, as he walked down the hall he kicked his heels. Oddly he wasn't thinking of the patent. No, he was thinking that Ota finally trusted him and that made him very happy.

Brad had finally finished talking.

Suzuki was complimenting him. Brad beamed at their words of praise. Henry lowered his eyes. Why didn't Brad understand? Suzuki was just playing the role of a civilized host. His fingers itched to slap Brad's smiling face. He was playing the part of the foreigner (gaijin) to the hilt.

He took a deep breath and tried to concentrate on the importance of the meeting for him. Suzuki and Ota were friends from university. It would be a good idea to have a drink with Suzuki before he left Japan—Suzuki was a good man to know. He would drop a hint to Ota tomorrow at lunch, and Ota would arrange the meeting. Ota would want him to meet Suzuki. Yes, that would be definitely right. For the first time he felt really relaxed; for the first time he really felt part of Japan.

Analysis:

Americans confront situations directly with questions based on observations. This deductive approach is considered appropriate in solving problems. Communication in Japan is inductive and a great deal more circumspect, both because of the indirect nature of the language and because of the concept of face. Henry's case reveals the Japanese approach to confrontation where a working relationship has been established in the "believe me" phase. Henry learns the valuable lessons of when and how to wait, observe, and insist.

From the start, Yukizaki considers Henry's questions about the makeup of the laboratory inappropriate. Since Henry is an outsider, his desire to verify his observations by asking questions is deeply suspect to Yukizaki. Yukizaki expects Henry to observe and understand the system at Yadi Electronics rather than ask questions that put Yukizaki on the spot.

Yukizaki's defensive response upsets Henry, and he begins to view Yadi Electronics as a jail. Henry is not cultivating a network of colleagues vital for information and support in a culture where direct communication is often difficult. Henry's isolation from his colleagues means that he cannot consult or seek advice. Henry has no inside group (nakama). *By isolating himself he has chosen to be on the outside* (soto). *Therefore, when he finds out about a meeting on his project, approaching Ota directly remains his only option.*

By doing so, Henry goes over the head of Yukizaki, who has seniority in the laboratory and takes the role of mentor by showing him the ropes. This action (gekokujo) *is disapproved of in Japanese society. Mentors are routinely assigned new employees in Japanese institutions and are responsible for the attitude and work of these employees.*

Henry puts both Yukizaki and Ota on the spot. Their evasive remarks are intended to let Henry know that although they would like to include Henry because of his work, it is simply not possible to do so. Henry forces the issue until Ota tells Henry that only insiders can attend the meeting because of marketing issues. By this admission Ota, his host, loses face, and Henry also feels ashamed.

Even after this incident, Henry does not appreciate the importance of building trusting relationships with colleagues. Although he works well as a team player, Henry is convinced that his ideas of doing full research instead of a demo for MITI will make a unique contribution to the direction of research at the laboratory. To this end, Henry prepares for a meeting, which he has proposed to Ota. But Henry's preparation includes only support for his ideas, rather than sounding out the group on his ideas (nemawashi), *which is necessary in Japan. After some time, Ota agrees to schedule the meeting. Henry is shocked by the dismissal of his ideas at the meeting. However, he is sensible enough to think more seriously about his behavior in regard to the MITI proposal. Henry has created a platform for his own ideas without either soliciting group support or providing a rationale outside himself, such as his obligation and concern for the company* (uchi). *He has failed to lay the groundwork* (nemawashi) *beforehand, and therefore his point of view is not taken seriously at the meeting.*

Henry uses all these lessons in his final battle to ensure that his name is mentioned on the patent. Although he approaches Ota on the patent issue, he waits for Ota to take the lead in the conversation. By creating tension through the use of silence and the use of a few key phrases ("patent should be interesting,"), Henry makes Ota aware of his desire to have his name on the patent. Ota has worked with Henry long enough to understand his concern. After Henry's statement "I am interested in the patent," Ota agrees to include Henry's name on the patent application. Henry's victory allows him to enter the "believe me" phase of the relationship.

Silence is used in a variety of ways to make a point. In Henry's case, it can mean disapproval or anger at a situation. This pulling back (enryo) disrupts the harmony of a situation without being explicit. In meetings silence often means the individual does not know how to proceed. The individual's group (ringi) may have given him a bottom line, and he is confounded by a situation. In the latter instance, the individual in question will appreciate some help in creating viable alternatives.

Just prior to Henry's departure from Japan, Ota orchestrates a meeting to widen Henry's and Brad's network at Yadi Electronics. Since Brad has never made it to the "believe-me" phase, his attempt to act as guarantor to another American is entirely inappropriate. Furthermore, Brad has not prepared anyone at the meeting for this introduction, so Ota risks losing face for not preparing Suzuki, his superior at corporate headquarters, adequately in advance.

As Henry prepares to leave Yadi Electronics, he does not think of the patent and the success of his work, but concentrates on how he can expand his present connections at Yadi Electronics, specifically focusing on his relationship with Suzuki. Henry will make a deeper connection with Suzuki by using Ota as a go-between, and he will use the power of subtle suggestion to make his request known. In this way, Henry will pass from the "believe me" phase into the "marry me" phase, where his networks will expand further and be continually nurtured.

Dr. EDWARDS: Inside-Outside

Dr. Edwards was very pleased as he stood on his laboratory steps watching Hiro Yabe get out of the car from Heathrow Airport. Yabe was the last of three Japanese scientists scheduled to arrive in Cambridge that year. Koto had come nine months ago. Nakajima, who stood by his side, had already been in the Edwards laboratory for six months. Dr. Edwards loved Nakajima, a brilliant young man with sparkling eyes and an extraordinary sense of humor. The exchange with Japan was in its tenth year and some of Dr. Edwards's best students had come from Japan.

"Yabe, *desu.*" Hiro Yabe bowed low several times.

"Edwards, *desu.*" Dr. Edwards had learned Japanese etiquette from his many trips to Japan. Hiro Yabe stood with his head bowed for several seconds. Dr. Edwards bowed, then stood straight. Yabe bowed again. Dr. Edwards lowered his head. Several moments passed. Dr. Edwards's head began to pound. He noticed Yabe had dandruff. The situation was getting awkward.

"This way," Nakajima said, quickly touching Yabe's sleeve. Dr. Edwards followed them and watched Yabe stumble. He must be tired, thought Dr. Edwards. He was surprised that Yabe seemed to be well over forty-five. He relied on his good friends in Japan to make placements. Curious, a man so old should be a contemporary of Nakajima. When he thought of Nakajima, he could not help but smile. He was extraordinary, and they were doing excellent work together.

Yabe went to work for Dr. Kendrick, an ambitious young assistant professor, who during the next few weeks repeatedly complained to Dr. Edwards that Yabe was incompetent. Dr. Edwards defended Yabe, saying that it was just a matter of time before he caught on. When Yabe locked himself out of the building four weeks later, Dr. Edwards was on hand to let him in. He followed Yabe to his laboratory and watched as Yabe began working. He picked up a pipette and dropped its contents on the floor. He picked up another and the same thing happened. Instead of cleaning up the mess, Yabe began filling a third pipette. Dr. Edwards brought him a rag and pointed to the liquid on the floor. Yabe bowed, accepted the rag, and began to wipe the floor. His arm motions were so wide that the liquid spread over half the floor. Exasperated, Dr. Edwards found another rag. In the end, Dr. Edwards cleaned the floor while Yabe ran for paper towels.

The next week Dr. Edwards was driving home from the Institute when he noticed smoke coming from Dr. Kendrick's laboratory window. He immediately parked his car, ran to the building, and axed the nearest fire alarm. Dr. Edwards learned the next day that Yabe had lowered hoods over two bunsen burners and left the building. The fire chief explained that the hood had ignited, and it would have been a matter of only a few more minutes before the whole room caught, then the floor, and of course, finally the Institute. "It doesn't take long," the fire chief concluded.

That day Dr. Edwards wrote a letter to Personnel explaining what had happened and suggesting Yabe be sent back to Japan. The letter was accepted without a need for explanation. Three days later Nakajima and Koto knocked on his door.

"Good morning, Dr. Edwards." Nakajima bowed low.

"Good morning." Dr. Edwards nodded.

"I would like to discuss the case of Yabe-san," Nakajima said firmly.

Dr. Edwards had not anticipated a meeting with Nakajima and Koto. News of the fire was all over the Institute and many people were relieved that Yabe was leaving. He wondered if he would have to pay Yabe's expenses back to Japan. That might be a problem, he thought, anticipating the question.

"We must quit," Nakajima said.

"Yes," Koto nodded.

Dr. Edwards hesitated. He couldn't believe his ears. Must quit, what the devil was Nakajima talking about? Nakajima was the most modern Japanese. He had British girlfriends, was a charming man and an aggressive scientist. Dr. Edwards used his English reticence and decided not to speak.

"We are responsible," Nakajima added quickly.

"I was not aware you were there at the time of the fire," Dr. Edwards said dryly.

"No," Nakajima answered.

"Then?"

"We are responsible for Yabe-san."

"Responsible? Did you get him drunk?"

"We should have taken better care of him," Nakajima answered and lowered his head. "If he goes back it will bring shame on all of us. We will have to quit."

Dr. Edwards frowned. "But I'm prepared to pay for his way," he said, wondering if their unreasonable stand was part of a ploy to win Yabe a return ticket to Japan.

"Dr. Edwards, you don't understand," Nakajima insisted. "We are responsible." Nakajima looked at him sternly.

Dr. Edwards lowered his eyes. The last ten years were going up in smoke: all the networking in Japan to make the exchange possible; all his work building and arranging the program; the excellent collaboration that had resulted. The end of all this made him want to scream, strangle Yabe, hit Nakajima. He cleared his throat and tried to think of Japanese etiquette. "What would you suggest we do?"

Nakajima smiled his brightest smile. "We should assign Yabe-san a caretaker. I will be that person. From this moment I will work in Dr. Kendrick's laboratory. I will be responsible for Yabe-san."

Dr. Edwards took a deep breath. Nakajima was his most brilliant student. Their experiments would change fundamental biology for years to come. He anticipated many years of work: great papers, keynote speeches at conferences. He was about to shake his head when Nakajima stepped forward. "I will be his caretaker," he repeated.

"You will be his caretaker," Dr. Edwards repeated. "I will make the arrangements." Nakajima smiled, but Dr. Edwards turned on his heels and left the room. He was sure to be sick if he stayed.

The next few months passed without event. He didn't see that much of Nakajima and heard no more rumors about Yabe. Late one day Nakajima appeared at his office. His face looked haggard. He slumped into a chair opposite Dr. Edwards. "I can't continue," he said in a hoarse voice.

"What do you mean?"

"Yabe is terrible. He lies, he cheats, he can't do science. I can't continue."

Dr. Edwards was about to make a sarcastic remark about responsibility, but Nakajima suddenly drew his chair close. His voice was intimate. "What should we do?" he asked.

"What should we do?" Dr. Edwards repeated.

"Yes," Nakajima nodded.

Dr. Edwards hesitated. Slowly he began to explore ideas with Nakajima. Suddenly they struck on a plan where Dr. Edwards would announce that grant money had been terminated for the project Yabe was working on. Yabe would be sent back to Japan because of a funding problem. "We have come to a good solution," Nakajima said with a satisfied smile on his face. "We have solved a great difficulty."

Dr. Edwards nodded. We have, he thought, and reached over to his cabinet and poured himself and Nakajima a glass of single malt Scotch.

Analysis:

Japanese have a reputation for functioning as efficient members of a group. For example, a corporate group's reputation is based on its history, its market share, and finally its attitude toward employees. Firms with the best reputation are the most sought after by new recruits who are then interviewed and tested before being hired. Once in a company, they are indoctrinated in corporate philosophy and their job rotations are designed to imbue them with the corporate culture. All of this causes the recruit to identify with the company and to view himself as part of a house (uchi).

The importance of the group and loyalty to the group is compounded by the vertical organization of Japanese society (tate shakai). Lifetime employment (shushin koyo) is the norm for more than a third of the workforce. These are prized jobs in Japan and entry to these companies is difficult. Employees are encouraged to be loyal in return for lifelong employment, where university graduates are promoted on the basis of seniority (nenko joretsu). Thus, employees understand that loyalty and obligation are calculated moves made with the expectation of security.

To reinforce the system, members of a company spend long hours together both in the office and after work. They understand that others in their group (nakama) *accept responsibility for its smooth functioning. Harmony is valued and the group endeavors to preserve the outward manifestation of consensus. Individuals are rarely singled out of a group for praise or blame.*

Although Dr. Edwards has been working successfully with Japanese in the "believe me" phase of the relationship, he is unprepared to deal with either the cohesiveness or the inside-outside nature of the Japanese group. According to Dr. Edwards's values, the individual must prove himself professionally and must be competent at all times. He is therefore unprepared for Nakajima and Koto's reaction to his plan to send the incompetent Yabe back to Japan. To Nakajima and Koto, Yabe's public disgrace reflects not only on their group in Japan but also on their sense of individual integrity. Once accepted, each member must work to help out others in the group. Loyalty to the group demands its preservation as a whole. The Japanese scientists perceive Yabe as their responsibility, and they must fulfill their obligation to the group by protecting him from the humiliation of having his contract publicly terminated. Nakajima and Koto understand their limitless obligations to the group, even if it means losing their own cherished positions.

Although both Japanese scientists are serious about their intention to leave the Institute, they also try to save the situation in a private meeting with Dr. Edwards. Both scientists declare they will continue to be vigilant about their colleague's behavior if Dr. Edwards will allow Yabe to stay at the Institute. Most importantly, this is a test of trust. Dr. Edwards is requested to bypass the rules in favor of his personal relationship with Nakajima.

Obligations are vital in building personal commitment, trust, and the human network that sustains Japanese business and personal relations. A thorough explanation of a situation is a common design to garner sympathy in the "believe me" phase of a negotiation or interaction. Dr. Edwards understands that he must comply with Nakajima's request to assign a caretaker for Yabe if he intends to keep his connection with the Japanese. Nakajima's willingness to express his point of view and the off-the-record nature of the agreement are evidence of his trust in Dr. Edwards and underscores Dr. Edwards's worthiness as a member of Nakajima's extended group. In the "believe me" phase, Dr. Edwards is no longer an authority figure who must be catered to but rather a fellow traveler, a consultant, a friend.

This insider behavior in the "believe me" phase becomes manifest later, when the tables turn. In desperation, Nakajima asks for Dr. Edwards's aid in terminating Yabe's contract. Nakajima and Dr. Edwards devise a face-saving plan: Yabe doesn't lose face due to incompetence, and Dr. Edwards's face is saved. The brilliance of the plan is that no one is to blame for Yabe's leaving. Termination of a grant is a neutral fact, which is an imperative in a culture so conscious of face and its linkage to responsibility.

In Japanese society, expulsion is more upsetting than any other punishment and is to be avoided at all costs. From childhood, the threat of removal from the group is used as discipline. In addition, Japanese are aware that the entrance fee of the best groups is high. The group protects its members fiercely, and this loyalty, in turn, increases the desirability of gaining access to the group.

By the end of the case Dr. Edwards has become a member of the "inside" group and passes through the "believe me" phase into the "marry me" phase by revealing his understanding that maintaining harmony in a situation takes precedence over other considerations.

MATT: *Nemawashi* and Consensus on Big Decisions

Matt Thomas, vice president of Trask Electronics, Japan, looked over a report about the location of a manufacturing plant. Matt was proud to see that Trask Electronics was doing well enough in Japan to expand its manufacturing facilities. In a transformation that had taken years, Trask Japan was now essentially Japanese. Matt was currently the only American manager at Trask Japan, and he'd had to study Japanese before taking this assignment.

Matt folded the report outlining the current debate about the location of the plant. Nomura, Trask Japan's financial officer, wanted the plant in Tokyo, and he had made his reasons known to Naito, president of Trask Japan, and to Doi, the powerful director of personnel. Matt was convinced the plant should be up north where Trask Japan could purchase cheap land and expand its facilities as needed.

"Good morning, Thomas-san." Naito stood in Matt's doorway.

"Good morning, Naito-san," Matt replied in Japanese. He was proud of his ability with the language; he was tutored every afternoon and could read about 80 percent of a newspaper and understand about 50 percent of a news broadcast. Language had gone a long way in creating a good relationship with both Naito and Doi. Though nominally a vice president, Matt was clearly the authority on this venture. He deliberately included Naito and Doi on every decision. It was also lucky he respected both men—people in positions such as president and personnel director could be powerful enemies in Japan.

Matt had especially learned to respect Doi's political ability. Doi was a University of Tokyo graduate who had been offered a job in a top Japanese company. However, Doi had spent some years as a child in California and wanted to work for an American company, insisting that he liked the American "way" with people. "You're more relaxed," Doi often said. Although Doi was bilingual, he always spoke to Matt in Japanese.

"I heard you wanted to see me," Naito said.

"Yes, Doi-san also."

"I'll send for him." Naito left the room.

Matt chewed on his pencil. The last time he tried to implement a change at the company it had taken months of conversation, using the famous Japanese method of planting ideas *(nemawashi)* among colleagues as a forerunner to building necessary consensus on an issue. He'd planted ideas with so many people, had met with so many groups, and had discussed issues so many times that in the end he'd lost sight of his goals. The Japanese system of consensus-building had left him fatigued and irritated. During the long months of continual meetings and conversation, he told himself over and over that Japanese companies couldn't really operate this way.

Once, after an extremely tiring day, Matt had brought up the *nemawashi* and consensus system with Ono, president of a major electronics firm. Ono nodded and smiled vaguely. It was the kind of smile, Matt finally realized, one gave an idiot or a small child.

Naito returned with Doi, who smiled and said, "You want to meet with us about the location of the new plant."

"Yes," Matt answered. "The new manufacturing site will cost at least fifty million dollars. It seems we have three choices: north, where we already have land; south, where we will have to purchase land at some expense; or right here in Tokyo, where we already have a high technology research center and an empty building. Any additional purchase of land in Tokyo will cost at least a half billion." Matt cleared his throat. "I want you to investigate the pros and cons of this situation."

"Of course," Naito and Doi answered in unison.

After the meeting was over, Matt placed a call to Philip Essex, president of Trask America. When he detailed the three choices before Trask Japan and his point of view that moving the manufacturing site north was the most sensible course, Essex agreed. Then Matt called two key vice presidents at Trask America, men who worked closely with Nomura. Matt sensed they'd already discussed the issue. They concurred with Matt on the advisability of the northern site.

At ten-thirty, Matt went to Doi's office. As he opened Doi's door, he remembered Ono's smile—this time it would be different, he thought.

Doi greeted him. "Good to see you. I have already been collecting some facts about the Tokyo site."

Matt was silent.

Doi pointed to some blueprints of the site. "The empty building here in Tokyo could be converted."

"Did you get this blueprint from Nomura-san?"

"Yes," Doi smiled brightly.

Matt lowered his voice. "Doi, I have decided that the site will be north. There are many reasons that I feel this is the correct decision, not the least being the price of land and the integrity of building a solid manufacturing plant away from the R and D laboratory. I feel this is the right long-term decision." Matt then proceeded to clarify the issue with a number of figures he'd collected.

As Matt spoke he watched Doi adjust to the information. Because many employees would have to be transferred, the manufacturing site was a major personnel issue, and Matt understood that Nomura and others in the company who opposed moving north would like to pitch it in those terms. "Nomura might need some help in under-standing the situation," Matt continued. "We have time. It takes time to understand. There must be many meetings at all levels in the company. The data you and Naito collect will be useful in explaining the move to others in a *ringi seido* [group consultation]. It takes time to understand an issue."

"Yes," Doi agreed. "It does take time."

Matt went to see Naito and made it clear he intended to move the manufacturing site north. Just as Doi had, Naito nodded in agree-ment to everything Matt said.

During the next few weeks Naito and Doi reported on the meetings that were taking place in the company on this issue. By the end of a month almost everybody of any importance was receptive to the idea that the manufacturing site be located in the north. However, Nomura still held out.

Late one Friday afternoon, a smiling Doi came into Matt's office. "Nomura just agreed that the manufacturing site should be moved north."

"That's good news," Matt said quickly. "How did it happen?"

"I told him the best Yamasaki Electronics manufacturing plant was in the same area."

Yamasaki Electronics was Trask's chief rival. In certain technologies they were involved in a neck-and-neck race. During the past year Nomura had been involved in organizing and financing several research projects that were directly competitive with Yamasaki both in the basic R&D area and in the manufacturing area. It was a standing Trask joke that Nomura began each day with the slogan "Smash Yamasaki."

"Nomura-san is a very committed man. He is to be commended," Matt said.

"Yes, very committed," Doi replied.

Matt was silent. Then he cleared his throat. "I didn't realize that the Yamasaki manufacturing plant was doing so well in the north."

Doi cleared his throat. His face reddened, and he looked at the ground.

"Well done!" Matt exclaimed.

Doi smiled.

Analysis:

As subsidiaries of foreign companies establish themselves in Japan, they increasingly look and behave like Japanese companies. Often subsidiaries will be staffed entirely by Japanese, with the exception of one or two foreign executives. In most essential ways, then, the subsidiary is run like a Japanese company despite rules and regulations written by the home company. In these situations, foreign managers are forced for the sake of efficient business to create their own networks and alliances within the subsidiary. They also must mediate problems between the home company and the subsidiary.

Foreign managers in this situation must work hard to accommodate Japanese customs. It is crucial they learn not only terms such as "go-between," "nemawashi," and concepts like consensus-building, but also how to apply them pragmatically in a corporate setting.

Having worked at Trask Japan for some years, Matt is in the "believe me" phase of the relationship. He speaks Japanese and has established relationships (ningen kankei) *with Naito, the president, and Doi, the director of personnel. Creating and relying on a team is crucial to Matt's effectiveness in the company. Every Japanese manager sees himself as an integral part of the whole. Executives play a different role in Japan. There is a common phrase that there are "no executives in Japan"* [juyaku ga inai]. *All managers of large firms were once members of the company union and, if they are university graduates, their promotion to management rank after about fifteen years is automatic, at which point they quit the union. High-ranking jobs are often reserved for those motivated, intelligent, and well-integrated members of the union. The Japanese management system encourages cooperation and an understanding of the people at every level of the company.*

Confronted with the problem of choosing a location for the new manufacturing facility, Matt involves his team. Informal meetings and consultations are an important part of this process. Japanese business managers, who have many more meetings than their American counterparts, believe these meetings consolidate the group and are vital in the consensus-making process.

Confident that Naito and Doi have understood the problem, Matt calls Trask America to ensure home-office support for a factory located in the north. Closing the "loop" with the mother company is vital in any initiative. Once Matt feels comfortable that he has Trask America's support, he approaches Naito and Doi individually with his decision. Matt entrusts them with the responsibility for collecting data to support his idea. Naito and Doi are to call meetings on this issue (nemawashi) with the understanding that as go-betweens they will orchestrate the discussion group's acceptance of Matt's plan. They are to report to him about the meetings that are held daily in the various sections.

Top executives in Japan like to keep above a situation. They oversee projects and are knowledgeable about issues. However, they rarely involve themselves in the day-to-day details of management. In this case, Naito and Doi are armed with arguments to persuade Nomura to support the move. Their presentations to the discussion groups assure that the logic of Matt's decision will be accepted. It is their responsibility to monitor the groups, focus the discussion, and report to Matt.

When Doi reports to Matt on his strategy for convincing Nomura of the advisability of Trask's move north, both Doi and Matt understand Doi has exaggerated Yamasaki's success there. Using the fact that Yamasaki is profiting from cheaper land prices, for instance, would be likely to rankle Nomura. Doi plays to Nomura's competitive nature and provides a rationale for him to accept and support Trask's move. *Matt has stumbled across the dichotomy between sincerity and truth in Japanese life. Doi is absolutely sincere and truthful* (makoto) *and has discharged his obligations to Trask Japan faithfully; however, to accomplish his goal, Doi has used a circumstantial truth* (koto to shidai ni wa). *This use of circumstantial truth is accepted in Japan when it helps a situation that commands a higher loyalty or obligation.*

Through using Doi and Naito as go-betweens, by making astute observations, and by networking skillfully, Matt has allowed Trask Japan to reach a consensus. Although the decision was made from the top down, there was employee participation at every level.

CRAIG: Using Good Old American Know-How

On the third night in a row that he'd worked at the Ultra Computer office past nine, Craig opened the large box that had arrived that afternoon from Hashi Electronics, Ultra Computer's Japanese joint venture. He'd received a fax that afternoon from Hashi explaining that "cosmetics" was the reason 90 percent of Ultra Computer's software disks had been returned. Cosmetic flaws indeed, thought Craig, the head of the joint R&D project. Japanese are perfectionists who expect perfection in appearance as well as performance. He'd tested the disks himself. They were 100 percent operational. When Ultra Computer's joint venture in Germany received the same disks, there was no problem. This was the third carton of disks sent back from Japan in less than a month.

Craig picked up the top disk and placed it under an examining light. Glue was splattered on the sides of the disk. He examined the disk under a magnifying glass and saw a scratch. The glue meant nothing, the scratch did not interfere with performance. Checking a few more disks revealed the same thing. Finally, Craig pushed the box away and dialed Tokyo.

"Yoshida-san, Craig Hensen here."

"Ah, Hensen-san."

Craig took a deep breath. "I see you still don't like our disks," Craig said, laughing nervously.

Yoshida cleared his throat. "Frankly speaking, there's a problem with most of the disks."

"Frankly speaking," Craig imitated Yoshida's tone, "there was one hundred percent accuracy."

Yoshida coughed. "I understand."

Craig tightened his grip on the phone. He'd learned from past experience that yelling at Yoshida was, as his father often said, like "banging your head against an open door." Craig's voice was deliberately soft. "Yoshida, the disks are perfect."

"No," Yoshida replied. "Not perfect. We cannot sell disks that are cosmetically not perfect."

Craig was silent. His anger had turned cold. He concentrated on Yoshida and the situation at hand. Yoshida had not changed his matter-of-fact tone of voice since the beginning of the conversation. Craig resisted the urge to complain that the situation was unfair— "unfair" was a ridiculous reply to Yoshida's even tone.

He'd had it with the Japanese, he thought again angrily. Even his unflappable father would have hit the ceiling with Yoshida. Craig had never seen his father lose his temper or judge a man harshly. "Always be a team player," he'd advised Craig when Craig went away to Hadwick College in New York. "Always put yourself in the other guy's shoes. Always do the best and most thorough job you can. And most important, always be your own man." Craig had remembered his father's words through his years at Hadwick, where it seemed that sometimes coming from a small Midwest town was a handicap. Easterners seemed more sophisticated, as if they had all the answers. After graduation, Craig eschewed job offers in Europe and New York for the simple life—he came home.

"Yoshida-san, perhaps your engineers and mine can work together on the cosmetics." Craig managed a light tone.

Yoshida laughed. "Good idea, work together on the cosmetics. Good."

"Do you think six engineers coming here for two weeks would be enough time?"

"Yes." Yoshida's reply was curt.

For the next two weeks Craig worked on persuading management at Ultra Computer to participate in his plan. They resisted, but softened their stand when Craig brought out a chart of the joint-venture rejections during the last year.

At the first meeting between Ultra Computer engineers and the Japanese team, Yoshida introduced the engineers and they presented their business cards. The Americans, who had no cards of their own to present, shook hands and tucked the cards away.

Craig began the meeting by describing the history of the disks and the purpose of the cooperative effort in producing goods that would be technically accurate and cosmetically perfect for the Japanese market. As his speech was translated, the Japanese nodded enthusiastically. Yoshida reiterated the same points, and the meeting ended on a positive note.

Since the initial meeting had gone well and since most of the engineers spoke English, Craig dismissed the translator. However, by the end of the week, the meetings began to disintegrate. It seemed to the Americans that the Japanese were incompetent. They nodded and repeated the word "yes" to everything the Americans said. The Americans in turn became frustrated by the lack of real communication. "We seem to be going in circles," Herb Brown, a project director, complained to Craig.

Craig brought back the translator for the next meeting. Bob, a young engineer, began with a complaint. "We have to do something. Here is the process," he said and pointed to several charts on the table. "You tell me why the capacity of the disks is so poor."

Sone, an outspoken engineer, answered quickly. "If this disk had been developed in Japan, there would be a different process."

The table was silent. Then the Japanese mumbled their support for Sone's comment. The Americans whispered to each other. Craig closed his eyes for a moment. The joint venture was about to go up in smoke. He looked at Sone's closed face and realized it was now or never. The Japanese would go back to Japan and report that Ultra Computer was incompetent. He knew the Japanese deeply resented the fact that research and development projects were funded from Ultra Computer America, a policy that had been implemented to ensure ownership of property and technology transfer back to the States. From the beginning, Americans tried to direct how the money would be used and also insisted that the new technology be transferred back. The Japanese resisted the latter, causing considerable acrimony on the part of the Americans, who felt they were not getting their money's worth. It was Japan first, Craig thought, as he watched Sone, but it was also jobs and self-respect.

"Sone-san," Craig began. "I wish there were a different process. We have invested several million dollars in this process. That means several lifetimes of all our salaries." He paused.

The group laughed.

Craig spoke quickly now. His serious voice and his intensity altered the mood. "This is the process we have," he continued. "This is the process we must improve together if we are to succeed." He waited for the translator to finish. "Together we will succeed. We will make the perfect product—perfect in all ways—we will all learn. That is what the Japanese mean by continuous improvement." He said the last words almost unconsciously, having read about continuous improvement in *Time* magazine. Sone and Craig exchanged smiles.

Using the framework that the process provided, the engineers discussed the various techniques available for testing the equipment.

Subsequent meetings also went well. By the sixth meeting Craig knew the project would be a success. When he called Yoshida, who had returned to Japan, Yoshida also sounded satisfied.

Once the Japanese engineers returned to Tokyo, only 50 percent of the next shipment was rejected. In the succeeding months, the rate of acceptance rose to 80 percent.

Craig and Yoshida decided to prepare for a second-generation project by having a Japanese team of twelve engineers work for two years in America on developing the product. Yoshida faxed Craig a list of engineers the day after their conversation. Craig was amazed by the speed with which Yoshida reacted. But he was also amazed because, although he'd specifically asked for chemical engineers, the list gave only the engineers' names and ages.

Craig called Yoshida and in a friendly tone thanked him for the list.

"You're welcome." Yoshida's voice was also friendly.

Craig paused. Then he cleared his throat. "Yoshida-san, are they all chemical engineers?"

"Not really."

"It would be helpful to know their disciplines so we can place them appropriately," Craig said. There was a long pause. Maybe Yoshida was dense after all. Many of the men on the list were over forty, others were barely out of school. Craig had heard of the difficulty of contending with the hierarchy of a Japanese company. "We make the rules," the president of Ultra Computer America had once said, "and Ultra Computer Japan ignores them. Try promoting a Japanese on merit. Try anything that's not part of their system."

Here was a pragmatic issue of where to place engineers to be effective on a project. Yoshida faced this problem every day in Japan, as did all R&D people. Didn't the Japanese want the project to work? You couldn't put a mechanical engineer on a chemical engineering project. Craig started to grind his teeth. "Well?"

"Yes, yes," Yoshida answered. "Such a list might be difficult."

"Difficult?" Craig asked.

"Yes." Another pause. "I will try. I will try," Yoshida said hurriedly.

The following week Yoshida sent Craig a second list, again consisting of names and ages. In response to Craig's requests, three further lists were faxed, all similar to the first. Finally, Craig exploded. He would give Yoshida a thrashing.

He called Japan. "Yoshida-san," Craig said slowly.

"Good to hear you," Yoshida said quickly.

"I want to talk about . . ."

"The engineers will be leaving soon," Yoshida interrupted. "They are excited about the project."

Yoshida was driving him crazy. Craig pressed his hand to his forehead. Suddenly, he realized the futility of an outburst. He wanted to call off the whole project—Yoshida was against it, and the concept of Japanese and Americans working together and learning from each other was clearly a pipe dream. Craig mumbled a terse good-bye. He'd call Yoshida later when he was thinking more clearly, he thought, as he hung up.

Craig came up with no solutions that day or the next. The Japanese were to arrive in less than a week, and he had no idea where to place them in the project. The managers at Ultra Computer were requesting information daily so they could finalize their plans. So far he'd put them off.

Craig placed a routine business call to Dr. Sugimoto, division head of the laboratory in Japan that worked on the disks. When Dr. Sugimoto had last visited Ultra Computer America, Craig had invited him to his home for a barbecue. Later, Craig heard through the grapevine that Dr. Sugimoto was very touched.

Their conversation was friendly. "Nakaguchi-san is looking forward to his time in America," Dr. Sugimoto said.

"Good," Craig said, encouraged by Dr. Sugimoto's warm tone. "He must be a good chemical engineer."

"Not a chemical engineer," Dr. Sugimoto replied.

Craig closed his eyes and waited.

"Mechanical engineer."

"In what area?"

Dr. Sugimoto provided the information. Craig asked about the other engineers on the final list. By the end of the conversation he had information on eight out of the twelve engineers. He not only knew their disciplines, but understood their backgrounds and their hopes for the project. Dr. Sugimoto offered opinions on which aspect of the project each engineer would be suited for.

Craig drafted a memo to all concerned American managers regarding the Japanese engineers. He also set up a time for a meeting for the American sections to divide up the Japanese engineers. Although many disciplines of the Japanese workers were inappropriate for the project, it was possible to make the placements on the strength of Dr. Sugimoto's advice about the Japanese engineers' personalities, backgrounds, and hopes.

As the joint development evolved, Craig grew more confident in his dealings with the Japanese in Tokyo and his handling of the team in America. He was aware from comments that the Japanese considered basic R&D a high-status profession. To the amazement of the Ultra Computer America engineers, Craig insisted on calling even production work "experiments."

Craig hired a bilingual secretary to take care of the Japanese engineers' needs. In many cases, the secretary had to help with personal matters such as payment of phone bills and car rentals. One engineer demanded that the secretary arrange new furnishings for his apartment. Aware that the Japanese engineers were status conscious among themselves, and that he was in the delicate position of host, Craig avoided any direct involvement in addressing these requests.

As the Japanese engineers began working effectively with their American counterparts, Craig began looking more closely at the economics of the joint venture. He found that although Americans paid for projects developed in Japan, they did not have much control. This became especially apparent when Craig wanted to terminate a project. The Japanese had placed a request for its extension with Bill Becker, a top Ultra Computer America company official. Since

Becker was interested in good relations with the Japanese in the joint venture and since the project had yielded some patents, he had signed off on the agreement.

Craig was disturbed by the obvious amount of planning on the Japanese end and the seemingly spontaneous reaction on the part of Americans such as Becker. He discovered that Japanese budgets, which were made up months in advance of their American counterparts, often used the lack of Ultra Computer's coherent fiscal policy to their advantage. Night after night, Craig analyzed various projects as they were handled in Japan and in America. Most Ultra Computer business units were spending more than 15 percent of their budgets on projects in Japan. Often, as in the case of Becker, the Japanese made their deals with American upper management. Consequently, business unit managers felt they had no control. He thought about complaining to Yoshida about Japan's techniques for securing their project budget. He remembered Yoshida's polite voice. It wouldn't work, he decided. Besides, Japan was doing nothing wrong. Craig called a meeting of the top managers of the American research section. He approached the topic of funding Japanese research carefully.

"We have no control," Herb Brown said quickly, "and we're paying the bills. It's a joke."

Craig listened as the business-unit managers complained about the lack of control over research they funded in Japan and the lack of return on their investment. It was clear they considered Ultra Computer's joint venture with the Japanese a liability. No one had made any real effort to plan or coordinate the research carefully or to cultivate relationships in Japan. As a result, many Ultra Computer business units tried to cut their research budgets in Japan. They were mostly concerned with juggling their budgets to reveal a profit that would enhance their careers, rather than help position Ultra Computer. Craig wanted a successful interaction with Japan. He also realized that he was the only business manager with enough information about Japan to plot a strategy for Ultra Computer's interaction with its Japanese counterparts.

"We have two problems here," Craig said gently. "The first is the problem that we aren't getting the most out of the joint venture." The managers mumbled their assent. "The second problem is that the

Japanese are getting their projects funded by this company irrespective of the plans of each business unit. They are using our lack of cohesion against us. Unless Ultra Computer America presents a unified front, the Japanese will continue to make separate deals at different levels and with different groups in this company. Ultra Computer America needs a uniform policy."

"How are we going to accomplish that?" Herb Brown asked.

"By giving an annual budget to the Japanese. Fifteen percent of each business unit and that's all. We will tell the boys upstairs. That will stop the individual deals." Craig knew it would take time for them to absorb the full meaning of the system. He'd chosen the amount of the percentage from his study of the yearly average of what most of the business units were investing in Japan. He watched the managers, many of whom had taken out calculators. The number was not too high or too low, Craig thought. They would find it acceptable.

Herb Brown laughed. "If I'm going to spend fifteen percent from my budget, I'd better find out how the money will be used."

The other managers agreed.

The new system went into place relatively smoothly. The Japanese were stunned at first, but seemed to recover quickly. The American business managers were now more invested in making their 15 percent work, and Craig encouraged them to spend time talking to their Japanese counterparts about funded projects. Craig was delighted with the outcome and also began to talk more regularly to the management at Hashi Electronics.

In the months that followed, Craig became aware of the amount and kind of work that was being done in Japan. He noticed that the Japanese often asked for documentation and that they were reassured when he explained his approach to a problem. Craig began compiling statistics on the various projects. He also understood that Japanese considered themselves the center of expertise in specific areas and were reluctant to have that technology transferred to Ultra Computer America.

Realizing he'd hit on a valuable tool with the Japanese in his casual mention of continuous improvement at their crucial first meeting, Craig read everything he could get his hands on about the subject. Craig paraphrased the theory of "continuous improvement," using it in conjunction with supportive documentation in dealing with Japanese managers. He was especially interested in an article stating that Edward Deming's system of statistical quality control was used in Japan. The article documented Deming's idea of identifying the problem, developing a plan, initiating a plan, and measuring the success. Craig was amazed. Deming's method sounded like the lectures his father had delivered on the back porch about the correct approach to confronting troubles. He began to incorporate Deming's ideas. When Japanese complained that projects developed in America were defective, Craig countered by faxing them control charts of all manufacturing processes. In addition, Craig documented "process research" and gave them an accounting of quality circles, the workers' input on quality control that was in place at Ultra Computer.

One spring night the phone rang at Craig's home.

"Hensen-san." Yoshida's voice sounded friendly. "I'm just calling about the new project. Thank you for all your trouble with the charts."

"No problem," Craig replied.

"Uchida-san, our president, will be visiting Ultra Computer America. He wants to meet you. You're famous in Japan, Hensen-san."

"I'd be honored to meet President Uchida."

There was a pause.

"You are like a Japanese," Yoshida said softly.

"Thank you," Craig answered quickly. There was another pause. He couldn't say more. Yoshida was paying him the highest compliment. He knew that. The hours of poring over details and proving to the Japanese again and again through documentation that Ultra Computer could be relied on had paid off.

The project's successful, but not because I'm Japanese, Craig thought. Yoshida, President Uchida, and the other Japanese would never understand that. The project works because Edward Deming's idea of continuous improvement is American. The project works because as an American I was brought up to do a job well, be a team player, and see the other guy's point of view.

Analysis:

With the increase in joint ventures, licensing agreements, and buyouts between the United States and Japan, more Americans work directly for or with Japanese. Many of these Americans have never been to Japan and many more know little or nothing about Japanese culture or business practice. Frustrations develop on both sides because of both ignorance and differences in approach to excellence and to building trust. Japanese managers complain that their American counterparts are sloppy and cannot be relied on. American managers feel Japanese are too demanding in terms of detail and documentation.

Craig's case begins in the "believe me" phase of the relationship. Craig has been working with Hashi Electronics for some time. He has established networks there and a good working knowledge of the company, especially its standards of excellence. Craig also understands that these standards differ from standards in America. In fact, until the time Ultra Computer disks are returned by Hashi Electronics, both Craig and Hashi Electronics feel comfortable with the suggestion of a joint R&D project.

To understand the tension between Hashi Electronics and Ultra Computer, it must be understood that Japanese develop products by meeting a series of specifications at all stages of development. Thus, Japanese consider a functional product only part of the criteria for its marketability. Americans, on the other hand, use the specification as a loose guideline and concentrate on the product's function. Consequently, Americans are less concerned with documentation and cosmetics. This difference of approach to standards of quality control affects every aspect of joint efforts between Americans and Japanese.

Once Craig initiates the joint development project a series of misunderstandings arise typical of a working relationship. First, because the American engineers do not have business cards, they cannot participate fully in the initial greeting (aisatsu) meeting, which establishes hierarchy and mutual acknowledgment of the other's institution (uchi) and the individual's commitment to it. Second, language also becomes a problem between the American and Japanese engineers. Many Japanese who can read English find understanding spoken English difficult. Japanese are usually taught English by other Japanese and have little opportunity in Japan to speak English. Answering "yes" often means just that they have heard the words rather than that they have any real understanding of the conversation. This lack of understanding of conversational English is compounded by the fact that Japanese use a vocabulary (in both Japanese and English) which is often vague and designed to maintain a harmonious tone rather than give explicit answers. Finally, the Japanese were convinced that Ultra Computer's development effort was based on technical incompetence and poor planning for their visit. In this case, their expectations of Ultra Computer's competence as a parent company are thwarted. Their feelings of hostility (uramu) *are a result of a trust or faith* (amae) *that has been betrayed.*

Craig considers the situation and does not react personally to the complaints of the Americans or to the accusations of the Japanese. He brings back the translator. At the next meeting he summarizes the history of the project, emphasizing the reasons for the current mode of development. His talk includes the Japanese engineers in the challenge of developing a "perfect" product, despite the constraints of the approach used in the R&D project. Craig does not enter into a debate, but rather explains a situation that demands full Japanese support. A historical approach establishes credibility, which in turn allows the Japanese to feel an obligation (on) *to the Hashi Electronics/Ultra Computer joint venture. Finally Craig mentions "continuous improvement," buzz words popular in Japan, to cement Japanese understanding and involvement.*

Although the initial project goes well, Craig again runs into obstacles on the second-generation joint R&D project. Yoshida will give only the names and ages of the Japanese engineers; it is impossible, given the hierarchical nature of a Japanese company, for Yoshida to provide a more extensive list. Yoshida feels he cannot be involved in the engineers' eventual placement.

While Yoshida understands Craig's dilemma, the Japanese engineers are chosen to go to America simply on the basis of seniority. When Yoshida says that the list "might be difficult," he means that internal politics of Hashi Electronics make Craig's request an impossibility. Words like "difficult" or phrases such as "I will try" are a softer approach than a straight refusal, and save face by creating the impression of an attempt to correct the situation. Yoshida expects Craig will understand that he is saying the task is impossible and will take the cue to gain access to the information through an "off-the-record" source. Again, what appears (tatemae) *to be Yoshida's unreasonable behavior is in fact dictated by a political situation* (honne) *that cannot be openly addressed. Accidently, Dr. Sugimoto acts as a passive go-between and gives Craig information.*

Once the Japanese engineers arrive, Craig uses a bilingual secretary as a buffer. In this respect, Craig assumes the role of the Japanese manager by not getting directly involved with the details of the everyday work world. Craig maintains his status as a manager through the use of his secretary (go-between) and thus does not demean his status as a leader. Although aware of all details, he manages from a distance.

Craig is also sensitive to Japanese hierarchy and status (kata-gaki) by assigning production work the high-status term "experiments." Ranking plays a major role in Japanese business, and basic research and development jobs are considered desirable. People use titles such as "bucho" and "kacho" conscientiously, and people are ranked by the status of the firm they belong to and the reputation of the group with which the firm is associated.

Finally, and most importantly, Craig uses all his information appropriately in the "believe me" phase to develop an integrated financial policy at Ultra Computer, one that funds projects at Hashi Electronics and will ensure that technology transfers back to Ultra Computer. In this way, although Craig's system inhibits the Japanese, it is logical in terms of Japanese standards of loyalty and therefore involves no loss of face. In addition, Ultra Computer's new policy is not personal. It can be explained logically in terms of integrating Ultra Computer's activities. Japanese strive for coordination in their own companies and therefore appreciate the need for such systems. Financial policies both in the government and in private industry are an accepted way of conducting business. Ultra Computer's decision is not personally directed at Hashi Electronics, but rather is a financial system that will enable Ultra Computer to manage and coordinate its operations. The system encourages more interaction with the Japanese in a controlled but mutually beneficial environment.

JEAN: Working as a Go-Between

Jean knew it was Harry on the phone. He'd called her twice the night before about the difficulties between the St. John's Hotel and the Japanese government. This would be another request for help. She just wouldn't get involved, she thought stubbornly, picking up the phone.

"Jean, you have to help out," Harry implored. "Your position as former head of the Pacific Rim Society makes you vital to a successful settlement."

"Harry, I haven't been head of the Pacific Rim Society for over a year now."

Harry answered quickly. "The Japanese trust you," he said softly. "Consul General Maekawa-san was just saying the other day how much he missed working with you."

"Flattery will get you nowhere."

Harry was undaunted. "The St. John's Hotel respects you also, Jean. You have held so many functions there in the past and they realize you are absolutely professional. That's important."

Jean listened while Harry rattled off her other qualifications as a San Francisco community leader. Harry's avoiding the real issue, Jean thought: no one—not even she—understood the complexities of the Imperial House of Japan, and that was the real point of the phone call. Jean waited.

"It's a touchy issue," Harry finally said.

Jean replied quickly. "Not for me—I don't want to touch it. The St. John's Hotel and the Japanese government both bit off more than they can chew. Even the crown prince has to pay his bills, Harry. I don't want to bring that bad news to the Japanese. You know the imperial household is fraught with politics. Whoever is involved will get smashed one way or the other."

"There is no one else," Harry insisted.

There was a long pause. Jean cursed her supposed position of authority in both communities. Harry was in a tight spot. As a businessman who did considerable work throughout the Pacific Rim, it was in his best interests to keep the Japanese consulate happy.

"The Japanese won't participate in the international festival until payment is settled," Harry continued. "As you know, I'm head of the committee for the festival. It's embarrassing. It's turning into an international incident."

Jean thought of all the times Harry had helped her in the past. She knew he was thinking of those incidents as well. "Okay, you win."

The following day Jean set up a meeting with the St. John's Hotel. Jean was aware she had to establish credibility and ground rules, and prepared notes about her conditions that night.

The meeting was held in the first-floor offices of Brad White, the manager of the St. John's. The people attending had been carefully selected according to their involvement with the case. White introduced Jean to the group, describing her work with the Pacific Rim Society and her current activities as a consultant. White defined the meeting as an information-gathering one (and only the beginning of negotiations with the Japanese government) and then gave Jean a quick history of the case.

At the request of the crown prince, St. John's had booked two floors, a total of fifty-eight rooms, for three nights. The entourage included the Japanese press corps, bodyguards, ladies-in-waiting, and others. In the end, the crown prince did not occupy the executive suite, White explained. He preferred a private residence and the entourage stayed only two nights. The St. John's was stuck with an unruly press corps and a statement by the Japanese consul that they were responsible for only two nights instead of three as stated in the invoice.

Jean nodded sympathetically to everything that was said. She shook her head when White described the noise, loud music, and three o'clock room service, and the generally obnoxious behavior of the Japanese press. "You have been wonderful," Jean reassured the St. John's staff. "This has been a really tough situation and you have handled it wonderfully. I congratulate you."

The staff was silent. White's mouth opened; he seemed to want more. Jean added that the Japanese were aware of the reputation of the St. John's. The Japanese government had had done careful research before selecting the St. John's, and the whole Japanese community was aware of the choice. Jean implied this was important for future business with Japan. White shook his head at this last statement.

Jean continued. "Please understand, the Japanese are in a sensitive situation. When it comes to the imperial household, it becomes very delicate. It is difficult for the consulate to handle properly, and equally difficult for Tokyo. I am not making apologies—I am simply stating a situation. Somewhere, someone did not do their homework. The crown prince's visit has been planned for over a year. The imperial house, the Japanese consulate, and other agencies have been working around the clock. Please understand." Jean cleared her throat. "I want you to know that whatever happens the settlement will be a fair one."

White stepped forward. His cheeks were bright red. "Some of the furniture was damaged," he said angrily.

"You have been wonderful," Jean repeated. "Simply wonderful."

The meeting ended abruptly. Jean smiled and shook hands with each person on the staff. After the meeting she stayed for some time telling White about the complexity of the situation and how professionally he and his staff had handled it thus far. White was mollified.

The next day Jean called Hamada, who was second in command to Consul General Maekawa at the Japanese consulate. She had worked with Hamada in the past and knew that he had asked Harry to solicit her as a go-between.

"Hamada-san, it's nice to talk to you."

"Yes, like old times," Hamada agreed. "Thank you for agreeing to meet with the St. John's Hotel. This is a very sensitive situation."

"I understand that," Jean reassured him.

"Consul General Maekawa is worried."

Jean was silent. Consul General Maekawa must be shaking in his boots, she thought. An incorrect estimate of this magnitude would not sit well with the Imperial Household Agency in Tokyo, not to mention the complaints the St. John's had about the behavior of the press. Sandwiches at 3 A.M., loud music, and furniture covered with cigarette burns were just a few of the hotel's complaints.

"Consul General Maekawa expects me to handle this," Hamada said, laughing nervously.

Hamada was an ambitious man. If Consul General Maekawa asked him to negotiate, Hamada would need a successful outcome on his record. She was sure that Hamada was trying to tell her that Consul General Maekawa was unaware of her involvement.

After a pause, Jean said, "I need to see you."

"Please come to the consulate," Hamada replied.

"I will call from downstairs," Jean replied.

Hamada's voice was warm as he said good-bye.

Late that afternoon Jean met with Hamada behind the coffee shop on the bottom floor of the building that housed the Japanese consulate. They discussed the situation. Jean told Hamada the overall outline for the agreement that she intended to put forward to the hotel. All losses would be split evenly between the St. John's and the Japanese government. When Hamada complained that Americans did not understand the honor of housing the crown prince, Jean changed the subject. When Hamada whined about the impossibility of the situation (given that the crown prince in the end chose to stay at a private residence instead of at the St. John's Hotel), Jean nodded sympathetically and began walking toward the door. "The St. John's admires you," Jean said firmly. "They respect the crown prince."

Hamada's face brightened. "Wait here," he directed.

Jean stood behind a column in the lobby to avoid meeting Japanese with whom she'd worked in the past on their way to or from the consulate. Ten minutes, fifteen, twenty. She was beginning to get edgy. Twenty-three minutes later, Hamada walked toward her. He bowed formally and said in a low voice, "Consul General Maekawa agrees."

Jean returned his bow and walked to the door.

Two days later Jean met with White and the rest of the St. John's staff. She began the meeting with a detailed description of the hotel's professionalism. Then she launched into a discussion of the expert handling of the complexities associated with the current case. She stressed what she described as the "well-known" problems of dealing with the Japanese press corps and the difficulties of the ambiguous language in the contract. Finally she spoke of the delicacy of doing business with the Japanese imperial house, especially when it involved any member of the imperial family.

"Now it is time to take the bill to Hamada at the Japanese consul-

ate," Jean concluded. "All losses will be split. Hamada will see that
the bill gets paid."

"What should we say to Hamada?" White asked cynically.

"You should apologize for the inconvenience."

White tapped his pencil on the table. " 'Inconvenience'? What?
Really, I'll look like a fool."

"Just the inconvenience," Jean repeated. "Don't make anything
specific and don't take the blame. Inconvenience is a good word, use
it."

White and his staff laughed. When Jean was sure they understood,
she turned to leave.

"Thank you," White said softly.

"It's not over yet," Jean replied.

"Of course, we want to host the festival," White said.

"Then take a present to Consul General Maekawa."

"What sort of present?"

"A drinkable one," Jean replied dryly. "Also bring information
about the festival."

"But they have the information."

Jean was silent. She turned away from the door and smiled
brightly at White's staff. Should she tell them the kind of champagne
to buy? No, they must know, she reasoned. "Expensive"—the word
popped out of her mouth. "Nicely wrapped." She finished and left the
room.

Hamada called about a week later. He wanted to pay a visit. He
would be there in twenty minutes. Jean sighed (it was Saturday), but
she agreed. When he arrived, Hamada bowed stiffly at the door. It
was a short deep bow, a bow of someone professionally beholden,
Jean thought. Hamada carried a beautifully wrapped present in his
hands. He bowed again and presented the present.

"I hope I'm not disturbing you," he said.

"Not at all," Jean answered. "Please sit down. I'll get some coffee."
She indicated a seat on the couch. Jean felt deeply content as she left
the room. Hamada's obviously large present was part of her reward
as the official go-between in the matter of the St. John's Hotel.

She handed Hamada a cup of coffee and watched as he carefully
poured his milk and added two lumps of sugar. "The festival will be

in August," Hamada said brightly. "Of course, the Japanese community will participate." He smiled. "Most of the Japanese community
thinks the crown prince stayed at the St. John's Hotel. The hotel is
becoming quite famous in Japan," he added and laughed.

Jean hesitated for a moment and then also laughed. She would
open her gift later, she thought happily. It would be a large gift, she
knew that. After all, she was the arranger this time. Hamada was
clearly on his way up. He must have received a lot of points with
Consul General Maekawa, and the Japanese government itself,
through their network, must be aware of his role. She needed some
influential contacts in the Japanese government for a current consulting job. Perhaps Hamada could help arrange a meeting. It was too
soon to mention the deal now. She would wait. When the time was
right and all the players were in place, she would definitely call
Hamada. He would be her go-between then. The situation had all the
trappings of "I'll scratch your back, you scratch mine." Except that
in Japan, nothing was left unmeasured, she thought. Everything
must be repaid in kind. Yes, definitely Hamada was the right man.

Analysis:

*Americans are confounded by the indirect communication of the
Japanese. Japanese relate through gesture that which is easily over-
looked by Americans, and their language is suggestive rather than
explicit. Even in the "believe me" stage of negotiation, where Westerners and Japanese have been working together for some time, misunderstandings occur. In addition, Japanese often feel that a straightforward description of a situation puts people on the "spot," and the
result is loss of face. As a result, disputes are often settled out of court
through the use of a go-between. Because of language and social
mores, go-betweens are an institution in Japan and are used in a
variety of ways, including initiating deals, facilitating negotiations,
correcting misunderstandings, and making settlements.*

*Working behind the scenes is common in Japanese business prac-
tice. Choosing the right go-between is often vital to the success of the
enterprise. The individual must be direct, have a sense of what is
appropriate and possible, and most importantly, be respected by all
parties involved. This means the individual must be in the "believe
me" or "marry me" phase of the relationship with the parties in-*

volved. Jean's former position as the director of the Pacific Rim Society brought her into routine contact with the Japanese government and the service sector of San Francisco, which makes her an ideal choice as a go-between.

Jean initiates the process by setting up a meeting with the St. John's to hear their "side" of the story. She prepares for the meeting by outlining acceptable ground rules. Japanese prepare for meetings in a similar manner. They often have a better idea before a meeting begins of their bottom line. At the meeting Jean explains the situation from the Japanese point of view while being sympathetic to the Americans. Explanation, rather than debate, is common among Japanese. Often, description of circumstance will take the burden off individuals, thus saving face and allowing for a more even-handed solution. In more personal situations, such explanations are designed to evoke a sympathetic response, which can also yield satisfactory results.

After the meeting with the St. John's Hotel, Jean calls Hamada, with whom she has worked in the past, to probe the situation at the consulate. She is conscious of Hamada's ambitions and is sensitive to the fact that he wants credit for the "negotiation." Her proposal to call from "downstairs" at the consulate lets him know she will remain behind the scenes. Jean outlines her proposal to Hamada of a fifty-fifty split, which Hamada then presents to Consul General Maekawa for his official approval. Here Jean has used her "ground rules" to help make a settlement. In keeping with the role of a go-between, Jean takes a back seat and allows Hamada to be the "official" negotiator.

Jean's acceptance of this behind-the-scenes role is important not only in being an effective go-between but also as an investment in Hamada as human capital. Hamada is now part of her network. His debt (giri) will be repaid at some point in the future. Japanese take obligations seriously and assign grades to them. Both Hamada and Jean understand that she is not only obligating Hamada by agreeing to be his go-between on a difficult case, but Hamada is incurring more obligation by allowing Jean to let him appear as sole facilitator in this transaction.

Although both sides reach an agreement, Jean's job is not over. If possible, she must facilitate a working relationship between the St. John's Hotel and the Japanese consulate. Jean urges White to pay a personal visit with a "nicely wrapped" present to the consul general's office and directs him to apologize for the "inconvenience." Face-to-face meetings are vital for a future relationship between the two parties. A general apology points to the situation but does not determine blame. It will clear the air and allow the relationship to move forward. Harmony is restored between the hotel and the consulate.

Lastly, Hamada pays his visit of respect. He also brings Jean a nicely wrapped present to show his appreciation of her adept handling of the situation. Jean, observing the traditional Japanese custom, does not open the present in front of Hamada, but she is aware of its cost. Gift giving in Japan is institutionalized. Neatly wrapped presents are presented routinely on office visits and larger gifts are given by companies to regular customers at fixed times of the year. However, this gift alone will not wipe the slate clean. Hamada is still in debt. As she serves coffee, Jean calculates how Hamada can repay his debt. She will talk to him about her problems some time in the future when she has fully planned her strategy.

ROY: How to Understand and Manipulate Exclusion

Roy arrived in Tokyo on a cold day in January. Professor Watanabe had met him at the bus station. He introduced him to Inose, who was to settle him in the institute dormitory. Roy slipped Professor Watanabe a bottle of whiskey while Inose was flagging a taxi. The professor seemed glad. By the time Inose had brought up the taxi, Watanabe had put the whiskey securely in his bag and was smiling benignly at Roy. Roy returned his smile and was momentarily grateful for his cultural training and his two years studying Japanese.

Roy was disappointed with the dormitory. He'd heard Japan was clean, but his room was filthy. The communal kitchen also looked as though it needed a good scrub. Inose helped Roy arrange his bedding. It would be all right, Roy told himself after Inose left. Professor Watanabe was friendly and Inose seemed eager to help.

Nonetheless, that night Roy slept badly. Japan was definitely not what he expected. Where was the hospitable Japan he'd heard so much about? he thought as he tossed uneasily on his threadbare futon.

The next morning Inose knocked on his door. Roy dressed quickly and after a perfunctory breakfast of hot bean curd soup and rice, they took a short bus ride to the laboratory. Professor Watanabe wouldn't be in until the afternoon, Inose explained, as he introduced Roy to the other members of the laboratory. Roy was surprised at the number of foreigners, including two Frenchmen, one Italian, an Austrian, several Koreans, and two Taiwanese. The foreigners stayed at one end of the laboratory, spoke English, and were barely civil to Inose. Roy was given a desk next to the Frenchmen.

Professor Watanabe came to the laboratory at one o'clock. He was friendly to Roy, urging him to relax, to get acquainted with members of the laboratory, to get over his jet lag, and take the afternoon off.

Although exhausted, Roy began assembling equipment for his experiment. He'd written Professor Watanabe about the work he wanted to accomplish while in the laboratory and had suggested several experiments. On the advice of Professor Allen, Roy's adviser, Roy had requested that he be placed at NKD after six months at the technical institute. Professor Allen knew Professor Watanabe had placed students at NKD and had some influence there. He had also written a letter on Roy's behalf asking Professor Watanabe to look into work at NKD.

"Inose-san," said Roy pleasantly. "Could you help me find this size pipette?" he asked, pointing to a medium-sized tube. "I'm afraid the storage room has run out."

Inose looked at Roy thoughtfully for a moment. His laboratory bench was directly across from Professor Watanabe's office and he seemed to be staring at the professor instead of listening to Roy. Roy repeated the request slowly.

"Professor Watanabe said you should relax today," Inose said. "The pipettes can wait. You should relax." He looked at the clock. Louis, one of the Frenchmen, and Hans, the Austrian, were preparing to leave. "Go for dinner," Inose said shortly.

Roy held his temper. His voice was soft. "I need to get set up. I've written Professor Watanabe from America about the project, we have very little time. I understand you are working on the same project. You know how much time the project takes."

Inose was still looking at Professor Watanabe when he answered. "Your health is important. The experiment can wait." His voice was soft but there was an abrupt clip to his words. He began flipping the pages of his notebook and scribbling some figures.

Roy backed away. He'd heard that assigned mentors were often paid for their work. He also was concerned about Inose's project being the same as his and wondered if he should mention his concern to Professor Watanabe. He'd seen this happen in America also. Some professors thought competition made the work go faster. Professor Watanabe was aware of the situation, he decided. He would just have to work fast and hard.

"The pipettes are in the third drawer of the storage room," a soft voice said in his ear.

Roy turned to face a tiny man with soft eyes and a huge smile. "I am Tamba," the man added quickly.

"I am Watson."

"I know," Tamba answered.

Roy grinned. Instinctively he recognized an ally.

During the next weeks, Roy organized his experiments and worked closely with Professor Watanabe. When Dr. Watanabe referred him to Inose for help, Roy went to Tamba. Although the quality of science in Watanabe's laboratory was good, the equipment and methods were out of date. Roy was careful to introduce new ideas as a logical outcome of fact rather than based on his experience in America or his own ideas. Dr. Watanabe listened and, as Roy's experiments began to yield results, included him in seminars.

At the end of four months, Roy was pleased with his results in the laboratory. Tamba was a good friend and because of him Roy had good working relations with several other members of Professor Watanabe's laboratory. In addition, his experiments had yielded good results. Although Inose was unhelpful, generally Roy felt that his laboratory experience was excellent. If Inose balked at giving him equipment, Roy quietly explained that Professor Watanabe expected the work done on schedule. Then he would pull out an elaborate schedule showing Inose what needed to be done. He ended the conversation with a mild threat: "If you're too busy, I'll make an appointment with Professor Watanabe—so please don't worry."

"Oh, no," Inose always answered. "You'll have the equipment tomorrow, no problem."

Sometimes, while lying under his quilt in his small dormitory room at night, Roy did still wonder about the dynamics of the laboratory. He was friends with Tamba but had never been invited to his house. He worked well with Watanabe, but again the relationship was entirely professional. He liked the other foreigners in the laboratory, but none spoke Japanese and they were bitter and alienated.

Roy also wondered about the Japanese reaction to issues of race. As close as Roy was to Tamba, when he mentioned the Japanese mania for small Black Sambo dolls, Tamba refused to discuss the topic. Another time, Tamba turned away when Roy repeated a fellow researcher's comment that Roy "must be a good dancer, like all blacks."

In Professor Watanabe's monthly group seminar on genetics, a paper was presented on racial types of hair. Professor Watanabe and others listened patiently during the paper but in the question-and-answer period dismissed the findings as unimportant. Their reasoning was that Japanese were all homogeneous. The seminar left Roy at a loss. When he tried to discuss the subject of race relations in America, Tamba and others looked embarrassed, paused, and changed the subject.

One weekend exactly four months after Roy's arrival in Japan, the laboratory was to go on a retreat in a mountain resort near Mt. Fuji. The weekend was discussed for days and the secretaries and Inose were busy with the last-minute details. Inose sent around a memo asking people if they wanted a foreign or Japanese breakfast. Roy noted that everyone was involved in planning the retreat and this made him curiously happy. The laboratory staff was to leave Friday night and Professor Watanabe was to arrive the following evening. The retreat sounded wonderful. He looked forward to the hot spring bath.

Roy rode to the retreat with Louis and with Kim and Ching, two Koreans in the laboratory. While it was a relief to speak English, halfway there Roy was sorry he'd accepted the ride. Kim and Ching were livid about their treatment in the laboratory. They'd been with Professor Watanabe for over two years and still had no defined project. Louis was also angry, and planned to return to France that spring. When Roy pointed out that Tamba had helped him, the others laughingly dismissed it.

Dead tired, Roy fell asleep almost immediately that night. He had sent in a card checked for a foreign breakfast and looked forward to a leisurely breakfast of bacon and eggs at nine. When he awoke the next morning his stomach was rumbling. The room was empty. Thinking he'd overslept, he dressed hurriedly and made his way to the dining hall. It was empty. Quickly he asked the innkeeper about breakfast.

"It was at seven-thirty," the innkeeper laughed. "Everyone was here."

"But a foreign breakfast at nine . . ."

"We don't serve foreign breakfast," the innkeeper answered.

Roy was silent. A seething fury took hold of him. Inose and the others had tricked him. He'd been purposely duped. Now everyone was gone. The schedule included a hike and a rowboat ride. Clearly he would not be able to locate the group.

Louis appeared suddenly and said hello.

Roy was silent. For a moment he was too furious to speak. "Where are the others?" he asked.

"Everyone who checked foreign breakfast is at the coffee shop across the street. You can get sweet rolls and coffee there. Don't be mad," Louis added. "This has happened before. Ching said in the last retreat, they lost him for two days."

Roy slowly ate his sweet roll. Where was his friend, Tamba? he asked himself. Were they friends? Who had thought up this plot? He was thoroughly enraged by the time he returned to the hotel. Inose had sent a message. They were to meet near a stream at twelve-thirty for lunch. The directions were explicit. Again amid jokes about the probability of a wild goose chase, the foreign group set off to find the stream.

By one-thirty they gave up and returned to the hotel. Roy retired to his room, pulled out the futon, and read for the rest of the afternoon.

At five Inose appeared. "Roy-san. I'm glad I've found you."

"Oh."

"Yes, didn't you get the note about the stream?"

"Yes."

"Well?"

Roy didn't answer. Inose stared at him for several seconds. "Dinner is at six-thirty."

Roy remained silent.

"Professor Watanabe will be there."

Roy stared at the floor.

Inose left.

At 6:25, Inose appeared again. "Roy-san, dinner is in five minutes."

Roy turned the page of his book. Inose watched him. Roy coughed. The quiet was giving him a tension headache. He was behaving on instinct and his observation that long pauses in conversation denoted disapproval. Inose walked to the door.

Inose appeared three more times. At seven forty-five Roy went to the dining room. When Professor Watanabe asked if there was a problem, Roy was silent. He ate quickly, drank no beer, and left at eight-thirty.

Although the incident at the retreat was never mentioned, Roy felt that Professor Watanabe was more considerate of him. His experiments continued to go well, and Roy worked long hours and did not complain. Six months after his arrival at the laboratory, Professor Watanabe arranged for his transfer to NKD. At NKD, one of the world's most successful, fastest growing high-tech laboratories, Roy was assigned to work under Mimatsu.

Roy's time at NKD went very well. Mimatsu provided excellent mentorship, incorporating Roy into the laboratory and into his home. Roy's work was interesting, and he received a patent for one project. When his stay at NKD, and in Japan, was almost over, he was given a good-bye party. These were his friends, Roy thought, looking around the room. He stood and bowed. The Japanese clapped. Roy flushed and turned to Mimatsu, his boss and mentor at NKD. Mimatsu's face beamed with pleasure.

"Roy-kun," Mimatsu said, "you did a wonderful job. Really great! You are an NKD man now."

For a moment, despite his six-foot-two frame and black skin, Roy believed Mimatsu. He flushed. "Thank you," he said softly. Then he turned toward his laboratory group gathered around him. "I made some chocolate chip cookies," he explained. "Please, I hope you enjoy them."

Mimatsu seconded the suggestion. "Please, try the cookies." His colleagues advanced slowly, giving a short bow to Roy as they bit into the cookies. They looked delighted and Mimatsu looked delighted. Roy took a deep breath. It had been a long road from Professor Watanabe's laboratory to this elite corporate laboratory. His last speech, which was delivered in Japanese, had been particularly well received. The cookies were one small part of the string of intimate gestures he'd learned to insinuate into every situation. He was leaving Japan with a patent to his name and a network of contacts from university professors like Professor Watanabe to superb corporate researchers like Mimatsu.

Mimatsu approached him with a cookie. "Roy-san, you must also try one."

"Thank you, Mimatsu-san," Roy said, accepting the cookie.

"You must give the recipe to Haruko-san," Mimatsu added, referring to his wife. "She's a very bad cook."

Roy laughed. Haruko had made several banquets in his honor. In fact, Mimatsu, Haruko, and their son had been the only Japanese able to make him forget he was a *gaijin*. "I'd be happy to give Haruko-san the recipe."

"Roy-kun, I hope you come back to Japan soon," Mimatsu said softly. "We made good science together. Professor Watanabe was my professor also. He said you are a very smart man."

"I will come back soon," Roy answered. "We'll make the best science together. Professor Watanabe is a very smart man."

They both laughed. But although Roy enjoyed the sudden burst of merriment, he felt suddenly forlorn, knowing that laughter was a spontaneous acknowledgment of their friendship, yet certain from his experience as a foreigner that they were laughing about different things.

Analysis:

Preparation paves the way for a smooth interaction in the "believe me" stage of communication in Japan. Work goals, when possible, must be considered ahead of time and must be made in consultation with people both in America and in Japan. In addition, colleagues and institutions should be involved to establish credibility. All this is vital in Japanese business, but is especially important for foreigners who plan to stay in Japan for a short time and need to use, rather than integrate into, the Japanese system.

Roy begins his tenure in Japan with good information on his laboratory, Professor Watanabe, and Professor Watanabe's connections to NKD. Professor Allen, Roy's academic adviser, knows Professor Watanabe and has written to him on Roy's behalf. This connection establishes Roy as an important link in Professor Watanabe's eyes. Roy has not only "prepared" by involving Professor Allen but has also outlined goals for his tenure in Professor Watanabe's laboratory. In addition, Roy speaks Japanese and understands the rudiments of Japanese customs.

This knowledge is of tremendous importance in allowing Roy to cope with the initial exclusion and the testing of a newcomer that routinely occurs in a Japanese work situation. Roy passes the first culture test by giving his present to Professor Watanabe in private. In Japan, larger gifts underscore debt incurred through obligation (giri) between individuals. Although gifts will ususally be exchanged between groups of people in public, elaborate or personal gifts will be given in private.

New hires in Japan are routinely tested for sincerity and commitment as well as technical competence. On his first day, Roy is encouraged to leave early and to "relax" so that he can recover from jet lag. Concerned about the schedule for his experiment, Roy ignores Professor Watanabe and Inose's suggestions and begins assembling his equipment. In this situation Roy's preparation and understanding of his experimental schedule motivates him to begin work. His attitude not only earns him respect, distinguishing him from the other foreigners in the laboratory, but also gains him a friend in Tamba.

Tamba helps Roy become acquainted with the laboratory and the equipment. However, his friendship presents an awkward situation for Roy because Inose is his designated mentor and is expected to take care of him. In reality, Roy is working on a project similar to Inose's and they are therefore competitive. Roy's instinct is correct in not complaining to Professor Watanabe about an obvious problem. He leaves the outward appearence intact, but is determined to deal with the situation through hard work.

A mentor relationship is crucial in work situations in Japan. All new hires in industry and academia are appointed a mentor responsible for showing them the ropes. If the relationship between the new hire and the mentor becomes difficult, new hires are expected to form other relationships that will have the same protective quality (sempai/kohai). *Part of an individual's success in a Japanese institutional setting is measured by his ability to form such nurturing relationships even in difficult situations.*

Although Roy's work is successful and he has made friends and connections in the laboratory, he still feels like an outsider, especially when Tamba refuses to discuss the issue of blacks in America. Japanese ethnocentricity becomes particularly apparent when, at a seminar, Professor Watanabe and others dismiss differences in racial types of hair as unimportant as Japanese are all homogenous. Japanese are deeply conscious of race. Entire sections in Japanese bookstores are devoted to titles on Japanese uniqueness.

All the tensions in the laboratory are manifest at the retreat, when the foreigners are excluded. The retreat provides Japanese co-workers

*a forum to vent any negative feelings about foreigners, and Roy is
savvy enough about Japan to express his anger indirectly by not
joining the group. His silence and politeness pointedly create distance
while at the same time do not overtly disturb the harmony (wa) of the
group. Professor Watanabe and Inose are forced to act by asking if
he is all right.*

*The retreat incident gains Roy respect in the laboratory. A number
of other factors also improve the situation: Roy has worked diligently
on his project and his results are good; he has made friends such as
Tamba without disturbing the order of the laboratory, which designated Inose as his mentor; and he has shown displeasure without
upsetting the group or putting anyone on the spot. As a result, Roy
leaves Professor Watanabe's laboratory for the NKD laboratory in
good standing.*

*Roy comes to the NKD laboratory under the umbrella of both
Professor Watanabe and his American university. In Japan these
letters of introduction are vital to being accepted in a group. In this
case Roy is immediately accepted by Mimatsu and is repeatedly invited
to his home. Mimatsu feels a bond with Roy because he was also
Professor Watanabe's student and he was placed in the NKD laboratory by Professor Watanabe. Mimatsu is not only acquiring a new
friend but is also repaying an obligation to his professor by befriend-
ing Roy. Thus, properly introduced, Roy becomes part of a network
and is more easily incorporated into NKD's working group.*

KEN: Manipulating the Japanese System

Ken picked up the phone and glanced at his watch. Two A.M.: the call must be from Tokyo. Doing business with Japan from the States was ruining his health. He glanced at his wife. Sarah, by now accustomed to these phone calls, had covered her head with a pillow. Sarah and he had had good times during Ken's three-year tenure as vice president of Semitex's joint venture with Hisashi Corporation. Tokyo had given them both a second wind. Friends he'd made at Semitex/Hisashi—such as Juba, the president of the joint venture—and businessmen in other Japanese corporations had guided him through some tough spots. The foreignness of Japan had also brought him closer to Sarah.

Even now Ken didn't pretend to know Japan. The layers of complexity were too much for him. Just when he figured something out, he'd realize there was a subtext he hadn't counted on. But Ken knew enough to be careful to have all the t's crossed, as Sarah put it.

"Hello," Ken said.

"John Williams here."

"John," Ken answered resentfully, thinking of the arrogant young engineer, who, because this was his third trip to Japan, thought he knew all the ropes. John never consulted Juba about any of his plans. More than once Ken had suggested John meet with Juba, but John complained Juba didn't speak English and balked when Ken suggested John learn Japanese, as he had done. Besides, John always ended the discussion with the fact that he was an employee of Semitex and therefore not officially accountable to Juba. An unguided missile, Ken thought.

"I wanted to run something by you."

"Good," Ken replied, trying to sound reassuring. Although Ken was now vice president and didn't work specifically with Japan, many colleagues still called him with specific problems on Japan.

"I want to buy the machines from Namba."

Ken snapped to attention. Namba, one of the largest *keiretsu* combines, was an influential financial powerhouse in Japan and indeed in the world. *Keiretsu* are the descendants of the prewar *zaibatsu*. The six main intermarket *keiretsu* in Japan control one quarter of the total Japanese economy. Ken thought of each *keiretsu* as a large wheel. The insurance company and bank were at the center. All around were the companies, each holding a small percentage of other companies. All *keiretsu* business was monitored by the *keiretsu's* own trading company. Mining, chemicals, department stores, computers: the list of companies went on and on. In a *keiretsu*, a self-sufficient unit supplied and bought from its own components, its capital was drawn from a central bank. At parties Japanese even drank the beer from a beer company in their own *keiretsu*. This was a difficult situation to break into.

Like all Japanese *keiretsu*, Namba Inc. was intent on capturing the international market. In addition, Namba Electric, a subsidiary of Namba Inc., was one of Semitex Corporation's most formidable competitors. If Semitex were to produce their own disks, that competition would intensify. This competition was not helped by the fact that Ken had never been able to establish any viable relationships in any of the companies that belonged to Namba.

"Any particular company at Namba?" Ken asked, trying to keep his voice casual.

"Namba Machine Supply Company."

Ken was silent. Namba Inc. owned a good percentage of Namba Machine Supply Company, Namba Electric Company, and Namba Trading. Namba Trading facilitated all of Semitex's transactions with all companies in Namba. These companies, as well as others, owned percentages in one another's stock. Namba was a typical *keiretsu* arrangement, a vast complex of ownership that underscored the description of Japan as a nation of hostages.

Ken spoke in a measured tone to disguise the extent of his anger. "You realize that Namba Electric Company is Semitex's chief supplier of disks. Buying the very machines that make those disks from a Namba sister company will obviously increase the tension between Namba Electric and Namba Machine Supply."

"Namba Machine Company wants to sell."

"Namba Machine Company wants to sell," Ken repeated. He tried to think clearly. John was not stupid, but he certainly upheld the philosophy that the best man should win. Ken knew John had done considerable research in determining that Namba Machine Company manufactured the best machine to make the disks. Most important, the Namba machines would ensure Semitex's self-sufficiency in making disks in the future.

On the other hand, John, who did not understand the Japanese system of consultation, had not talked with Juba. Juba's advice had been of invaluable help to Ken while he was vice president of the Semitex/Hisashi joint venture.

This was new territory for Semitex, Ken thought, but busting through the iron guard of the *keiretsu* intrigued him. No one had ever made one *keiretsu* company a competitor of another *keiretsu* company.

"Okay," Ken said quickly. "Buy the machines. Send the purchase order through this office. I'll make sure the lawyers go over the contract with a fine-tooth comb."

"Done," John answered.

"Done," Ken repeated and fell into bed. That night he tossed and turned.

When he received the purchase orders for the machines the next morning, John had his lawyers look them over before sending them to Namba Trading Company. A week later Ken received confirmation that Namba Trading Company had processed the purchase order.

Two weeks after that Ken received a phone call from Ozu, a manager at Namba Trading Company. Ozu's tone was apologetic. "We are having a little trouble with NE," he said, using the abbreviation for Namba Electric.

Ken was aware that NE was a powerful company in the Namba *keiretsu*. NE was an innovator of disk technology and must have worked hard on the details of the machine. President Saba of NE had great influence with Mori, president of Namba Inc. Ozu was in a tough spot, Ken thought.

"Of course this is an internal problem," Ozu added.

"Of course," Ken reiterated. Namba Electric must be really raising hell to warrant this phone call, he thought. Namba Trading had processed the purchase orders, which meant it was a done deal. Ken wondered who at Namba Trading or Namba Machine Supply had squealed to Namba Electric. Privately, he cursed John for refusing to consult with Juba; then he cursed himself for not insisting John do so. He'd not listened to his own maxim of "Be careful." Everyone knew *keiretsu* were closed shops. Semitex was reaching into the heart of Japan without advice, without having anyone on the inside, without a clear strategy.

By the time Ken put down the receiver he felt ill. Ozu's soft voice and formal tone left him shaken. The situation was too important to delegate. A senior manager like Ozu would expect to negotiate with someone of Ken's stature to underscore the seriousness of the situation. Ken needed to consult Juba, who was well respected in the Japanese business community and knew all the players. He'd joined Semitex near retirement age after vast experience in Toho Electronics, a major Japanese electronics firm that had an interest in the Semitex/Hisashi joint venture.

Ken composed his fax to Juba carefully, pointing out John's lack of knowledge of Japan in proposing to buy machines from a sister company of Semitex's chief competitor, Namba Electric. He made it clear that he himself had authorized the purchase order for the machines from Namba Trading Company and that Namba Trading Company had processed the purchase order.

An hour later Ken received a call from Juba. Ken carefully explained the situation again. "Namba Trading Company processed the order for the machines. They must honor their promise."

There was a long pause.

Ken said, "Perhaps Imai-san, president of Namba Trading Company, should know our position."

"I'll call Imai-san," Juba volunteered. "But it is you who must come to Japan and meet with Namba."

"I realize that," Ken said.

The meeting took place within the week in a formal meeting room at a Namba office building in Tokyo. Ken, Juba, and two others were present from the Semitex side. Namba Trading was represented by Yagi, a vice president, and Hogen, manager of U.S. sales; Yagi explained that President Imai was ill and could not attend the meeting. Namba Machine Supply sent Taba, a vice president, and Hori, a member of the technical support staff; its president, Kumamoto, was also supposedly ill.

Ken opened the meeting. He deliberately kept his tone crisp in what he liked to describe as his "all out there approach."

"As you can see I'm not Japanese," Ken began.

The Japanese nodded. Yagi from Namba Trading murmured his approval and the other Japanese followed.

"While I've lived in Japan many years, I don't profess to be Japanese," Ken continued. "My approach is to be myself and to deal with you honestly and directly. Please excuse my direct approach. I cannot beat around the bush. So if I'm too direct, I apologize."

The two vice presidents, Yagi and Taba, nodded in solemn agreement. Ken was pleased that the introductory speech had prepared them. He took a deep breath.

"John Williams, one of our finest engineers at Semitex, has been involved in a worldwide study to determine the best machine to make disks. He has spent the last year traveling, writing voluminous reports, and developing a system for determining the best machine. John has done a fine job. He has determined that Namba Machine Company produces a machine with the most up-to-date technology."

Ken paused. The Japanese faces were expressionless.

"John came to me and asked if I would approve doing business with Namba Machine Supply, a sister company of Namba Electric, Semitex's competitor, and I said 'yes'. I made that decision myself. I made a commitment to Namba Machine Supply and subsequently Semitex placed an order with Namba Trading Company. Namba Trading Company countersigned and accepted the order. We have planned our business activity on our commitment and on your commitment." Ken lowered his voice. "In many parts of the world it might be okay to change your mind, but not in Japan. I made a commitment—you made a commitment. You must honor this. You're Japanese."

The room was utterly silent. Ken glanced at Juba. He was staring relentlessly at the table. Taba and Yagi also avoided eye contact. It was hard to tell whether he'd said enough. For the first time in many years, Ken felt uncertain.

He took a deep breath and continued. "I know Namba Electric has developed much of the technology used by Namba Machine Supply. I know also that this is cause for concern. However, I am sure that Namba Electric would rather Semitex buy the machines from Namba

Machine Supply than from Yamahashi Electronics. This way our engineers will be working together and there will be technological feedback as well as a continuing capital investment for more research support at Namba. For Namba Electric, for Namba Machine Supply, and for Semitex, this is a win/win situation."

There was dead silence as Ken took his seat. He hadn't realized his hands were shaking until he tried to pick up a piece of paper; its rattling set his nerves further on edge. Across the table, Yagi and Taba looked pained—Yagi drew in his breath and scratched his head while Taba crossed one leg over the other and frowned. Minutes passed by, yet the room remained quiet. Ken had never been in a room where the silence had gone on for so long. Five minutes and counting. The tick of the clock dominated the room. He stared across the table—waiting—waiting—six minutes, seven minutes, eight minutes, nine minutes, ten minutes.

"We appreciate very much your talk," Taba of Namba Machine Supply said in a stressed tone. He paused and his face reddened. Then he reiterated Ken's comments in an abbreviated form. The staccato sound of his voice echoed off the polished wood table. He talked around the situation for a while without adding anything new. By the time he finished, his face was the color of a freshly picked apple.

Juba spoke slowly. "I agree with Semitex's position. I am a Japanese, and we Japanese have to keep our agreements. Everything in this matter was done in a straightforward manner. The purchase order was agreed on by the two parties. The order was signed and countersigned. The Japanese way is to honor that. I have worked with Semitex and Ken for many years now. That is important."

Ken stared straight ahead. He was grateful for his proficiency in Japanese, because the translator had given only a generalized version of Juba's talk.

Yagi from Namba Trading concluded the meeting. "We owe you an answer. Frankly speaking, we don't yet know what that answer will be. In every country there are some people who have yet to learn the elements of global business. They are narrow-minded. I can't tell you what the decision will be. We understand your points. We might even agree with your points. But you understand this is a decision that must be made from within Namba."

.　.　.

Two weeks later Yagi of Namba Trading, accompanied by two other
Namba Trading vice presidents, came to Semitex America. In a short
meeting Yagi outlined Namba's decision. The purchase order for the
three machines that Namba Trading had processed would be honored. However, Yagi made it clear that any commitment beyond that
was out of the question.

Ken realized that Semitex had passed only the first test of the
relationship. Without a continued supply of machines Semitex
would have grave problems in the future.

Therefore, Ken drew up a new purchase order for another machine. Then he flew to Japan and met briefly with Yagi. Ken reiterated that he understood the decision was an internal one at Namba.
However, he also clarified his hope that Namba Inc. would finally
make a policy decision about the machine order. Then Ken proceeded to a brief meeting with Mori, Namba Inc.'s president, in which
Ken recounted the importance of commitment, global business strategy, and the win/win notion for Semitex and Namba.

A meeting to announce Namba's decision was scheduled a week
later at one of Tokyo's most elite golf clubs. President Imai of Namba
Trading Company and President Kumamoto of Namba Machine
Supply Company were present, along with four other Japanese. Ken
brought Togo, a Japanese with whom he'd worked at the Semitex/
Hisashi joint venture. First, Ken, President Kumamoto, and President Imai played golf. The five other Japanese waited inside the golf
club. Their conversation was pleasant and noncommittal. Ken worried because he could not read the situation. At least he was sure
they would be pleased with the gifts he had brought: golf hats
commemorating the Masters Tournament (it had taken all his pull at
the Augusta National Golf Club to get these).

The private room where the meeting was held had pictures of
various tournaments on its walls. Ken opened the meeting. "I know
the decision has been made. Please be patient while I express the
whole story once again, just to be sure that what I understand to be
the case is in fact true, and to hear from both your companies that
Semitex has nothing to fear from Namba ever again."

President Imai, President Kumamoto, Togo, and the four other
Japanese listened patiently while Ken described the situation. When

he was through, President Imai nodded. "We at Namba have had many meetings in which we discussed this story," he said. "It is the decision of Namba to do business with Semitex."

President Kumamoto's face had reddened through President Imai's talk. Now he spoke quickly. "I would like to say we had meetings with President Mori of Namba Inc. last week. I offered to resign Namba Machine Supply Company if the decision was made that we can do no business with the outside world and Namba Machine Supply Company has to remain an internal supplier."

Togo patted Ken's arm as soon as President Kumamoto's speech was over and whispered, "Everything is okay. Semitex doesn't have to worry."

President Imai presented Ken with two Japanese dolls. Imai and Kumamoto seemed genuinely pleased with the golf hats. President Imai commented on his knowledge of the exclusive Augusta Tournament and the difficulty Ken must have had in obtaining the hats. The meeting closed on a good note.

The next day Ken met with President Saba of Namba Electric Company. President Saba was reserved. Ken repeated the history of the machine purchase and his idea that Semitex's purchase of the machines was in fact a win/win situation for Namba Electric Company because the coordination and exchange of information with Namba Machine would ultimately fine-tune the disks produced by Namba Electric as well. President Saba's face paled as Ken finished his speech and he held up his hand. "I won't talk about this," he said bluntly. "Namba Machine Supply Company is an independent company and they have their own business policy."

Ken stared at the floor. President Saba allowed the silence to continue for several minutes before suggesting lunch. The conversation at lunch was general. After several beers President Saba seemed more relaxed. Ken discovered that Saba was an expert sailor and that he would be visiting America that summer. Privately he make a note to charter a sailboat. He knew of a lovely wooden boat that slept six. Yes, an overnight sail would help. He knew of a wonderful chef that specialized in oysters. President Saba would like that.

Analysis:

Japan has been regarded by the outside world as a black box, difficult to understand and impossible to penetrate. Trade barriers and a complicated distribution system make market access difficult. This situation is compounded by the keiretsu *organization of having many different companies under the same umbrella. Since they are involved with industries most central to the Japanese economy, their combined sales total 40 to 50 percent of those industries.* Keiretsu *groups practice a "one set principle," which means that usually a trading company represents all the major industries within the* keiretsu *to the outside. The presidents' council* (shacho kai), *which meets once a month, is also instrumental in developing group strategy. Finally, the member companies of the* keiretsu *are interwoven financially in a number of ways: borrowing from a group financial institution, the mutual holding of ownership shares, and the fact that the cross-ownership of shares among companies in the* keiretsu *group formalizes the supplier/buyer relationship among the companies. Again, all aspects of the* keiretsu *organization and tradition can work to exclude the foreign company that would like to buy or to sell goods, buy shares, or lend money to a member company of a particular* keiretsu, *especially if there is a perceived conflict of interest.*

This relatively closed situation compounded with Japan's intermittent but long periods of isolation—the last one (the Tokugawa Era) ended just a little over a hundred years ago—have reinforced a self-conscious attitude on the part of Japanese. Japanese spend a great deal of time defining Japan and Japanese behavior. Shinto myths legitimize this scrutiny. "Like a Japanese" (Nihon teki) *is a phrase used commonly in conversation to define and redefine characteristics of the Japanese such as sincerity, commitment to group, and obligation. Bookstores abound with literature classified as the theory of being Japanese* (Nihongin ron), *which portrays Japanese mental and physical characteristics as unique. Japanese underscore their feeling of tribal homogeneity with references to themselves as "We Japanese"* (ware, ware, Nihonjin), *"Our nation"* (wagakuni), *or, of course, "It's characteristic of an island nation"* (yapari, shimaguni no koto de aru).

In many periods of Japanese history, various aspects of this sense of "oneness" of the Japanese people and Japanese values have been emphasized and used pragmatically by the Japanese elite. For example, during the Meiji period, the Kamakura Period's Bushido code of absolute loyalty was evoked to tie a mobile workforce to large companies. In business today, the Japanese way (or approach to business and tasks, commonly known as "Japanese business practice") is used repeatedly in negotiations with the West. It is vital that Westerners also learn to manipulate Japanese values and business practice where appropriate in their negotiations with Japanese.

Having lived there, Ken is acquainted with both Japanese economic structure and Japanese values, and he has a working relationship in the "believe me" phase with many Japanese. He knows John's suggestion that Semitex buy disk-making machines from Namba Machine Supply will be an internal conflict of interest for the Namba keiretsu. Ken is also aware that John has acted on his own without consultation (sodan) with Juba, head of the Semitex/Hisashi joint venture. Juba has an excellent knowledge of intimate details and important people in Japanese business. Ken understands that, as an American, John is inclined to act alone and rebels against the Japanese system of consultation. Used to working in an American business environment, John has no understanding of the expectations in the "believe me" phase of the relationship in Japan. Japanese use consultation in a variety of ways. Often consultations are used as a self-protective device to involve people, and generally build a network familiar with the issues of a particular situation. However, in this case, contrary to Ken's usual pattern, Ken does not insist on consulting Juba. Rather, although annoyed by John, Ken is intrigued by the possibility of using John's energy to break into the keiretsu.

Only when Ken receives a concerned call from Ozu, manager at Namba Trading Company, does Ken realize he and John can no longer act alone. He cannot approach anyone at Namba for help or advice because he has not established any relations, and a phone call out of the blue would be dismissed. This need to establish relationships before serious business can begin is typically Japanese and involves the preparation in the "know me" and "trust me" stages of the relationship.

First, Ken prepares Juba by faxing him a letter that honestly de-

scribes the situation. In the follow-up phone call with Juba, Ken makes it clear that he takes full responsibility for the agreement and that the approved purchase order for the machines must be honored. Juba offers to be a go-between in the situation. From Juba's point of view, this problem must be solved through a series of discussions. He has worked with Ken and trusts his judgment.

Japanese are very conscious of sincerity. In this situation Ken must take responsibility for what transpired. It is also important that Juba, as a go-between, have an accurate accounting of the situation and know Ken's objectives and strategy.

Ken uses this well-considered approach in his negotiations with Namba. As with Juba, Ken prepares the Namba officials for his approach ("If I'm too direct, I apologize"). Once having established the ground rules, Ken recounts the history of the situation and accepts responsibility for sending the purchase order to Namba Trading Company. History puts the meeting in perspective. The creation of a track record in Japan is important in establishing credibility and determining the stage of involvement. Here Ken makes it clear that the relationship has been sanctified by Namba Trading Company.

Ken also makes it clear he expects Namba to honor its commitments and begin working together in the "believe me" phase. To emphasize his point, Ken evokes Japanese honor in terms of commitment, "You must honor this; you're Japanese." Ken's use of Japanese morality in this situation is effective. Japanese are trained to think of Japanese spirit and character (yamato damashii) as unique. Yamato is an ancient word for Japan and also for peace. Damashii means "heart" or "soul." Together these words sum up Japanese values. This religious outlook toward Japan is compounded by a feeling of obligation (on) the Japanese feel toward Japan and being Japanese. Ken's challenge is felt deeply by the Japanese. The ten-minute silence that ensues as a result of Ken's speech reveals the extent of the conflict at Namba. Silence demonstrates Namba's discomfort with the situation.

The initial phase of the case is settled two weeks later when Yagi announces that Namba Trading Company will honor the approved purchase order for the machines. Ken realizes this is an important first step. This incremental approach to problem solving is typical of Japanese business practice in this phase of the relationship.

Ken prepares for the meeting carefully. His effort in obtaining golf hats from the Masters Golf Tournament in Augusta will complement the setting and will communicate forethought.

Although the meeting is a victory for Ken, he must now attend to unfinished business with President Saba of Namba Electric Company. Even though President Saba does not want to discuss Namba Machine's decision, Ken's point is to pay respects to Namba Electric and set the tone for future business. Ken's personal visit is an apology that goes a long way toward wiping out the past. By the end of the lunch Ken feels some harmony has been reestablished and thinks of a plan to go sailing, which may put President Saba under some obligation to Ken and Semitex. In Japanese fashion, Ken has used this victory over Namba Electric to extend contacts within Namba for Semitex.

MARRY ME

The importance of continually nurturing your business relationships cannot be underestimated. Contracts are important and must be honored. Japanese expect that, once established, your relationship with a person or institution will continue to develop and that people involved will become resources for extending business relationships.

Entry into the "inner circle" of Japan comes with the expectation that you and your institution will become part of a certain network. Emphasis on humans as a resource is part of the basic structure of Japanese society and must be taken seriously. Passing to the inside demands loyalty, and with it comes responsibilities and obligations that must be met consistently. Alex does not understand this important principle and nearly loses a valued part of his Japanese network. Mizumoto builds and depends on his networks throughout his professional life. The duty of insiders includes being willing to nurture, incorporate, and include other insiders whenever possible. Once Steve reaches the "marry me" phase he is incorporated into an extended network of business relationships that are carefully orchestrated by his mentor.

To understand nurturing in the context of a long-term business relationship, the cases in this section are analyzed in terms of all four stages. This means that you will be able to follow each case's progress through the need to prepare, respect, and use ritual; scrutinize, test, and understand each other's attitudes and motivations; develop networks while negotiating or working with Japanese; and finally nurture the existing relationships and understand the privilege of being within the inner circle. The investment of time and energy as in the case of Arthur indicates the level of commitment and involvement that are requisite in the "marry me" phase.

MIZUMOTO: How Networks Function on the Inside

Mizumoto groaned and glanced at the clock. Six o'clock. It seemed just a moment ago that he put his head on the bean pillow. He pressed his hand to his temple. Too much sake, and he shouldn't have had the beer. "For old times' sake," Yoshio had insisted as he ordered the fifth round. Old times' sake, Mizumoto smiled. Yes, he'd known Yoshio from college days. They'd frequented the hot springs *(onzen)* together, belonged to the same fencing *(kendo)* club, and finally joined Sanke Company, where they had worked side by side for the last thirty-five years. Mizumoto's closest colleagues were as important as family—maybe even more so.

Yoshio was an important ally. As a young man Yoshio had been advanced as quickly as Sanke's seniority system allowed. Earlier, at the University of Tokyo, Yoshio had cultivated professors in touch with the most current research. He was invited to professors' homes and taken to dinner with the dean of engineering. While other students were bewildered by Yoshio's political sense, Mizumoto understood that Yoshio made everyone feel good. His accepting attitude allowed people to take themselves and Yoshio seriously without being obligated. Later Yoshio was asked by Sanke to court professors on government committees. In time, Yoshio was Sanke's own representative on the committees.

Because of these unique interactions with professors from the University of Tokyo, Yoshio was still considered useful to Sanke Company. When most employees were contemplating retirement, Yoshio was enjoying new authority and used it to help Mizumoto by arranging for him to represent Sanke in a joint venture with the American company TEX. Later, Yoshio arranged for Mizumoto's appointment to represent TEX on the MITI committee.

Mizumoto smiled when he thought of his first days at TEX. Winslow, TEX Japan's president, was a nice man who was at a total loss in dealing with Japan. Because Mizumoto wanted the joint venture between Sanke and TEX to work, he subtly began to advise Winslow. Winslow learned to be on time for meetings, to speak only when he could substantiate his data, to use transparencies and good translators, and, most importantly, to listen even in areas where he was an expert.

Gradually, Winslow began to trust Mizumoto and ask his advice on important matters. Now Winslow was practically a Japanese, although Mizumoto never let Winslow know how good he was. Mizumoto became indispensable to Winslow and was offered a job as Winslow's assistant at TEX. Sanke was pleased to have Mizumoto make the move from the joint venture to TEX itself, since he was nearing retirement age. Mizumoto's presence strengthened Sanke's relationship to TEX and to the foreign business community.

"Anata," his wife called from the kitchen, using the intimate form of address. "It's past six."

When he stood up, the tatami floor felt cold. He still slept on the tatami floor, refusing to heed his children's pleas for central heating. His children slept in beds; he shook his head sadly as he thought of them—they would not be up for hours. He and his children misunderstood each other entirely. The new Japanese—Mizumoto's generation called them the "new breed" *(shinjinrui)*—were heartless and aggressive and had no sense of obligation *(on)*. The younger generation called Mizumoto's generation "dinosaurs."

Whether he had given them too much, or too little, he was not sure. Certainly, they had all the material rewards of a hardworking Japan. But in the end all those piano and art lessons had taken away their initiative. Santaro, his beautiful son, had dropped out of junior high school, only to finish high school at night because of his shame at being a year older than the rest of his class. He refused to study for the university exams and took odd jobs in restaurants to support himself. Even though they lived in the same house, their paths seldom crossed. Yoko, his bright daughter, had entered a good high school but had decided to play. She hung around coffee shops during the week and went dancing on Sunday afternoon at the various band jams held in Tokyo's parks.

The washroom was really cold. He splashed water on his face quickly and brushed his teeth. The bottle of hair formula sat next to the sink. He combed the sticky liquid through his hair. Winslow and the other foreigners at TEX let their hair go gray. TEX had no formal retirement age. Mizumoto's contract read, ". . . shall be hired as long as the company finds the person useful." He'd heard foreigners say they never knew how old Japanese were, as he touched a new age line on his cheek. If that were true he might work until he was seventy. He intended to be incredibly useful.

Breakfast was always the same, miso soup, rice, and a few pickles. He didn't like fish in the morning. *"Anata,* are you going to be late today?" his wife asked.

"Mmm," Mizumoto replied absentmindedly.

"Should I plan on dinner?" she asked with a veiled look in his direction.

"No, I don't think so." He raised his soup bowl so she would not see his expression. When he thought of his wife he was filled with an unspeakable sadness. She was a good woman, but years of hard work, their unruly children, and his long assignment in Germany had estranged them. He knew she felt the same alienation, which was part of his pain. Her curiosity about his dinner plans only added to his desperation. She did not want him at home in hopeless retirement. No dinner plans meant no business plans. "Garbage bags," Japanese women called retired men. He was sure his wife had given him the title.

He did not think to tell her about Yoshio's suggestion that he represent TEX on the MITI committee. They had never really talked. The first person he'd told was Fumiko, a hostess he'd known for the last twenty-five years, who had been delighted. "The first foreign firm on a MITI committee and you brought it about," she kept saying. "Are you sure your foreign company understands the importance of the committee? After all, it wouldn't yield any immediate results. Foreigners don't understand the importance of being in such situations. They want results."

"Winslow-san understands. Winslow-san is more Japanese than you think," he'd answered in a wary tone. Fumiko's intelligence always made him happy but uneasy. He pinched her hand. "Fumiko, let's plan a trip to Kamakura." Fumiko's eyes brightened as she refilled his sake.

He glanced at his wife. When they had met, her quick wit and bright smile had been big attractions. She was a pretty young woman and many people still described her as beautiful. But as the years went by and their situation soured, he resented her good looks. Recently her interest in his new success made him unspeakably sad. "The soup is good."

"You are going to dinner tomorrow night as well?"

"Yes," he snapped angrily. She lowered her eyes and he immediately regretted his anger. "The soup is good," he repeated softly, this time trying to apologize. After all, he thought, she was only trying to encourage him to be successful.

It was seven-fifteen when Mizumoto left the house for his ninety-minute ride to the city. At the station he picked up a comic book *(manga)* on how to play golf. He noted a new foot position. Every Saturday Yoshio invited him to an exclusive golf club in Tokyo. At the club they met businessmen from other companies. Yoshio knew everyone and introduced Mizumoto to business people he thought Mizumoto would find useful. Mizumoto always had lunch with at least two members of his old gang.

During one such meal more than a year ago, Yoshio had told Mizumoto about the MITI committee headed by Professor Sabe, who had been a teacher of his at the University of Tokyo. Yoshio suggested that Mizumoto represent TEX on the MITI committee. In the meantime he would work on Professor Sabe.

It had taken many months for Mizumoto to convince Winslow of the importance of the committee. While Winslow repeatedly stressed how he trusted Mizumoto, he didn't see the value to TEX of a study committee (organized by MITI and headed by a University of Tokyo professor) seeking to prove that the field TEX was already heavily invested in was indeed the wave of the future. Winslow felt the committee would take months of Mizumoto's time and was further alarmed by the fact that this was just the first step. If the MITI committee's report convinced the MITI Finance Committee that this area of research was worth funding, then TEX would have to contribute a team to the consortium to work on a ten-year project.

In the end Winslow's greatest concern, however, was TEX headquarters in Milwaukee. Winslow said, "They won't go for this kind of a long-term investment, Mizumoto-san. Milwaukee has to turn a profit every quarter. They will see this as a drain.

"Milwaukee won't want to share information with other companies, either. It will sound political," Winslow continued. "TEX doesn't talk to other companies. I'll have to do some fast talking."

Mizumoto had tried to look sympathetic. Winslow was convinced, Mizumoto decided—he just needed arguments for the home office. "You are a fast talker, Winslow-san." Mizumoto said.

"Milwaukee will ask what TEX will get out of it," Winslow replied. "I can't even tell them they'll have exclusive patents." Mizumoto nodded as if he were to blame for the fact that all ten companies on the MITI committee would participate in the consortium and would have joint patent rights; in addition, because it was a government committee, other companies would also have the right to the patents.

"Don't the Japanese have any notion of what is meant by an original idea?" Winslow asked. "I know you're going to tell me for the hundredth time there is no such thing as an original idea."

"Japanese have the idea of not falling behind," Mizumoto responded. "This MITI committee is the Japanese way of making sure the research pool is large enough to make Japan competitive."

"Mizumoto-san, really, what can I tell Milwaukee?" Winslow asked, anxiously rubbing his hands.

Mizumoto smiled. In succeeding discussions he'd laid out reasons Winslow could use with Milwaukee. The committee would open up additional networks for TEX, including the University of Tokyo and MITI. The consortium determined the direction of research in this area. TEX would work on joint projects with competitors, it would hear about new information and research sooner, and the Japanese would see that TEX would be around to contend with in the future. (As it turned out, Mizumoto had been proven right. TEX already had learned of several new research projects and was pursuing joint ventures with Japanese companies in those areas. Now that TEX was on the inside, the government, the universities, and even other companies had an interest in things going right.)

It had also taken time for Yoshio to persuade MITI, Professor Sabe, and the other members of the committee to allow a foreign company in. Both Mizumoto and Yoshio agreed that five years ago such a move would have been impossible.

Mizumoto checked his watch as he got off the train. He was ten minutes early. The MITI meetings were being held in a government building in downtown Tokyo. Most of the committee members had already seated themselves at a long table. As Yoshio greeted him formally, Mizumoto wondered if he too had a hangover. Mizumoto bowed briefly to the nine committee members he knew. He exchanged name cards with the two he hadn't met.

Yoda was the member of MITI who was responsible for guiding the discussion. As expected, Yoda was immediately assertive and obviously brilliant. MITI always got the University of Tokyo's best; Mizumoto had heard that Yoda had been number one in his class at their law school. Yoshimoto, the technical man from the Japanese government, was quieter. He would counsel on technical details.

Everyone fell silent as Professor Sabe from the University of Tokyo took his seat. He was a thin man with a long face. Of all the men on the committee, only he had let his hair go gray. He nodded briefly to the members of the committee. Introductions were not necessary—everybody knew Professor Sabe. He was responsible for the makeup of the committee, his contacts were vast and deep in each company, and in fact he'd trained most of the men sitting around the table. The committee was part of their deep obligation to him and his to them.

Professor Sabe cleared his throat, indicating it was time to begin. His voice was reedy and his language formal. "Today we begin the serious work of proving beyond a shadow of a doubt to the MITI Finance Committee that this project should be funded. We have called together the members of companies who we feel are committed to this project and who have shown their commitment through spending numerous hours preparing the necessary reports so that this project will be considered. Spirit is the most important Japanese trait, and this committee will be judged not only on its hard work and commitment but on that very Japanese quality—spirit. I have full confidence that, as we go forward and assign different parts of the report to different companies, that Japanese spirit will inspire your effort to prove that this project is the right investment for the future of Japan. You will write the project's history, the current state of the industry, the current state of research, and how that research will be leveraged in the future into valuable products for Japan, which in turn will open up new areas of Japanese research."

Professor Sabe looked around the room. He inhaled deeply, and scratched his head. Then he looked up and smiled. "Now we will introduce ourselves. Please begin by describing your history and your particular interests, as well as your company. We all know each other, but by next year we really will be together. That is the Japanese style." His smile widened.

When Yoda finished his statement, he glanced significantly in Mizumoto's direction; Mizumoto lowered his eyes.

Nishi, the man from Tabi, began his introduction. He was a thin man with a long neck and huge eyes that reminded Mizumoto of an ant. His bulging eyes flicked in Mizumoto's direction.

Mizumoto panicked. They were right: TEX was an American company, on this committee only because of American government pressure that Japan "open up." Professor Sabe had described the meeting taking place with the Japanese spirit. Mizumoto's presence was an invasion. He didn't belong.

By the time Mizumoto was next to speak, his skin was clammy. He looked at Yoshio for reassurance, but Yoshio stared at the table. Then Yoshio raised his pencil and began gently tapping his notebook. *Tap, tap, tap*—the eraser hit the paper again and again—*tap, tap, tap*. It was the signal they had used at school to reassure each other before a test. At Sanke Company meetings, they had tapped the paper to indicate that, no matter how things looked, the proper groundwork had been laid and the meeting would go all right.

When it was Mizumoto's turn, he bowed briefly. "Mizumoto, who belongs to TEX," he began in a low voice. The room was silent except for the tapping, which continued through Mizumoto's description of his history at the University of Tokyo, his employment at Sanke Company, and finally his current position at TEX. Mizumoto sucked in his cheeks and ran his fingers through his hair. The tapping stopped.

Professor Sabe cleared his throat and announced that they would now move on to the main order of business: this MITI committee that was to advise the Finance Committee on the advisability of investing in the project.

Analysis:

Japanese place great emphasis on networks and on people as a resource for those networks. The Japanese university system provides fertile ground for relationships. The academic program at the university is relatively uncompetitive, leaving time and energy for students to join clubs and to socialize. The relationships formed during this period are often retained throughout life. In addition to these friendships, students also become attached to a professor, with the understanding that the professor will recommend the student to a desired company.

This network involving university, company, and government is reinforced by the dominance of elite public university graduate hires (i.e., the University of Tokyo) in influential government departments such as MITI and in the most powerful companies. MITI, for example, is staffed approximately 80 percent by University of Tokyo graduates. Japanese refer to this as "rule by school cliques" (gakubatsu). The rate of employed (shushokuritsu) is discussed openly.

Once accepted into a company, the new hires form a strong bond during training, which lasts throughout their tenure at the company. Year clubs (nenbatsu), groups of all the people who entered the corporation in a particular year, help cement the bond. In addition, company employees refer to themselves as part of the household (uchi-no kaisha), emphasizing the importance of the company rather than the job.

Mizumoto's relationship with Yoshio, a friend from the university and a colleague (the same class of new hires) from Sanke Company, illustrates these bonds. Mizumoto muses over Yoshio's career as a networker both at the university and at Sanke Company, which has gained him tremendous authority and prestige. In Mizumoto's case Yoshio has helped facilitate his being hired by TEX.

Foreign subsidiaries often hire senior executives such as Mizumoto who face retirement and are in the "marry me" stage of their professional relationships. When Japanese retire at fifty-five they often look for employment elsewhere. Not only do these men have tremendous business experience, but they also bring with them a vast network of associations dating from their contacts with professors, other univer-

sity students, fellow new hires in the company, and—as they ma-
ture—contacts in industrial and professional associations.

It is again through Yoshio's contacts with MITI that TEX is invited
to join a MITI study committee. MITI is being pressured by the United
States to "open up" and consequently has chosen TEX as its first
foreign firm to sit on a MITI committee. Mizumoto understands the
significance of the committee in terms of networks and knowledge of
the future funding directions of R&D projects in the field.

Mizumoto must first convince Winslow, president of TEX Japan, to
join the study group, despite the fact that the MITI study committee
will not result in a short-term profit. The committee will begin by
studying the project and submitting a report. If the MITI Finance
Committee decides to fund the research on the basis of the report, a
consortium will be formed. As a member of the consortium, TEX
must invest money for ten years in this R&D project. At the end of this
time the patents will be public property.

Professor Sabe's opening remarks on the spirit of Japan under-
score the nationalist tone of the committee. As Mizumoto had ex-
plained earlier to Winslow, the research consortium exists so firms
can pool their resources in important designated areas, ensuring
that Japan will not fall behind. Although it is understood that these
firms are competitive (and will remain so), there is a common goal:
Japan comes first. The orchestration of research in key areas is
beneficial to the companies involved in that they have an "inside"
view on the direction of funding of research. In addition, companies
strengthen their networks within the government, other companies,
and the university.

The meeting begins customarily with a self-introduction (jiko sho-
kai). Each person is expected to give his educational and professional
history. Traditionally, self-introductions are used as a means to intro-
duce members of a working group. There will be no surprises at this
meeting. Although Mizumoto is uncomfortable, everyone is aware
that he represents the American company TEX and they are also
aware that the TEX presence on the committee signifies a new devel-
opment in Japanese business.

The case of Mizumoto underscores the networks that exist in the
"marry me" stage of Japanese business. Mizumoto's mature relation-
ships at Sanke and his understanding of the intricacies of the connec-

tion between Japanese business and government create an opportunity for an American company like TEX to participate in the matrix of business and government connections that make up the Japanese system. Mizumoto is a resource not only because of his understanding of the business but because of his real ability to create a window on Japan for TEX.

ALEX: Using Japanese as Guides

Luminous in the reddish haze of Tokyo's early morning sun, the Micro Communications Building was at the end of a small lane. Tokyo before the morning rush was beautiful, thought Alex, quickening his steps. The tiny washed streets made the city look like a miniature village. A thousand villages linked by the most complex subway system in the world. Yet these villages—this Tokyo—had more energy than New York, Washington, and Boston combined. Alex was delighted to be part of it. He'd wanted an overseas assignment for some time and had worked hard for his new assignment as sales representative at Micro Communications. His engineering background had been a determining factor in the promotion.

The central clock read 7:30 as Alex entered the building. Todd James, Micro Communications overseas manager, would not be in the office for another hour. Alex relished the time to read his electronic mail and collect his thoughts. Todd—Mr. Japan Know-it-all—irritated him, correcting him at every turn. Everyone in Japan seemed straightforward to Alex, but Todd insisted on making a mystery out of common business practice. Twenty years of being an overseas manager had made Todd incredibly territorial and uptight. Well, Todd was just going to have to get used to sharing the turf, Alex thought.

Todd greeted him when he stepped out of the elevator. "Good to see you. I got here early hoping to meet. Come into my office. We've a lot to discuss."

Todd led the way to a large corner office. One side looked out onto the elegant tile rooftops of the Imperial Palace; the other provided a view of a maze of streets, stretching to the sea, that made up some of the most wealthy business and entertainment districts in the world. Todd had bragged about his view all the way from the airport. By the end of the ride Alex tried to reassure Todd, "I'm here to explore new opportunities with your help." "Micro Communications thinks with my engineering background and your Japan expertise that will be possible." Todd grunted.

Now Todd handed Alex a sheet of paper. "It's a proposal from TDI. They need some technical help on a job that Chiba Motors has proposed."

"Chiba Motors, that's big."

"Yes, and so is TDI."

Alex followed Todd's gaze. The red glow of the morning sun tinged the curved roof of the Imperial Palace.

"Uchida-san, my old friend at TDI of seventeen years, brought me the proposal."

Alex waited.

"Uchida-san thinks it will be big. Twenty-five million anyway. Six million at least in annual revenues. Chiba Motors needs a complete communications system between Tennessee, Los Angeles, and Tokyo. That means fax-telecommunication, video distribution networks, teleconferencing, interactive computer modeling—the works. Managers in Tennessee are in trouble and need constant communication with Tokyo at all hours of the day and night." Todd paused. "I can't tell you the importance of delivering such a system to Chiba Motors."

"TDI?" Alex questioned.

"They will be our partners all the way. Understand?"

"Sure."

"All the way," Todd repeated. "We meet Uchida-san tonight in Shinjuku."

That night Alex had trouble finding the restaurant in Shinjuku and arrived ten minutes late. Todd and three Japanese were already seated around a low table drinking sake. Uchida had an impressive face. The strong lines around his mouth gave him a look of authority. The two other Japanese, Kato and Shimizu, were in their late twenties.

Todd introduced Alex by talking about the first time he'd met Alex at Micro Communications R&D Center in Ohio five years before. Then Todd mentioned the number of letters he'd received from Alex over the years and the subsequent times they'd met at Micro Communications R&D conferences, the most recent one being a communications meeting in Hawaii. When the introduction was over, Alex was irritated that Todd hadn't mentioned Alex's earlier work as an engineer for the Defense Department and for Micro Electronics Corporation. Nor had Todd spoken of Alex's considerable achievements in marketing. Todd was more competitive than he'd imagined, thought Alex.

The evening progressed slowly, and Alex was dumbfounded by the endless chitchat. If Todd's assertion about Uchida's proposal was correct, they were wasting precious time. Each time the conversation waned, Alex expected Uchida to interrupt with an outline of the proposal. By ten o'clock he was dizzy from alcohol. The evening was almost over and they were still smiling and talking about a recent sumo match. It seemed that Uchida routinely rented box seats and took Todd to the games. He watched Todd smile and down another cup of sake. Todd's face was completely relaxed. Alex wondered why Micro Communications America wanted Todd on the job. He didn't seem effective. The expert on Japanese culture and small talk, Alex thought. There was a pause in the conversation. Uchida sipped his sake slowly and nibbled at some pickled shrimp. The silence lengthened. Alex had an urge to laugh. The evening was ridiculous—a total waste.

Uchida spoke slowly. "The proposal from Chiba Motors Company might be interesting."

"Yes," Todd replied softly.

"The technology might create some problems."

Alex spoke quickly. "I've worked in network design. In fact, I've taught network design for over two years both with the Defense Department and with Micro Communications." Alex then proceeded to describe several projects in the area. By the end of his discourse Todd looked pleased.

"Good," Uchida said shortly. "Please come to my office at four P.M. tomorrow. We will discuss the problem in more detail."

Uchida's office was on the thirtieth floor of the TDI building in downtown Tokyo. Seven TDI managers briskly presented their cards before Alex and Todd were seated. Uchida's tone was pragmatic as he opened the meeting and introduced Fujisaki, a manager with a systems engineering degree from MIT, an MBA from Stanford, and two years' work experience in New York City. Fujisaki presented the Chiba Motors proposal using detailed documentation on each point.

Halfway through the presentation, Alex shook his head at Todd. The Chiba Motors proposal was impossible: the technology simply didn't exist, and Alex could see from Todd's incredulous expression that he agreed.

When the lights went on after the last transparency was shown, Todd cleared his throat. He spoke slowly, describing the risk of such a project to both TDI and Micro Communications. "All we have is pieces of the technology. It would be our job to put it together. Maybe we can, maybe we can't." Alex agreed, outlining some of the problems.

Fujisaki responding by showing more transparencies. Uchida did not take part in the discussion—he stared at the desk for some minutes before closing his eyes. The discussion continued for half an hour.

By the time the meeting ended it was well after six. Uchida's face was blank as he said good-bye. Todd was still shaking his head. The TDI managers stood stiffly behind Uchida, except for Fujisaki, who was putting the charts back in the folders. Fujisaki smiled at Alex. "Nice to meet you."

Fujisaki was the kind of urbane, aggressive, modern Japanese Alex had read about. He needed to cultivate that kind of Japanese—more in touch with the real world than either Todd or Uchida. Japanese called them "new human being." Alex said, "Fujisaki-san, your presentation was very insightful."

Fujisaki reddened and looked nervously around the room. Todd, Uchida, and the other engineers had left.

"Let's have drinks. I know a nice place nearby."

"Good idea," Fujisaki agreed.

The bar Alex chose was Japanese style, with small tables that sat neatly over a hole in the tatami mat. Alex took charge and ordered several bottles of sake, beer, and a large assortment of hors d'oeuvres. Fujisaki appeared relaxed and joked about the early fall and the difficulty of the subway. Alex laughed, poured sake, and reminded himself once again that Japan was not that complex. Just like the books said, Alex thought, noting Fujisaki's flushed face—a few drinks and you could really do business in Japan. How many times had he heard from Todd and others that big deals were made after 9:30, sitting on a tatami mat in a small, smoke-filled room. Alex felt elated.

"Fujisaki-san," Alex said, "tell me the real story about Chiba Motors. I don't believe all that stuff you showed on the view graph. It doesn't make sense."

"Doesn't make sense?" Fujisaki's face reddened and he scratched his head.

Alex nodded and poured another round of drinks. "Yeah, no one can make that proposal real. The technology doesn't exist. Todd's a pain in the neck, but in that respect he's right."

Fujisaki put down his glass. He stared at Alex with wide, incredulous eyes and his cheeks reddened.

Fujisaki was paying attention, Alex thought. He was on a roll. "Listen," he said brightly, "you tell me the real story and I'll fix it so we both look like princes. What do you say?"

There was a long pause. Fujisaki lowered his eyes, returned his chopsticks to their holder, and folded his arms across his chest. He remained motionless for several seconds. Alex waited—he was certain Fujisaki would give him the story. Just a matter of time, Alex thought, as the silence lengthened. Fujisaki seemed deep in thought. Suddenly he raised his head. "I must go now," he said hurriedly. "The trains will stop soon." Slightly dazed, Alex stood as Fujisaki hurriedly left the restaurant.

The next day Alex left for Hawaii on a business trip. His mood was good as he left Japan. Todd took him to the airport, so they could talk more about Chiba Motors. Alex had several ideas on the technology that Todd seemed to appreciate, and by the end of the ride Alex felt rather fond of Todd.

Much later, lying on the Waikiki beach, Alex began to feel uneasy. Fujisaki's flushed face haunted him. By the time the sun was sinking into the ocean Alex was sure he'd made a dreadful error. At seven he called Japan.

"Hello, Fujisaki, Alex here." The pause confirmed Alex's suspicions. "May I speak bluntly?"

The silence lengthened.

Alex took a deep breath. "I'm sorry about the other night. I spoke out of turn. Too many drinks and too much business. I hope I didn't cause you any discomfort."

"Not at all," Fujisaki said quickly.

Alex hesitated. Had he said enough? Fujisaki's tone was formal.

There was nothing more he could do, he decided, and after a few pleasantries, he terminated the conversation.

That night Alex received a call from Todd. "You nearly lost it, buster."

"What?"

"It's just lucky you didn't call me before you called Fujisaki to apologize or you would be through in Japan."

"What are you talking about?"

"TDI is what I'm talking about. Uchida-san called this morning and told me all about your interaction with Fujisaki. Then he called me this afternoon just after you apologized and wanted to know if the apology was generated by a conversation with me. I assured him this wasn't the case. I want you back in this office on Monday. We are going ahead with the Chiba Motors deal. It's too much money to pass up." Todd paused. "I'm giving you to Uchida to train. I hope you're worth his time and energy," Todd added dryly.

For the next months Alex worked in the TDI offices with Uchida and a select team of engineers. Their express purpose was to prepare for the upcoming meeting with Chiba Motors. Every aspect of the technology had to be appraised and evaluated. Solutions to technological problems were to be worked out. Uchida anticipated the information would be packed into a three-hour meeting. The task was awesome.

Typically, Uchida arrived at the office by seven-thirty. He went over the prepared documents and then discussed the schedule for the day. Alex was amazed at the extent of Uchida's knowledge of engineering problems. Uchida's staff was impressed with Alex's expertise as well. Take-out lunches and dinners were ordered in from a local restaurant.

By the second week his nerves were raw and there was an acid taste in his mouth. Toward the end of the third week he became short-tempered. Uchida's demands for details were incessant. It seemed as if Alex was under the control of a sadistic, anal-retentive taskmaster. One bright winter morning, he took a short walk around a temple near his home. He sat on the stone temple bench and reread a letter from his fiancée, Ellen. She was ready to call off their engagement unless he returned to America at once. Alex shook his head. How could he explain? Ellen would never understand that

Uchida and the fifteen-hour days were all for the Chiba Motors presentation. She'd think he was insane. Seated on the cold stone, Alex felt his old life slipping away—Ellen, his ambitions, all seemed distant, even trivial. His forehead was wet with perspiration. He must be going mad, he thought.

That morning he arrived at the office twenty minutes late. Uchida tapped his pencil on the table as Alex entered the room. "We have a series of questions that need answers," Uchida said in a brisk tone, glancing at the clock.

"Question one," Uchida said. "What is the distance of the proposed Chiba Motors Telecommunications Center in L.A. from the fault line?"

"What?"

Uchida repeated the question.

"This is absurd, Uchida-san. I have been researching answers fifteen hours a day but this question is absurd. Who cares? Right, who really cares? You've got to be insane to even think up a question like that."

Alex coughed. There was dead silence in the room. Uchida's face was impassive. He nodded as if agreeing with Alex. The silence in the room lengthened. The clock ticked on. Suddenly Alex hated Uchida—he was sick of the endless detail. His fiancée had been right—he needed his own life. The apathy of the morning dissolved in fury. He'd never been so enraged. His heart pounded as he jumped to his feet, turned on his heels, and left the room.

Two hours later he was sitting in the library taking some notes. His head hurt, and he didn't want to think about the phone call Uchida had surely made to Todd. To hell with it, he thought for the hundredth time, he was glad to have set limits. The situation was out of hand. The question about the L.A. building's distance from the fault line showed Uchida was also losing it.

"Hello," Fujisaki said, putting his hand on Alex's shoulder.

"Hello," Alex replied.

Fujisaki sat down. "How are you doing?"

"Fine."

"Good."

"It's been a lot of work?"

"Yes."

"Very tiring."

"Yes."

"Uchida knows how difficult this is. He knows the many hours you are spending in the library doing research.

"That last question—"

"Yes, it is so difficult," Fujisaki said. There was a pause. "But perhaps it would be best if we had that information. Chiba Motors has a reputation for liking detail." Pause. "But I understand that this is difficult. It is so difficult. Do you have trouble sleeping?" his voice softened.

Alex tried to think clearly. He felt irritated and pleased at the same time. It was an uncomfortable feeling. "I'll answer the question," Alex replied.

During the next month the pace did not slacken, and Alex had several more outbursts. But each time, two to three hours later, Fujisaki or another engineer approached him with a gentle explanation of the importance of the information in the overall structure of the Chiba Motors presentation. As time passed, Alex accepted more and more requests. The endless days and the meals of rice, pickled fish, and vegetables were becoming normal. Alex rarely ventured out of the building. His world had shrunk to the library, the planning sessions, and the mock presentations. Uchida's insistence on detail had become a challenge.

Uchida and his engineers did not ask any questions at Alex's last mock presentation. Concerned, he stood for several minutes at the blackboard waiting for the barrage to begin. Uchida stared at the floor and the silence lengthened. Suddenly Uchida was out of his seat, moving across the floor quickly. His hands were around Alex's shoulders and his grip was surprisingly strong. Over Uchida's shoulder he saw the surprised looks of Fujisaki and three Japanese engineers. The silence in the room lengthened. Alex was breathless. At last Uchida broke away.

The next evening Todd informed Alex that he had been promoted to director of sales in Japan. When he walked into the office at seven-thirty the following morning to start the briefing, Uchida smiled at him.

"You had good news last night," Uchida said. "You are now director of sales."

Alex blinked. Was his phone bugged? Todd had called to tell him late last night. Before that the promotion was top secret. Todd had sworn him to secrecy.

Uchida grinned and pounded the table with his fist. "Tonight we will celebrate. Tonight you will be my guest at *bunraku* [puppet theater]."

That night Alex met Uchida at a small Japanese-style restaurant on the Ginza. He was sitting next to a beautiful middle-aged Japanese woman dressed in a kimono, whom he introduced as Midori. Midori poured sake for both men. Alex noticed her apricot fingernail polish as her tiny hand grasped the bottle. A tortoiseshell comb framed her bun at the nape of her neck.

"Midori is a patron of *bunraku*," Uchida explained. "She knows more about the puppets than the masters. Often she will visit Osaka, the home of *bunraku*, just to see a certain play."

"You're flattering me," Midori laughed and poured more sake. Uchida translated.

As the evening progressed Alex learned that Midori and Uchida had known each other for the past thirty years. Every Thursday, rain or shine, even at times like these, when he was under pressure, Midori and he would meet at this restaurant before attending *bunraku*. Alex noted the easy atmosphere between them—Midori teased and Uchida laughed. He wondered about Midori, but felt he could not ask. By the time they left for *bunraku*, Alex had forgotten the fifteen-hour days. He lost himself in the darkened *bunraku* theater, and as Midori explained the role of the master puppeteer in a mixture of broken English and Japanese, reality merged with fantasy and Alex allowed himself to dream.

The morning of the Chiba presentation was the first warm day of spring. Alex, Uchida, Fujisaki, and four other engineers from TDI met at the Chiba Motors office at nine o'clock in downtown Tokyo. They were led to a conference room equipped with an overhead projector and a blackboard. Alex and Fujisaki were scheduled for a two-hour presentation. Alex began to worry when he saw that Sakamura, the senior managing director of Chiba, was present. All told, twenty-one other Chiba Motors managers, ranging from the factory floor managers to people in communications and data processing, were in attendance.

Uchida introduced Alex, Fujisaki, and the other TDI engineers. Alex's was the first presentation. He stood at the blackboard and began to talk about the project in general. A middle-aged woman in a dark blue suit translated. Sakamura began the questioning. "You are aware that Chiba Motors has purchased a communications building in Los Angeles."

"Yes," Alex answered quickly. "I believe in Santa Monica."

"That is correct," Sakamura answered. "How far is the Chiba Motors communications building from the San Andreas Fault, and what would be the impact on the building of a major earthquake?"

As Alex began to answer, he didn't dare look at Uchida.

The questions did not stop at the end of two hours. Chiba Motors wanted to know detailed questions about software interfaces, hardware options, and the installation process. Alex drew diagrams and equations on the blackboard. The questions were as good as Uchida had anticipated. By one they were still coming fast. They ordered a take-out lunch.

At two Alex again took the stand. He felt ill with fatigue by the time Sakamura stopped the questioning at seven. This time TDI and Alex were hosted by Chiba Motors in a nearby Japanese restaurant. The atmosphere was relaxed. Alex tried to catch Uchida's eye for a reaction, but his expression was blank.

"You have the natural speaking voice of a Japanese," Sakamura said.

"Thank you," Alex answered.

"Do you like Japanese women?"

Alex nodded his head, affirming that he'd heard the statement without agreeing or disagreeing.

"Do you have a Japanese girlfriend?"

Again Alex bobbed his head as if considering the statement.

Sakamura smiled and filled Alex's sake cup. For the rest of the meal he seemed in exceptionally good humor. Uchida also smiled, poured sake, and seemed generally pleased.

After dinner Alex, Fujisaki, and four engineers from Chiba Motors met in a hotel room. They outlined a time schedule for the project that included technical exchanges and product articulation process. By the end of the meeting Alex was satisfied that he had a good working relationship with Chiba Motors. In the next few weeks Alex attended many similar meetings on technical details with middle-management engineers.

It was late spring when Todd dropped the news that TDI had lost the bid to Nanri Corporation as equipment suppliers to Chiba Motors. Todd had already received a call from Sone, the general manager of Nanri Corporation. Alex listened carefully to Todd's recommendation that he immediately be in touch with Sone. "After all our work, we don't want to be left out," Todd said. "Nanri Corporation will need the same expertise as TDI in making the communications network happen. We have experience in this area, but unfortunately some of our competitors have the same expertise. I have checked on Nanri Corporation and from my sources they will need some help. We don't want them to approach another company," Todd finished.

Sone seemed to have expected Alex's call and they set up a meeting for the next day.

During the next few weeks Alex met repeatedly with Sone and his group of engineers. The communication network system was slowly falling into place. Alex was pleased with the progress and was also pleased to be back in Micro Communications offices. Memories of Uchida and the back-breaking days of work faded as the blueprints were being drawn up. It was all worth it, thought Alex. He was his own man now. Communications with Sone and the other engineers was a breeze after working with TDI.

On a Friday afternoon three weeks after he'd begun working with Sone, Alex received a phone call from Micro Communications engineers in America. They wanted technical information about the network that Alex and TDI had developed. Alex felt pleased as he dialed Uchida's number. He missed the old boy. Perhaps they could combine dinner and business, he thought, remembering the small Japanese restaurants they frequented in Asakusa.

"Hello, is Uchida there?"

"Who may I say is calling?"

"Alex James."

"Which company?"

"Micro Communications."

"Please wait a second." Mozart played on the telephone.

"I'm sorry, Uchida is out just now."

"When will he be back?"

"We're not sure."

"Let me speak to Fujisaki."

"Just a minute, please." Mozart again was heard.

"Fujisaki is also out."

"Do you know when he'll return?"

"His secretary is not sure."

Alex asked for several other engineers, but they were all out.

He shrugged off his letdown, returning to the latest set of diagrams that Sone and his group of engineers had delivered.

During the next week Alex frequently tried to reach Uchida and the other engineers at TDI for the information Micro Communications America urgently needed. Uchida and his engineers were always either out or busy with a meeting. By the middle of the second week, Alex was calling twice a day.

At the end of the second week he received a phone call from Sakamura of Chiba Motors. His tone was formal as he expressed concern about the project. Chiba Motors was concerned about the latest blueprints. Had Alex been in touch with Micro Communications America? Was there some engineering problem? Alex reassured Sakamura that everything was under control. Immediately after hanging up, he again called Uchida. Uchida was in Osaka for the day.

Alex walked slowly to Todd's corner office. He glanced briefly at the view of the Imperial Palace. Todd's grand view depressed him.

"Alex, what can I do?" Todd's tone was cheerful.

Alex explained the situation. It was a relief to talk. Todd would understand. It was those enigmatic Japanese, Alex thought furiously, as he ended his speech with a description of the latest phone call from Sakamura.

"You are either oblivious or a fool," Todd's voice was quiet.

Alex stared at Todd's white face.

"You mean you didn't include Uchida and TDI in the conversations with Nanri Corporation?"

"Nanri Corporation got the job," Alex said. "They won the bid for the job with Chiba Motors over TDI."

Todd stared at Alex. It was a look of utter disdain. "You're an ass. We are in solid with TDI. Do you understand what that means? Nanri knows that we work closely with TDI. Even if they lost the contract, you just don't put Uchida on an ice block. You should have talked it over with Sone. He might have had some ideas. You should have definitely talked it over with Uchida," he paused. "I'll call him."

A week later Alex received a call from Uchida. His voice was cheerful. He wanted to have dinner that night. Was Alex free? They agreed to meet in Asakusa at a small restaurant that specialized in blowfish.

Alex was greatly relieved to see that Uchida had reserved a small room and was alone. He'd ordered a complete dinner including sake scented with the tail of the *fugu*. The conversation was general and lighthearted. Uchida was his most charming. He related stories of his uncle's time in Borneo during the war. "He loved the natives of Borneo," he stated emphatically. "Whenever anyone criticized them, my uncle yelled and said, "I starved just like them, and by the end of the war my legs were as skinny as theirs. Good people." Uchida laughed and poured more sake. Alex smiled, feeling briefly like a native from Borneo.

It was ten o'clock by the time the meal ended. Alex's mouth tingled from the *fugu* fish. Nothing important was discussed. Perhaps that's how it should be, he thought, looking affectionately at Uchida's smiling face.

There was a long pause. "I've enjoyed the past two weeks," Uchida said.

"What?"

"Yes," Uchida nodded. "I have enjoyed the last two weeks very much."

Alex was silent. "Why?" he asked.

Uchida threw back his head and laughed. It was a boyish laugh, one that came from the belly. The clear sound filled the room. "I enjoyed seeing you squirm, Alex-san." Then Uchida laughed again, this time catching Alex's eyes. Alex laughed too.

Analysis:

The case of Alex opens with his lack of understanding of the preparation necessary in the "know me" and "trust me" stages of a relationship with the Japanese. Alex only superficially understands Japan and the Japanese. He is confident of his professional qualifications and fully expects others to be aware and appreciative of his achievements as well. This arrogance reveals itself in his competitive relationship with Todd, as well as in his assumptions about the role he should play at meetings with the Japanese.

Alex is late for his initial meeting with Uchida and TDI. Lack of punctuality in Japan shows a lack of commitment and is a sign of disrespect. In this case Alex should have called the restaurant and let the participants of the meeting know he was running late. Alex feels the tone of the dinner is too informal given the serious intention of the meeting, and he is irritated by Todd's introduction, which describes the history of their relationship rather than Alex's credentials. In the "know me" and "trust me" stages such introductions are common. History is the best introduction in Japan. Self-introductions are also based on personal and professional history, with emphasis on professors and other mentors. A track record of the individual's relationships confirms that the individual can be trusted.

At the end of the meeting the conversation becomes serious and Alex lets TDI know his credentials. It is common for business in Japan to be discussed in the late evening after several hours of drinks. Japanese are interested in a friendly tone in business.

Again in his first business meeting with TDI, Alex does not understand Japanese etiquette in the "trust me" phase. He compliments Fujisaki on his presentation, which singles Fujisaki out of the group and sets up a special relationship between them. Fujisaki is nervous that others might observe this interaction. Alex's apologetic phone call after the bar incident saves him because it is a gesture that reveals Alex's true character. In the early stages of a relationship, Japanese are conscious of sincerity and believe that choice is the best indicator of character. Often a newcomer to a situation will be offered several choices in order to test his dedication and his sensitivity to nuance. Alex's unsolicited apology allows him entry to the "believe me" phase of a relationship with TDI.

The incident in the bar also highlights the intricate system of social control in Japan. Fujisaki consults with Uchida about the incident in the bar. Uchida then relays his concerns to Todd. In this manner all parties have been informed.

Uchida prepared for the Chiba Motors presentation by concentrating on detail. Like many Japanese managers, Uchida's background is in engineering and therefore his questions reveal good knowledge of the technology. This is a common strategy for business meetings in Japan. The attention to detail is commitment and this commitment in turn reveals sincerity.

In the "believe me" stage, Alex is accepted as a member of the group. His tantrums are tolerated. Fujisaki acts as a go-between for Uchida by approaching Alex some hours after the outburst and coaxing him to accept the work load. In these sessions Fujisaki does not try to explain Uchida or to chastise Alex, but rather empathizes with Alex. This method of encouraging Alex to accept the situation is common in the "believe me" phase of a relationship where the person is already an acknowledged member of the group. The same coaxing and sympathy is used by adults with children to accept situations.

Finally after a particularly long day Alex enters the inner circle of the group with a spontaneous hug from Uchida and an invitation to the theater. Uchida's show of emotion is instinctual and typically Japanese. His invitation to bunraku *merely underscores the reality of an already intimate relationship. The meeting with Chiba Motors goes beyond everyone's expectations in terms of length and detail and Alex finds that he is tested on his commitment.*

Alex has clearly passed the test with Uchida and has entered the "marry me" phase of the relationship. However, at this stage the relationship needs to be continually nurtured. Alex does not include TDI on his contract with Nanri Corporation. For Alex, TDI has lost the contract with Chiba Motors and is no longer a "player." However, from Japanese standards this is not how "insiders" play the game. Uchida expects to be consulted and included as much as is reasonable. Uchida does not confront Alex with his lapse in judgment but reacts in a passive-aggressive manner by remaining unavailable when Alex needs his help. In desperation, Alex resorts to using Todd as a go-between and relies on Todd to be direct with him. Finally Uchida's invitation to dinner makes clear his commitment to Alex is contingent on Alex's continued nurturing of the situation. The "marry me" phase merely underscores the description of Japan as a country of "networks." The case illustrates that understanding how those networks are maintained is as important as acquiring the networks in the first place.

STEVE: Networks to the Inside

Steve leaned back on his desk and folded his arms around his chest. There was a rapid knock. Ed Brown entered the room, his face pale, and glanced nervously at the papers he held in his right hand. Ed's straightforward manner reminded Steve of himself when he'd first come to Japan—a Texan, cheerfully cut-and-dry, always ready to tackle a new situation, win, and then remind others in a thousand ways of how he'd done it.

"Steve," I've got something here," Ed said, handing him papers. "We're in deep . . . ten thousand parts—all defective, every last one of them. These are just the first reports"—he nodded at the papers— "When the rest come in, well, our name is mud here and in Japan."

Steve felt his blood pressure rising, and his head began to hammer. How could such a thing happen? He'd given orders that all the parts be checked. Ed was talking about calling the company lawyers and lawsuits.

As Steve reached toward the phone, he suddenly imagined Osumi's face. "You are in the castle now," Osumi had toasted at a meeting last week in a small *yakitori* bar. "To the castle." Steve had smiled at his mentor as he lifted his sake cup. If it weren't for Osumi and his own stubborn curiosity, he'd still be another frustrated American businessman. It had taken five years to get to the "castle." No one stateside would believe that Steve had allowed himself to be led for five years on a quest for some Japanese pie-in-the-sky. Ed was still talking about lawyers.

"Come back in twenty minutes, and we'll discuss what to do," Steve said. "Don't call any damned lawyers until I say so!"

When Ed left the office, Steve closed his eyes. He needed time to collect himself. His mind flashed back six years.

It was in late July, just six months after his arrival in Japan, that Steve first met Osumi. Steve remembered how puffed with importance he'd been. He had built his reputation at TRIX as a trouble shooter and had often been sent to branch offices to turn things around. He saw his assignment as president of TRIX Japan in the same light. The reports read, "Japan was not moving . . . Japanese only wanted licensing deals . . . TRIX barely breaking even . . . little market penetration . . . low market share." TRIX sold its merchandise to the Fortune 500 in America. It had a world-class reputation for innovative technology. His marching orders were to cut dead wood, streamline, make things efficient, turn a profit every quarter.

It was in that spirit that Steve and his assistant Nomura arranged for a meeting with Osumi of Sanko company. TRIX had been doing business with the Sanko foundry for years. The books showed little or no profit. It was time to cut the cord. Nomura didn't protest, merely observing that Osumi was a powerful man.

"There's not a damned thing Osumi-san or Sanko can do about it," Steve replied. "Our contract is up for renewal."

Nomura was silent.

It was stiflingly hot that morning as Steve left his house. "I'll be home for dinner," he promised his wife, Emily, at the door.

"Promise?" Emily replied.

Steve looked at her worn face. "Promise," he repeated firmly. Emily was a good wife. He'd told her when they married that he intended to go right to the top, but the journey would be difficult. These days he was gone six out of seven nights at business dinners and Emily was left alone to arrange the children's lives in a culture totally different from her own. His two boys, who fought constantly, were definitely not making a good adjustment.

"It's a day trip," he said softly. "I'll be back by seven." Emily had that fragile look she got when she was about to cry. He turned on his heels and walked swiftly to the car.

The meeting in Osaka was held in Sanko's small meeting room, with two couches covered in a Victorian-looking floral brocade separated by a coffee table topped with three small doilies. There were some pictures of horses on the wall. He'd heard that Osumi liked horse racing. Suddenly Steve was curious to meet this important man.

Five minutes later the door opened. Steve checked his watch. Two o'clock on the button. Japanese were remarkably punctual, he thought, as he stood, following Nomura's lead.

Osumi was a small, bright-eyed man dressed in a nondescript gray suit. He presented his business card with authority. "Osumi desu."

Steve sat on the couch where Osumi indicated.

"Did you have a pleasant journey?" Osumi began the conversation slowly. His English was good, and Steve immediately relaxed. He fingered the folder and waited.

But Osumi continued discussing the weather for another fifteen minutes. Steve was getting edgy. He'd never heard so much detail about typhoons. He wondered if Osumi was making a point. If that was the case, Steve was sure missing it. Finally there was a pause.

"I am here to discuss the renewal of the contract."

"Good!" Osumi's face brightened.

"I have the figures here of business between the TRIX and Sanko companies for the last two years. In fact I have the figures for the last five years," Steve began.

"Good!" Osumi repeated.

Nomura coughed.

Steve opened the folder. "As this chart indicates, TRIX company has broken just above even for the last two years. Before that TRIX made only a tiny profit," he said, handing the pages to Osumi.

"I see," Osumi repeated and looked at the charts closely with great interest.

Steve let Osumi pour over the charts, watching him nod as he understood each point on the graph. The meeting was going well, Steve thought. Just let Osumi take time with the figures. TRIX's decision about the contract renewal would be obvious from what was on the charts. Osumi's face was curiously still. Steve was sure Osumi grasped the point.

Steve smiled. "Under the circumstances I don't believe it advisable for TRIX to sign a new contract."

"I understand," Osumi said.

Nomura coughed again.

"Good," Steve said, returning the pages to their folder. Osumi smiled and talked traffic patterns in the late afternoon and the best route to take to the airport. Then he stood. The meeting was over. Just over an hour and a half, Steve thought. Wonderful!

"Osburn-san," Osumi addressed him softly.

"Yes," Steve smiled and extended his hand.

Osumi bowed and half extended his own. "Shall we have a drink and some supper? I know a nice place quite close by."

Steve hesitated. He liked Osumi, but he'd made a promise to Emily. If he left now, he'd be only half an hour late.

"We'd love to have a drink and supper," Nomura spoke firmly. "Thank you for the invitation."

There was an awkward pause. Steve heard himself agreeing and Osumi finalizing the details.

Osumi took them to a small restaurant near his office. The room was divided into sections and customers sat on the floor around tables. The serving girl brought sake and Osumi talked of nothing in particular. The effect of the sake was beginning to numb Steve. He stopped glancing at his watch.

Suddenly Osumi turned to him. "Osburn-san, please excuse my bluntness. You're making a mistake. Frankly speaking, stopping business with Sanko is a mistake TRIX will regret."

"What do you mean?" Steve stammered, suddenly sober. "I thought we agreed in the meeting at the office that terminating the contract was a good idea. What mistake?"

Steve looked at Nomura for help. Nomura's face was blank. It dawned on him that Nomura must have known something was going to happen. Was Nomura in on the plot? Steve didn't know what to think.

"The foundry business is noncritical," Osumi replied. "It's a perfect business for building a reputation. Once you have done well here and shown you're a good person to do business with, then it is time to move you closer to the inner moat of the castle."

"Inner moat? Castle?" Steve was feeling like an idiot. On the one hand, Steve wanted to let Osumi know he was TRIX's golden boy, the disciplined hell raiser, first on his University of Texas football team and good enough to get into a top business school without work experience and an engineering background. On the other hand, Steve was just plain curious. What the hell was Osumi talking about? What castle?

Realizing it was useless to quiz Nomura, Steve was silent on the plane back to Tokyo. Steve would probably never know whether Osumi and Nomura had talked beforehand. He rather doubted it, but Nomura had read the meeting differently, that was for sure. Nomura understood Japan in a way that Steve couldn't fathom. Steve felt alone and depressed.

Nevertheless, by the time they arrived in Tokyo, he was definitely curious. He wanted to know what Nomura understood. What did Osumi mean by "castle"?

During the next year, Steve met frequently with Osumi, mostly in small restaurants and bars near Osumi's Osaka office. They discussed their current contract and general business strategy and Osumi listened carefully to Steve's description of TRIX's business portfolio in Japan. The most important discussions always occurred when the evening was almost over, leaving Steve with a feeling that there was more to be said. There certainly was more to be learned. Osumi patiently explained the networks and alliances that made up the Japanese business world. He used institutions and people effectively.

For instance, one night the following spring Steve explained TRIX's frustration at not being able to get a market share in Japan. "Licensing technology to Japanese companies is not a viable business strategy," Steve said, "but that's all Japanese companies want from TRIX. I am no closer to turning that around for TRIX than when I first came here."

"Have patience," Osumi said. "If you build trust, TRIX will be ready for the next step."

"I'm ready now."

"Have patience."

One night they dined at Osumi's favorite restaurant, the same one he'd taken Steve to the day they met. *"Kampai,"* Osumi said, lifting his sake cup.

It was past ten and Steve also raised his cup, thinking it was the last drink of the evening. *"Kampai,"* Steve replied.

Suddenly Osumi leaned across the table. "Would TRIX like to supply TAN company?"

Steve grinned. "I thought TAN's suppliers were all sewn up: Sanko, HONGO, NKR."

"One company would have to drop as a supplier," Osumi replied. "TRIX would take that place."

"Are you trying to tell me . . ." Steve began. Osumi's face was blank. Steve held his tongue and lifted his glass. He needed time to think. One of the largest, most successful firms in Japan, TAN was an industrial conglomerate with fingers in virtually every sector. Of all the Japanese companies, TAN was reported to be the most insular. Only the best Japanese companies supplied TAN. To be a supplier to TAN meant you had passed every Japanese test, jumped though every Japanese hoop. In short, to be a supplier to TAN would mean tremendous honor and prestige for TRIX. TRIX would cross that moat.

Osumi's face still had a faraway look. "TAN must agree. TAN must help NKR understand that they must give up the business with TAN. Also TRIX and Sanko must work closely with NKR to help them understand."

Yes, thought Steve, good thinking, Osumi. NKR is going to buy this like a cold morning in hell. Voluntarily give up a huge business. The only contact TRIX had with NKR was through one licensing agreement for technology. Although Steve had been promised a business deal between TRIX and NKR, his overtures had always been rejected. NKR wanted only technology. Either Osumi is losing it, or I'm hearing things. NKR would never be convinced to give up a huge business, especially to a foreign company.

"I know Kato, a top man at NKR," Osumi continued. "Kato works closely with MITI on market access issues in Japan. I think he is the person we should approach first."

During the next year Osumi and Steve had many dinner meetings together with Kato, always in small Japanese restaurants in downtown Osaka. There was much discussion of business, especially the relationship of suppliers to TAN. Kato entered into these discussions with enthusiasm. Steve never brought up NKR's licensing agreement with TRIX. He knew NKR's licensing contract was up for renewal within the next couple of years.

Two and a half years after the meetings with Kato began, Steve received a call from Kato. He and a team from NKR wanted to meet at a small Japanese restaurant in downtown Tokyo. Immediately Steve consulted Osumi as to what would be discussed. Osumi felt it was the right time to talk about the relation between TRIX's licensing agreement with NKR and market access to TAN. Steve decided to bring three TRIX people: Nomura, Oda (Nomura's assistant, who acted as a translator), and himself.

NKR had reserved a private room at the restaurant. Steve bowed and presented his business card to the NKR men he didn't know. He was given the seat of honor, opposite Kato, with his back to the scroll. Kato began to discuss crowding in Tokyo and the miserable heat. Steve joined in cautiously. The conversation was conducted in English and Japanese, with Oda translating. Steve thought of the 2 ½ years of preparation. It could all go down the drain in a night. He suddenly realized he was glad that he was one of those men who got drunk only when he wanted to. There would be plenty of sake tonight and he needed his wits about him.

About an hour into dinner, Steve decided to bite the bullet. He was not sure this was the right time. According to custom, the hosts should bring up business, but no one had mentioned business and it seemed entirely possible that the dinner would be over with nothing accomplished. Then both TRIX and NKR would be back to go-betweens. Osumi had repeatedly told Steve to follow his instincts; this made him brave. "Kato-san," he said. "TRIX is aware of the enormous pressure on your industry from MITI to give foreign firms more access to the Japanese market."

Kato smiled. "Yes, enormous pressure," he agreed. The other NKR men also nodded as if this was a brilliant but worrisome observation. Their faces remained expectant. Steve felt he was on the right track—Nomura hadn't coughed.

"TRIX would like to help with this problem of market share," Steve continued. "TRIX is in a good position in Japan. We have done business here for years and feel it is time to move into the Japanese marketplace, direct sales."

The four NKR men looked at their plates. There was a long silence. Steve knew the NKR men were thinking of supplying TAN and the "trade off" licensing agreement with TRIX. Regarding the renewal of the licensing agreement with TRIX, Steve was sure the incentives from MITI, Sanko, and HONGO must have been tremendous for NKR to give up its business as a supplier to TAN. He wondered if TAN had also given NKR something. Suddenly Steve was certain that they were involved also. The thought made him feel weary.

Steve wondered if he should mention TAN. After all, TAN was on everyone's mind. The NKR team was still silent. Had he done something wrong? Kato looked pale, and the others were staring at their plates. Steve wanted to look at Nomura but did not dare. Maybe he would have started in a straightforward way about the NKR–TRIX licensing agreement. After all, business was a trade-off.

Steve picked up a pickle. His forehead was perspiring. He kept eating. Nomura began eating also. Perhaps he hadn't said enough. He'd seen Kato be very direct. Maybe he should lay it all out, let everyone know the situation. A little hard ball never hurt.

Kato began to speak. "Perhaps TRIX would be helpful as an example of a foreign firm getting good market access to Japan. Perhaps that is possible." The other Japanese nodded and murmured their assent.

"Perhaps TRIX would be helpful . . ." Steve repeated Kato's phrase. He wasn't really sure. Had Kato agreed? Should he mention the licensing contract just to make sure? He was beginning to feel ill. Nomura coughed. Steve bit his lip and remained silent.

The next morning he called Osumi. "Your call is ten minutes late," Osumi laughed.

Steve was silent. He tried to gauge Osumi's voice.

"The dinner was a great success. You're moving closer," Osumi said. "It's time you met with TAN."

"Osumi-san, isn't it time you discussed it at your board?" Steve said in exasperation. Osumi was silent.

"My president doesn't like to discuss problems at the board meeting," Osumi's voice was soft. "He expects facts at the board meeting, not problems." Steve had never heard Osumi's voice so deliberately soft. "Do you understand?"

That day Steve flew to Osaka and took Osumi to the best French restaurant he could find. By the end of the meal Osumi was relaxed, toasting Sanko and TRIX.

Shortly thereafter, even before the first official meeting with TAN, Steve and Osumi began working with the technical people from TAN. The meetings were small, and engineers from both companies worked intently on the product.

Finally, five years after Osumi and Steve's initial meeting, TAN, TRIX, Sanko, and HONGO met at TAN headquarters. Engineers from both TAN and TRIX made brief presentations. The meeting was cut-and-dry and Steve sensed that all details had been worked out earlier. Everyone agreed on the supply strategy to TAN.

A knock brought Steve back to the present. He knew it was Ed with his list of lawyers. What a fool, Steve thought. It had taken five years to get into the castle—five years of meetings and dinners, of making connections and creating trust—and a man like Ed could blow it in five minutes.

Steve would be leaving Japan soon. Emily wanted to go home, and the children were going to college. He'd promised Emily just a couple more years. He needed to start training someone, someone who was aggressive, smart, and intuitive.

"I've got a list of lawyers," Ed stuck his head in the door. "I haven't called anyone."

"Good," Steve said. "Come on in, Ed. I'm going to make a bunch of calls to all those affected, and I want you to listen."

"Listen?"

"Yes, and take notes. Then I want you to clear the decks for a dinner meeting tonight."

"With?"

"The first person I call."

"But I promised my wife. You know we've just arrived. We're in ..." Steve waited.

"I'll call her," Ed said, picking up a notebook and pencil.

"Good," Steve replied. TRIX would stay inside the castle, he thought, looking at Ed's bewildered but curious expression. Yes, Ed could learn, Steve decided.

Analysis:

In Japan a network of give-and-take relationships between upper levels of business management, government bureaucrats, and the Liberal Democratic Party determine a great deal of Japanese business practice. Managers from the largest Japanese companies sit on MITI committees that discuss a series of issues from government-funded research to market access, production, and trade friction. In turn, some government bureaucrats join private industry upon retirement. Big business funds the Liberal Democratic Party and expects favor-

*able treatment. Together these professionals try to coordinate Japan's
complex economic and industrial policies. To the outside this complex
matrix of relationships has given Japan the reputation of a "black
box" known as "Japan Incorporated."*

*As with any system, "Japan Inc." is by no means immune from
interest groups. Politicians and bureaucrats are susceptible to pressure from labor, small business, agriculture, public opinion, press,
opposition parties, and even the United States government. However,
the voice of lobbyists alone is insufficient to bring about change.
Interest groups, whether Japanese or foreign, not only must understand the relationship among government, industry, and bureaucracy, but also must have personal access to key people in these institutions.*

*Steve's case reveals the importance of building a relationship with
key people in order to gain access to this system. Instinctively, Steve
not only understands but is intrigued by the process of building trust
with Osumi. His journey with Osumi takes Steve five years, in which
he goes through the four distinct stages of a relationship with a
Japanese. As the relationship with Osumi deepens, so does Steve's
understanding of Japan, Osumi's trust in Steve, and his willingness
to make Steve part of the system.*

*The case opens in the "know me" stage of the relationship. Steve
intends not to renew TRIX's business with Sanko. Although Steve is
prepared for the meeting with Osumi in terms of etiquette and careful
documentation, Steve's agenda is clear: TRIX must get out of a
nonprofitable situation. He is confused by Osumi's insistence on discussing the weather as a preamble to business. Osumi is maintaining
the Japanese custom of establishing a suitable entrée through small
talk before actual business begins. Osumi would like the meeting to
continue in the same tone, no matter what the differences and no
matter how hard the bargaining. The office meeting ends on a cordial,
agreeable tone.*

*In the restaurant, however, Osumi's reasonable tone disappears,
and he uses vague language to express his feelings that TRIX should
remain in business with Sanko. It's customary in Japan to use office
space to discuss official business; in that light, Osumi's request that
Steve and Nomura join him for a drink is also an invitation for a
potential off-the-record meeting. Alcohol provides a cover for this*

*off-the-record talk. Traditionally in Japan alcohol allows for behavior that is otherwise not permitted. In a sense alcohol can provide a loophole in the business system. Alcohol, often called the source of life (*inochi no moto*), is considered a permission slip to be more open and start a bonding process. It is considered a positive contribution to humanity and its effects are also seen in the same light.*

*Osumi initiates a mentor relationship with Steve and expects this relationship to develop into a friendship that will equalize over time. He is impressed with Steve's negotiation skills and his willingness to be patient (*nintai*) through the meeting. Steve is open-minded enough to accept an invitation for a drink even though the meeting in the office had supposedly ended dealings between TRIX and Sanko.*

In the months that follow, Osumi and Steve meet frequently and enter into the "trust me" phase of the relationship. Hal explains that TRIX wants market share, not licensing agreements. Osumi counsels patience and continues to act as Steve's mentor, explaining the intricacies of Japanese business practice. Finally, when Osumi thinks Steve is ready, he suggests that TRIX take the place of NKR as a supplier to TAN. To Steve's amazement Osumi introduces Steve to Kato, who is a manager at NKR and also sits on a MITI committee that works on market access issues.

Thus, through a mentor relationship with Osumi, Steve is introduced to the upper levels of management of "Japan Inc." and enters into the "believe me" phase of the relationship. Steve is aware that NKR's renewal of a licensing agreement with TRIX is not enough to make NKR drop out as a supplier to TAN. Another factor is MITI's pressure on NKR to "help" with market access to American companies, which will alleviate pressure from the United States. Finally, Steve understands there must have been other trade-offs among NKR, HONGO, Sanko, and TAN. Steve begins to comprehend the delicate orchestration of influence and pressure between the Japanese bureaucracy and the upper levels of Japanese business management. He also is aware of the impact of the lobbyists (including the United States itself) on Japanese government and business. The relationship between influence groups, the Japanese government, and business determine not only the players but also how the game is played.

Steve's entry into the Japanese system in the "marry me" phase is based on his relationship with Osumi, which has taken years of build-

ing trust. Only once does Steve try to short-cut the endless meetings with Osumi by asking him to bring the matter of TAN up with the SANKO board. Almost immediately Steve realizes his error of questioning his mentor's judgment by trying to make a deal official before there has been adequate preparation. Steve corrects his mistake with an expensive dinner of atonement. Osumi remains an important go-between. To make public his role or to formalize the back-room politics of the deal with NKR and TAN is inadmissible in this situation. Steve must learn that Osumi's integrity is bound up in his role as go-between. In this situation Osumi is playing the role of guarantor (hoshonin). The guarantor accepts full responsibility for all actions of the person he is introducing. His sense of understanding of situations and ability to orchestrate those situations for everyone's benefit is crucial to carrying out his role with dignity and self-respect. Steve must show his trust by patience and by working with Osumi as a team.

Finally TRIX and TAN meet to formalize their relationship. TRIX has crossed the moat to the castle. It has taken five years for TRIX to become part of the inner circle, with close Japanese business partners, and for Steve to understand the Japanese business-government network. Therefore, when Steve is faced with a problem he does not march straight to his lawyers; instead, he calls on the loyalty of his go-betweens and his business associates to correct a difficult situation. For Steve, as a member of the "castle" in the "marry me" phase of a relationship, terminating business or even the threat of terminating business is not a viable business strategy.

ARTHUR: Success Through Interpretation Rather Than Confrontation

Arthur straightened his jacket and tucked the wool scarf around his neck. He hadn't expected December in Tokyo to be so raw. The narrow streets were like wind tunnels, he thought miserably, as he peered out the taxi window. The car stopped and his door swung open. Arthur handed the money to the white-gloved taxi driver.

The memory of the taxi driver's spotless, pressed white gloves irritated Arthur as he entered the government building. Arthur was a no-nonsense New Yorker; at home, grimy cabs were part of the landscape. He loved his family and his work. Arthur never felt better than when seated on the bleachers yelling at a local baseball game. He was proud of the fact that he and his son Allen never missed a game.

Arthur's down-to-earth personality had earned him respect at General Aviation. In fact, he'd been chosen for the job of negotiating General Aviation's contract with the Ministry of International Trade and Industry (MITI) because of his good common sense. Dr. Sharp, president of General Aviation, had talked to him personally about the job. "Your engineering degree, your MBA in business administration, and your experience with NASA in Washington make you the right man for the job, Arthur." Arthur had protested briefly that he knew nothing about the Japanese. "No one knows the Japanese," Dr. Sharp snapped. "Even the Japanese are confused by this contract."

Sharp explained quickly that MITI had already negotiated contracts with the three key players in the Japanese jet engine business at 65 percent equity participation. Ten percent was reserved for Japanese National Laboratories. Now they were inviting foreign key players to join the consortium at 25 percent participation: General Aviation; TRD, an electronics company also from the United States; BTU, an aerospace company from Britain; and Tandeau, a French aerospace company.

Arthur waited patiently while Sharp rattled off the figures. He had been briefed on the material, but Sharp knew that. Sharp must be worried about having such a small part of the pie, Arthur thought.

When Sharp switched abruptly to the politics of the situation, Arthur listened carefully. He knew that General Aviation and TRD were also bidding for the RMX contract to supply jet engines to the Japanese military. The RMX contract had been in all the newspapers. MITI was aware of the potential complications of inviting the same two American players to be part of this consortium. Arthur was more concerned about General Aviation's contract with the U.S. government to develop a jet engine that would allow planes to travel at twenty-five times the speed of sound.

"Won't the U.S. government be more than a little annoyed if we go with the Japanese?" Arthur asked.

"Frankly, I believe there is a chance that U.S. funds will run out, and I believe the Japanese idea of a jet engine that will go five times the speed of sound is good," Dr. Sharp said. "We are lucky MITI has had relations with us. As you know, General Aviation has contacts with MITI from previous participation in a consortium with Japanese industry, which was funded by MITI. Other foreign firms also have good contacts in Japan. For instance, BTU and Danko Heavy Industries have plans to do joint ventures."

When Arthur politely reiterated his question about a conflict of interest with the U.S. government, Dr. Sharp said it was part of his job to see that there was none. Arthur knew the people in Washington to speak to about this, Sharp insisted.

The interview ended with a warning from Sharp. "The Japanese have the money, Arthur. They will do this project with or without us. We have a lot more to lose if we keep on the outside. Your job is to create a win/win situation for General Aviation, in Japan and in America. This is a first, Arthur. You are breaking ground."

It had taken all of Arthur's imagination to create a meaningful dialogue with the American government. He had numerous meetings with the Department of Commerce, as well as other agencies, to convince them that General Aviation's approach was to bid on development of a technology that currently did not exist in America. To make matters easier, Arthur had also initiated the complete physical separation of the two projects. General Aviation staff working on the Japanese joint venture (the jet engine five times the speed of sound) were moved to the Midwest; those working on the American project (the jet engine twenty-five times the speed of sound), remained in California. Despite all General Aviation's efforts to avoid conflict of interest, the *New Economic Times* had run a scathing article charging that "the jet engine industry, in which we are clearly ahead, is being turned over to the Japanese."

Arthur took a deep breath as he approached the meeting room on the second floor. Tempers were high on both sides of the Pacific. It was up to him, and he felt pretty much at sea.

The room was nearly full of people gathered around a long table. The MITI representatives, who, according to Arthur's briefing, had initiated the idea, sat on one side of the table, with teams from two affiliated offices: the Agency of Industrial Science and Technology (AIST), which coordinated technical aspects of the program, and the New Energy and Industrial Technology Development Organization (NEDO), which was responsible for implementing the project. The foreign companies sat opposite the Japanese officials. To the right of the table were rows of chairs to accommodate an audience made up of Japanese company participants and representatives from other interested companies who were watching that MITI did not give any extra concessions to foreign companies. Arthur had heard through the grapevine that when Japanese companies had protested foreign involvement, MITI had called them in and had read them the riot act, saying whoever wanted to leave should do so. All the companies remained, and now the Japanese companies watched from bleacher seats.

The meeting was called to order by Kondo of NEDO. "Thank you for coming," he said slowly, for the sake of the translator. "We are here today to discuss the proposed contract between General Aviation, TRD, BTU, and Tandeau and MITI." Slowly Kondo outlined the history. Arthur had heard from other Japanese that Kondo was sympathetic to America. He never knew what to make of that remark. It sounded as though the Japanese were trying to reassure him.

Arthur sat next to Jim Brown, attorney for General Aviation. Jim was a good lawyer and an old friend. They had worked together on a number of situations. "I don't think they like the fact that I'm here," Jim said, nodding at Ikeda, the senior MITI representative with a stern expression.

"They'll have to get used to it," Arthur answered, thinking of the impossibility of trying to explain to Dr. Sharp and others at General Aviation that he didn't want to bring a lawyer to a major negotiating meeting. Like most American corporate attorneys, Dr. Sharp's lawyers prepared contracts that protected the company from litigation. Everyone present knew that U.S. business culture made litigation all too common. He looked at the solemn faces of Mori of AIST and Kondo and Ikeda. Dr. Sharp needed to attend these meetings, he thought. There was clearly another agenda in Japan at these meetings—one that Arthur couldn't figure out. All the foreign companies were of different opinions. Were the agencies directly competitive? If so, could he turn their animosity to his advantage in the negotiation? He knew the players but that was clearly not enough. Understanding takes time, he thought.

The other foreign companies also had lawyers. BTU had brought technical and contract people. TRD had technical people but was making noises about not participating fully because of intellectual property issues. Arthur was pretty sure they would elect to participate solely on a consultant basis. Tandeau had technical people and seemed intent on full participation.

Kondo cleared his throat. "I have copies of the contract," he explained.

Arthur watched Ikeda; he was a small, powerfully built man with an easy smile, especially in a Ginza bar. Like most MITI officials, Ikeda had spent time abroad and spoke English well. While Arthur had cultivated him since his arrival in Japan, he still felt at sea. After the meeting he had an appointment with Ikeda. It was depressing, he thought. He might just be wasting time. He wasn't certain Ikeda was the right person. For one, Kondo of NEDO was in charge of the meetings. In addition, Mori of AIST knew the technical details better than anyone. Despite this knowledge he had no idea who the point man for General Aviation should be.

"You will note that the contract is being passed to you," Kondo said, as a young man placed a bulky document in front of Arthur. Arthur fingered the pages. The members of the Japanese companies straightened their backs. Similar contracts were passed to them. Yabe, manager of Japan Aircraft Company, whom Arthur knew slightly, was doubled over the pages. Other Japanese were following suit. The only sound in the room was the rustle of paper.

In a methodical tone Kondo began going through the document. Jim was scribbling notes, as were the other lawyers. The technical people were also making notes. Arthur watched Kondo, who had a particularly blank expression.

One by one, the foreign companies began to question the document. They didn't understand the royalty system or the budget system. Kondo nodded at each question as if it were totally reasonable. Then he explained the point in a quiet tone. If the point was too technical he turned the question over to Mori of AIST. The meeting went on in this vein for several hours. The room became stuffy, and Arthur found it difficult to concentrate. The questions from the foreign companies lacked focus. They didn't know enough about the system, and the Japanese knew it.

"Royalty agreements in the U.S. are quite different," Jim said.

"I understand," Kondo answered.

"We own the product of this research," Jim continued.

"In Japan that is not the case," Kondo replied. "Royalties are calculated by a mathematical formula. Turn to section six." The formula Kondo referred to was a complex one incorporating four different variable rates, known as the basic rate (high if substitutes weren't available), the utilization rate (calculated from NEDO's investment and the cost of commercialization), the up/down rate, and the development rate.

A murmur of protest went up from the foreign companies. The room was tense. The lawyers from BTU spoke together quickly. Their punctuated British accents carried across the room. BTU's Senior Counsel Williams spoke up. "What is this up/down rate? I've never seen this one before."

Kondo waited patiently until the room was quiet. He explained that the number would be based on current socioeconomic factors.

"And how do you calculate those factors?" Williams interrupted.

"We understand how things currently are."

"Well, that's rather handy," Williams answered quickly.

Kondo nodded.

Williams continued in a slightly cynical tone, "Who are 'we'?"

Kondo explained that a government committee decided the up/down rate.

"And who makes up this committee?" Williams said. Stone, the TRD counsel, smiled and shook his head. Williams's points were in agreement with TRD's strategy of not bidding on full membership in the consortium because of what appeared to TRD to be the arbitrary nature of the royalty issue. Jean-Paul Rouée, Tandeau's counsel, also shook his head. Jim stopped taking notes. Again Williams questioned the criteria for the decision.

Arthur winced. Williams's tone was getting nasty and the Japanese weren't engaging in any sort of meaningful debate. Williams was well known as a brilliant wit in the jet engine business, and never failed to engage his opposition in a lively exchange. Kondo's face was impassive and Ikeda was pale. The Japanese companies seemed only mildly interested in Williams's points. The meeting read like a rehearsed script. In fact all the meetings in this room had the same tone. The Japanese gave curt answers to questions, all of which they seemed to have anticipated. When the foreign companies argued, the Japanese replied with patience, as if the bottom line had been reached beforehand.

The debate on the up/down rate lasted two hours. Although Williams was speaking loudly by the end of the meeting, Kondo, Ikeda, and Mori never varied their tone.

Arthur was tired and thought of canceling his meeting with Ikeda, but the fact that TRD, BTU, and Tandeau were also meeting with other Japanese corporate or governmental officials rankled. General Aviation must also have its meeting, he thought wearily, as he reached the meeting place. Ikeda waved to him. "I know a nice place quite close by," Ikeda said.

Arthur walked briskly beside Ikeda. They stopped on a narrow lane outside a restaurant with a red Japanese lantern with a black lacquer base. Its elegance contrasted with the brightly lit signs on the street. Ikeda pushed the frosted glass door to one side.

"Welcome," a woman in a kimono said softly and bowed.

Quickly Ikeda removed his shoes and beckoned Arthur to do

likewise. The woman led them to a private room, bowing again before closing the door. Immediately Ikeda relaxed. Arthur smiled. Ikeda never ordered in restaurants; the most he said was "the usual." Arthur figured that Ikeda must be a regular in at least fifty restaurants in the city. Ikeda handed him a hot towel, motioning for Arthur to follow his example as he buried his face in his own towel and rubbed the back of his neck. The room was quiet for several seconds.

An older woman holding a tray of beer and sake opened the door and bowed before entering. She began serving drinks, making small talk about the weather. Ikeda translated, then he spoke of the weather. Arthur relaxed. All their meetings had begun with the same small talk. At first it had irritated him. After all, he was on an important mission, he was supposed to take a short trip to America in two weeks' time, and there were issues like the up/down rate to be settled. Still, during the last month, Arthur had grown more patient with Ikeda and easier on himself. At each official meeting he recognized his lack of understanding of how Japan operated. The afternoon meeting nagged at him.

"Ikeda-san, I don't understand the formula."

"Yes," Ikeda nodded and quaffed his beer.

"Please explain."

Ikeda shook his head. "The fiscal year of Japan ends in April, but the budget for the next year is set in September."

Arthur wanted to know more about the formula, but Ikeda's stern expression stopped him.

"We have to organize our finances by then," Ikeda continued. "That means a real time pressure. The Japanese ministries will want to go over your books with auditors."

"That would cause problems," Arthur said. "General Aviation does not permit outsiders to go over their books."

"That procedure is required in contracts by agreement with the Ministry of Finance. It's just a rule." Ikeda's face was composed. "We must work this out so the timing of the finances is right."

For the next hour Arthur went over General Aviation's fiscal system.

He is trying to understand, Arthur reasoned. He is dedicated to the project and really wants this to work. Ikeda's time abroad had been a crucial training ground to analyze and learn from other nations' systems. Bureaucrats are educated as generalists—most go to the University of Tokyo and most graduate with a degree in economics or law, although very few became lawyers. However, the rigorous legal training and time abroad enabled MITI officials to apply the lessons learned from cases, such as the jet engine consortium, to the future. Talking to Ikeda was really like conducting an intense consultation in which situations were explored in order to find a mutually beneficial solution. He is the best trained detective in the world, thought Arthur. He is disciplined and curious. Methodically, he is finding out how we work, not just so General Aviation and MITI can work together, but so MITI can find solutions to problems they might encounter with other foreign companies in the future. Arthur felt a grudging respect. Ikeda's openness to learn and adapt was a lesson, he thought. General Aviation could use someone like Ikeda.

By the time green melon was served, Arthur felt drained. Ikeda sipped his tea and urged Arthur to eat. Arthur tried to concentrate. Although he was sure Ikeda was trying to help, he was still curious about the up/down rate in the royalty formula. Why wouldn't Ikeda discuss it? Had the Japanese companies made a private deal with the government? Should he ask Ikeda directly about his concerns? Surely, Japanese companies did not allow the government to decide their royalty payments based on a government committee's response to current socioeconomic factors. "What about the up/down rate?" Arthur asked abruptly.

"Mmm," Ikeda's expression was thoughtful. "There are probably many items in the contract that you question."

"Yes," Arthur said quickly. "Perhaps we could go through them."

"Possible."

"Maybe a letter outlining concerns would be helpful." Arthur tried to keep his voice steady.

There was a long pause. "Yes," Ikeda suddenly agreed. "That might be helpful. Tomorrow I will propose this at the meeting."

Arthur felt curiously light-headed. Of course a letter would help, he thought. He would talk to TRD, BTU, and Tandeau about it. They had worked together long enough on joint projects and understood enough about one another's fiscal systems to agree on points of concern in the Japanese contract. It would be good to cooperate and pool resources rather than having each company negotiate with the Japanese independently.

At the meeting the next morning, Ikeda proposed the idea of the letter of understanding on the contract. The Japanese approved immediately. Arthur had an uncomfortable feeling that the Japanese officials had discussed the idea before the meeting. But when? Ikeda must have gotten home at twelve. Surely there hadn't been a midnight conference call. Arthur felt uneasy, then overwhelmed. Again the feeling of being lost took over. He pressed his hand against his forehead and tried to relax.

The foreign companies worked intently on the letter for the next two months. The official meetings continued, as did the off-the-record meetings with the various Japanese agencies. However, the foreign companies concentrated their efforts on the letter of understanding.

When Arthur was in Japan, he saw Ikeda and they continued to work on coordinating the fiscal year of the Japanese ministries and companies with that of the foreign companies, particularly General Aviation. Ikeda also urged Arthur to propose that General Aviation and other foreign companies join a research association that was being formed by retired senior technical people. This association, which would last only the life of the project, was to act as the project manager to the consortium. Its mandate was to review the technical proposals submitted by companies and send recommendations to AIST for final approval.

Arthur brought up the idea of joining the research association with the upper management of General Aviation and with Jim Brown. Both Jim and the upper management were not sure of the immediate benefits because General Aviation had never been involved in a research association. The association would require more time and an investment of personnel, but it was the best way to ensure the two-way flow of technology requested by the U.S. government. After many discussions, General Aviation decided to join, contingent upon satisfactory limitation of cost and risk to the company. Nevertheless, negotiations dragged on, and the Japanese were irritated by General Aviation's inability to act. Ikeda seemed especially disappointed.

During this process, Arthur also began spending time with Kondo of NEDO. At first their meetings were brief and formal, but as drafts of the letter were circulated, their interaction became more frequent. Arthur was also aware that Ikeda and Mori had a special line to

Kondo. Kondo's authority seemed to rest on his character. The Japanese officials called Kondo with their problems and were aware of Kondo's discussions with Arthur. Arthur suspected Kondo informed Ikeda and Mori of new developments, even before Kondo informed his own boss.

Arthur's conversations with Kondo were similar in tone to the ones with Ikeda; however, unlike Ikeda, Kondo often ended an exchange with a philosophical statement. One morning, after a night of barhopping, Kondo called Arthur at his office. They discussed a draft of the letter of understanding by the foreign companies. At the end of the conversation, Kondo said, "I would like to discuss with you the corporate game and the color of pink."

"The color of pink?" Arthur was incredulous.

"The color of pink," Kondo replied firmly. "We listen to the interpreter and hear what we want and vice versa."

"You mean that we all have rose-colored glasses?" responded Arthur.

"In the corporate game," Kondo continued, "if both parties want something long enough, they will achieve their goal." Before Arthur could reply, Kondo said good-bye.

Later, Arthur tried to understand Kondo's statement. What had Kondo meant by the color of pink? Was Kondo implying that Arthur was impatient or narrow-minded? Kondo had been abrupt about the content of the letter of understanding. He repeated, "Please understand our system, please understand our system," when Arthur brought up the auditing and royalty issues. Arthur shook his head—he was getting too sensitive. Kondo was just probably irritated at the long, tiresome, official meetings where nothing seemed to happen, Arthur decided.

Arthur was in a bad mood. Two more months had passed, and nothing had changed. The foreign companies had worked over the contract and presented many drafts of the letter of understanding at the official meetings. All drafts had been ignored. Although Arthur had a good rapport with Ikeda and Kondo, and he was beginning to understand the Japanese contract, General Aviation hadn't made much progress. All this was bad enough, but Arthur knew that the program was under a time constraint. General Aviation's Japanese advisers in Tokyo claimed that budgetary issues had to be settled before final inputs to the next Japanese fiscal year were negotiated with the Finance Ministry in September.

One cold evening in March Arthur went to a cocktail party hosted by TRD at the Imperial Hotel. He wondered how the others felt. Everyone had been working so hard on the letter of understanding that there hadn't been much general discussion.

The cocktail party was held in a small, cozy reception room with soft couches and a round glass table. Only the foreign companies were invited. Glen Walker, vice president of international strategy at TRD, greeted him at the door. "Good to see you, Arthur."

"Nice to be here." Arthur replied.

Williams was talking about his most recent dealing with MITI. His clipped British voice sounded less than amused. "I am sure that MITI is the correct agency to concentrate on. They are directly under the prime minister's office and AIST and NEDO answer to them. Besides, they proposed that we join the consortium. Any originator is bound to be important."

"MITI might be the one, but nothing has really changed," Arthur said. "Every meeting is the same. The cast of characters is always smiling, but none of our concerns in the letter of understanding have really been addressed. I meet regularly with MITI, as I'm sure all of you do."

There was a glum silence.

"Well now," Williams said briskly. "I'm sure something will break soon. It can't just keep going in this way, now can it?"

Walker shook his head. "You know, when I look around the room I see the best in the jet engine business. I mean it. We are the best: no one can touch us, and our research and our technology make us unique. Not too many industries can still say that. The Japanese need us, damn it."

"Hear, hear." Jim Brown raised his glass.

"Then why are we scrambling?" Walker asked. "If the world's best is really in this room, why not make that work for all of us?" Walker's face reddened as he finished the sentence.

The room was quiet. The men stirred their drinks uneasily. They were waiting for someone to take the lead. Arthur watched Jim's face carefully. Jim was a solid, polished, all-American type from Michigan who always carried a neat briefcase. Arthur liked Jim and knew he was a real stickler for the law. The law was against the formation of cartels. This could be viewed as "le grand cartel," Arthur thought. The four jet engine companies assembled were not only the best, but they had also done business and joint ventures for the last thirty years. There was little they didn't know about one another. As fierce competitors most of all, they understood one another with a mix of suspicion and trust. Collectively, they neither truly trusted nor truly understood the Japanese side.

Arthur's thoughts turned to the Japanese. How would they take one set of demands from the foreign companies? The Japanese had asked the foreign companies to work together and address critical issues in the contract. In doing so the Japanese had set the stage for what had transpired today. Even the off-the-record meetings with Ikeda, Mori, Kondo, and others had helped change Arthur's attitude. Arthur knew that other foreign companies had been affected by the constant dialogue with the Japanese and by the letter of understanding. The foreigners in Japan were constructing their own system. It was, as his son Allen often said, "awesome." In this room was a grassroots beginning to an American trade policy. While the government was still debating the issue of free trade, General Aviation was making history.

The Japanese had been negotiating independently with each of the foreign companies. They might take to the hills if the foreigners presented a united front. Arthur said, "We know the contract cold."

"Cold," Williams agreed.

"We all have about the same problems with it," Arthur continued.

The men waited. They knew what he was going to say. Williams was smiling; even Jim was smiling. They faced him, their bodies frozen. Arthur noted the ice in Williams's drink had holes. He had always wondered about ice cubes with holes. The silence lengthened. He cleared his throat. "We should present a united front," Arthur said softly. "We need to spend today and tomorrow drafting our requirements."

"Yes!" Williams stood.

Walker, Jim, and the rest concurred.

That night and for a good part of the next day, the foreign companies worked on their demands in the General Aviation office.

The letter of understanding had given them a good sense of problem areas. They tackled the financial area first because their fiscal cycle made that most pressing. Then they looked at the area of intellectual property. The requirements the foreign companies came up with were:

FINANCIAL PRINCIPLES

1. Each Company will use its own standard company accounting procedures and systems.
2. NEDO shall have audit privileges through an independent auditor, as permitted by each company, at NEDO's expense.
3. Cost reporting shall be to each company's standard method.
4. Each company shall recover its full costs, with negotiated fee.
5. Financial treatment of directed changes shall be the same as the basic contract.
6. Exchange rates shall be fixed annually.
7. Payments shall be made to the participating companies every six months.

INTELLECTUAL PROPERTY RIGHTS

1. Results (including know-how and patents) generated under the contract are to be jointly owned.
2. Each party can use and disclose its own results (whether patented or not) without accounting to NEDO for any and all purposes.
3. Each party can license its own results without accounting to NEDO but licensing of jointly owned patents will be subject to royalties agreed with NEDO.
4. Each party will have access to the total results generated.

The next day, Arthur read through the principles again. He straightened his back as he picked up the phone. Knowing that both MITI and AIST used Kondo as a clearinghouse and as a transmitter of information from one agency to another, Arthur decided that this time he would also use Kondo. Once Arthur had asked Ikeda about Kondo's background. Ikeda had merely said, "Kondo is a person who understands." When Arthur tried to question him further, Ikeda just nodded and smiled.

Arthur was also attracted to Kondo's humanity. Kondo usually ended conversations by saying "We will find a way." Well, thought Arthur, the letter of understanding had not gone anywhere—maybe this was the way.

"Kondo-san," Arthur kept his voice deliberately cheerful, "how are you?"

"Good," Kondo's voice was warm.

There was a slight pause.

"I'm calling about the meeting this afternoon."

Kondo was silent.

"The group feels strongly about the same issues in the contract." Arthur paused. "We have put together a list of requirements in the area of finance and intellectual property that would allow foreign companies to sign the contract. It is a very simple list," he added, thinking of the lengthy letter of understanding on which they had labored. He tried to imagine Kondo's reaction. Kondo had an unusually expressive face. When angry or disappointed his face was still, but if pleased his eyes shone, and he walked with a bounce.

"I see," Kondo's voice was soft. "This may be a very useful idea. Thank you for calling me."

At the meeting that afternoon, Arthur handed a copy of the list to Kondo. As agreed by the foreign companies, Arthur asked that he be permitted to make opening remarks on their behalf. "As requested yesterday, the foreign companies prepared a list of the principles that reflect their most critical concerns. I am responding with our consensus position. Matters associated with accounting and finance and with intellectual property rights are the most critical issues to the foreign companies."

Following the translation, he continued. "Until progress is made toward our position in these areas, further face-to-face discussions will be of limited benefit." Although the Japanese closed their eyes, they nodded and seemed to be listening to the translation. Ikeda scratched his head. Kondo followed suit. Ikeda and the translator spoke briefly in Japanese. The foreign representatives were silent. No one knew what to make of the situation. Kondo resumed the meeting with questions about this new list of financial requirements. Throughout the meeting, Arthur was aware the Japanese had not altered any position stated in the contract.

After two seemingly endless hours of discussion, Leon Wolf, the TRD lawyer, walked over and whispered in Arthur's ear with an air of irritation. "They didn't understand, you need to repeat our position so that they realize how important it is to the continuation of the negotiations."

Arthur answered quietly. "Perhaps you should repeat them, at the end of the meeting." Wolf nodded.

As the meeting neared adjournment, Wolf requested permission to speak. He reiterated Arthur's point with one small change. "Until there is movement toward agreement in these areas, agreement is not possible," Wolf stated emphatically.

Breaking from the procedure of awaiting translation for the first time in the negotiations, Kondo responded addressing Wolf directly. "Arthur-san said progress, you said movement, what do the foreign companies mean?" Shortly thereafter the meeting was adjourned.

In the taxi Arthur thought about the language barrier. If the use of a single word, such as movement versus progress, could create misunderstanding, how could he reach closure on the fine points in the contract? Who was going to do the literal and cultural translating? On the other hand, the Japanese had understood the message well enough that they feared that the fate of the negotiations could depend on just one word. Dr. Sharp was right. He was at a frontier. God, what if he failed? What if the contract was never signed? What if the contract was signed and it was all a misunderstanding?

That night at dinner Arthur and his General Aviation colleagues questioned whether their efforts had been for naught.

On yet another trip to America the next week, Arthur worried about the General Aviation negotiating team he'd left behind and wondered when and if serious negotiations, as he knew them, would begin.

For the next months the small, off-the-record meetings intensified between the Japanese and the foreign companies. In addition, Arthur spoke frequently on the phone with Kondo. Most of their talks centered around General Aviation's accounting system and the adjustments necessary to coordinate General Aviation with the Japanese fiscal year. Kondo seemed intent on going over General Aviation's financial system again and again. When Arthur returned to Tokyo in late April, he was bone-tired, and his team was suffering from serious morale problems. The financial people resented explaining General Aviation's fiscal system and, moreover, the lawyers resented the lack of passion at the negotiating sessions. Arthur was sick of being polite. The intimate atmosphere of the off-the-record meetings made all of them feel like dupes. He would put his points to Kondo straight, he thought, as, accompanied by his financial manager, Frank, he walked down the small Ginza street to their usual meeting place to begin yet another round of talks.

Kondo was already there, sitting at the small table talking to Iwasa, NEDO's financial man. The bar was small and noisy. Guitars hung overhead and the plaintive twang of country-and-western music filled the room. He remembered Kondo's fondness for America and that he collected original posters of 1930s films and other pieces of Americana. Mrs. Kondo had spent two years in America during high school and now worked as a translator. Watching as Kondo tapped his finger to the music, Arthur wondered if the Japanese government had taken his love for America into consideration when they picked him for the job.

"Kondo-san, Iwasa-san," Arthur and Frank greeted them.

"Hi," Kondo replied in English and smiled.

Arthur ordered a beer. The evening always started the same way. Kondo would ask him general questions about his day, where he'd been, who he'd met. The questions were always casual and when Arthur chose to remain silent, Kondo never pressed the point.

By ten o'clock Arthur was tired of chitchat and was growing annoyed. Every pore wanted a confrontation. He was sick of the rehearsed script, the small talk, going over the same material. He wanted an honest, face-to-face New Yorker–type discussion. He took a deep breath. "Kondo-san," Arthur began, "last night we were talking about General Aviation's accounting system."

Kondo nodded. "Yes, we must have our auditor go over General Aviation's procedure. That is the Japanese system. NEDO must explain everything to the Ministry of Finance. Your financial people will explain everything to our financial people. We will come to America."

Arthur was silent. He was about to protest when Kondo lifted the beer bottle and nodded. Arthur lifted his glass and Kondo filled it for him. Then with traditional Japanese courtesy Arthur did the same for Kondo. *"Kampai,* NEDO, *kampai,* General Aviation," Kondo smiled. "Together Arthur, great things will happen," Kondo said and sat back in his seat.

Arthur was momentarily silent. "I am sorry about the requirements for the foreign companies," Arthur said.

"I like the requirements," Kondo answered.

"You do," Arthur confirmed.

"Yes, of course, it makes our job easier," Kondo replied. "Now everything is simpler. The requirements were a good idea."

Arthur thought quickly. The requirements were the logical outgrowth of a system. Kondo and the other Japanese were used to that. It was clear to him again that the Japanese were in a learning mode. General Aviation was trying to make an important deal, but the Japanese government was both making a deal and using this as a study of how to make such deals. They must have a file on foreign financial systems and royalty-right expectations a mile high, he thought uneasily. The realization both elated and fatigued him.

Arthur took a deep breath. "Kondo-san, let Frank explain the General Aviation system," Arthur said. "Then you will understand our difficulty."

Kondo's face brightened. "Yes, please," he replied.

Slowly Frank explained the General Aviation's bookkeeping system and the impossibility of allowing anyone from the outside to see the books. The breakouts would reveal the competitive labor and overhead rates and other numerous fine details, he said.

Instead of answering the specific questions Kondo and Iwasa asked, Arthur and Frank explained the system again. The atmosphere was one of genuine goodwill. Arthur felt alive for the first time in weeks. He buried his desire for debate and instead adopted the Japanese technique of avoiding confrontation. Purposefully, Arthur avoided denying Japanese information outright. Instead of saying "no" he used the word "difficulty," referring again and again to the system. Kondo tried to find loopholes in the system. Arthur summarized the discussion. He kept his voice soft. Kondo was responding, he told himself. There was no debate; the system was responsible for the impasse.

Arthur continued to use this technique of explanation in all his meetings with the Japanese. Negotiations were moving forward.

Kondo and Mori planned to come to America in early July to talk to General Aviation's financial people. Frank prepared for the meetings carefully, faxing Kondo numerous documents that validated his explanation of General Aviation's system. Arthur was both elated and frustrated. The negotiations had progressed, yet the basic situation remained unchanged.

In any event, the crucial meetings in the United States were frustrating. Arthur felt negotiations had reached an impasse. The Japanese questioned the auditors, but clearly wanted to examine the books. By the third day, the Japanese were still friendly, but it was clear that no one knew what the next step would be. Mori and Kondo stayed for the weekend.

Arthur sat in his study and tried to think of tourist attractions for his visitors. His small town in Wisconsin had very little to offer. He thought of the maze of bars in Tokyo and briefly felt embarrassed. There wasn't even a decent movie playing in town. They'd already been to Chez Nous, the local French restaurant, twice.

His eleven-year-old son interrupted his thoughts. "Dad," Allen said, "you promised we'd go to the baseball game tonight, remember?"

Arthur sighed. The last year had put an unbelievable strain on his family. At first he thought the nightly long-distance phone calls from Tokyo would suffice. But that proved difficult. His wife tried to be understanding. The kids needed his attention. Until the past year he'd prided himself on being able to spend lots of time with his family. He loved being a coach for Allen's baseball team and helping his wife with the Boy Scouts. When other parents complained, he was silent. He enjoyed his children and their activities. He'd once heard Allen bragging to his friends that Arthur and he were pals, that they never missed a baseball game. Now he would have to renege on his promise to Allen. "Allen, come here," he said gently, thinking that if he continued working with Japan, Allen would grow up hating the Japanese.

"When do we leave, Dad? We should get there early."

Arthur tugged the baseball cap over Allen's forehead. "Well sport," he said. "I have guests."

"We can get tickets," Allen said quickly. "I'll call."

Arthur opened his mouth to protest, then hesitated. Why not? he thought. The Japanese love baseball. Kondo was always asking to see pictures of Arthur's children. "Okay, sport, you're on. I'll need two extra tickets."

The baseball game was held at the local high school. The night lights were on despite the fact that it was broad daylight. Girls in short red-and-white striped skirts took their tickets. Boys in the same colors ushered them to their seats. The crowd was excited and Allen squeezed Arthur's hand. Allen's eyes were bright as he took his seat.

Allen sat between Kondo and Mori. He jumped up and down, pointing to the different players in the hatch shell. Arthur bought everyone paper baseball caps from a vendor. By the time the game began, Arthur had relaxed. The Japanese seemed to be enjoying themselves, and Allen was in heaven. By the end of the third inning Kondo and Mori were cheering with all the others. Allen bought everyone Cokes and hot dogs.

When play resumed, Kondo turned to Arthur. His eyes were bright with unshed tears, and his face was flushed. He held his hot dog in one hand, the other hand rested on Allen's head. "It has always been my dream to eat a hot dog at an American baseball game," he said. "Thank you."

Arthur had forgotten Kondo's infatuation with America. Mori was also moved, but Kondo was transported. Arthur reached around Kondo and affectionately pulled at Allen's baseball cap, silently thanking him for saving the day.

A week later Arthur received a phone call from Kondo. He thanked Arthur for his hospitality and especially for the baseball game. His tone was warm but not gushing. Arthur responded in kind. "I have an idea," Kondo said.

Arthur waited.

"There is the idea of side letters."

Arthur was annoyed. The foreign companies had spent the whole winter writing a letter of understanding without much in the way of results. "What is a side letter?"

Kondo explained that a side letter expanded and interpreted the language of the contract. Arthur would send him a list of the problem areas in the contract (mostly the areas of finances and intellectual property) that conflicted with the requirements of the foreign companies. Kondo would create a side letter that would reinterpret the language of the contract to the satisfaction of the foreign companies. The side letters must be absolutely confidential, Kondo said. They must never be published, and never mentioned in public.

Arthur took a deep breath, remembering the watchful expressions of the representatives of the Japanese companies at every official meeting. "I'll start working on this right away," he said.

For the next month both Arthur and Kondo worked eighteen-hour days, honing in through long phone calls on the fine details of the contract and the interpretations and expansion on points to be addressed by the side letter. Every point was discussed with the other foreign companies in conference calls. Then Arthur, Jim, and the others wrote their "interpretations" of the contract in English, which Kondo refined and then translated into Japanese for inclusion in the side letter. Kondo was especially concerned about the formula used to determine royalties. Arthur had explained that, because the American government demanded no royalty payments for its project with General Aviation, it was impossible for General Aviation to give a more favorable situation to a foreign government. Kondo seemed sympathetic to this point of view, but had no solution.

Under the complex formula the Japanese had proposed for determining the royalty rate, Kondo now explained, any result of less than .005 would be rounded off to zero. Knowing the costs of developing an engine from his years at General Aviation, Arthur then realized that this would be the case with this jet engine: General Aviation would have to put so much money into development that it would receive no royalties from the finished product. Arthur also told Kondo that it would be impossible for General Aviation to divulge its commercialization costs, another figure used in the formula. This policy of keeping the price of a component secret was important to General Aviation.

In September, General Aviation sent its delegation to Japan. Kondo was delighted that spouses were included. Mrs. Kondo acted as the translator and guide for the wives, even inviting them to her home. Coincidental with General Aviation's financial people being grilled by the Japanese, trust was being established. There was a real effort to understand each other's financial systems, to develop trust through one another's families. By the end of the meetings, a series of pen-pal relationships had been set up between the children of the Japanese and the children of the managers of General Aviation. Kondo sent videotapes of his children's school to Arthur. Their children, who were a comparable age, soon became pen pals.

The relationship was working like a well-oiled machine. For the first time, Arthur was part of a system, and he began to realize the extent of the connections among the Japanese. However, when Arthur made his next trip to Tokyo in October, the foreign companies began having disagreements among themselves. BTU and Tandeau, the European companies, didn't want to use the royalty formula. They were concerned that close scrutiny of the figures would reveal government subsidies and this would create controversy in the United States and in the current GATT negotiations. The foreign companies and MITI were to meet at the Imperial Hotel at 9:30 P.M. to discuss the subsidy problem. Ikeda approached the group gingerly. "It might be better if we met at the MITI office," he said.

Arthur was confused. Why had Ikeda insisted on meeting at the MITI office? Everyone was tired and he had been looking forward to a drink. At the office the Europeans immediately expressed their concerns about revealing their commercialization costs. Arthur let them have the floor. BTU proposed the idea of "notional value": the companies would make an estimate of expenses predicated on reasonable assumptions of what each particular item cost. Then this estimate would be presented to the auditors from the foreign companies (the involvement of foreign auditors had been agreed to earlier). While the auditors could not divulge the actual research and development estimates in their report, they could indicate if the Japanese estimates were in the ball park. This figure would then be used in the royalty formula for commercialization. Having funded Japanese investment in a private program on this same basis, MITI seemed to accept the idea. They reviewed the formula. The meeting broke up after midnight.

The next day Arthur met Kondo for lunch. Kondo looked exhausted. "We met with MITI last night," Arthur said.

"I know," Kondo answered.

"Oh, you talked to Ikeda-san this morning?" Arthur answered, thinking again that news in Japan traveled fast.

"No, last night."

"Last night?"

"Yes, Ikeda, Mori, and I talked until three in the morning."

Arthur smiled. Kondo spoke cheerfully for the rest of the lunch about the formula and the concerns of the foreign companies, but Arthur was numbed by Kondo's revelation. Had Ikeda planned the briefing telephone calls for that night? Is that why he wanted to use the MITI office? No three government agencies in the United States would have had a briefing session ending at three in the morning. In fact, the American agencies were hardly in touch with one another. The obvious dedication of the Japanese bureaucracy was unsettling. Ikeda's planning made Arthur feel inept.

The side letter concentrated on the issues of use of notional value and the freezing of the co-efficient in the up/down rate. Dr. Kawamura, president of NEDO, sent the side letter to General Aviation and the three other foreign companies. A cover letter explained the side letter as a document that expanded upon and interpreted the contract. It also stated that "you can rely upon this letter."

Arthur personally took the letter to Dr. Sharp. Dr. Sharp's philosophy was to cover his bases, and Arthur knew that he countersigned everything. This side letter would not stand up in court and both he and Arthur knew that. Arthur was prepared to fight. Kondo and he had put too much into the side letters for Sharp to reject them now. He thought of the hours of phone calls to Tokyo, London, and Paris, as well as the eighteen-hour days going over the nuance of each word with the other foreign companies. The concept of the side letters must be accepted by Sharp. Both he and Sharp knew that any dispute in the contract would have to be settled in Tokyo District Court.

"Arthur," Dr. Sharp's tone was friendly.

Arthur sat in the large leather chair opposite Dr. Sharp's desk and waited.

"I hear you have the side letter." Dr. Sharp broke the silence.

"Yes," Arthur answered quickly.

"I hear that it's from Dr. Kawamura. He's an important man. I'm told he is very powerful."

"Yes," Arthur said. Sharp was good, he thought. Dr. Sharp smiled. Arthur returned his smile and waited. This was a first for General Aviation. Litigation was the company's second name. A fleet of lawyers was on call, warning the company at every moment not to touch anything that wasn't absolutely fail-safe. Side letters weren't in the least fail-safe, he thought. Sharp knew that too. Sharp must be also thinking of the Japanese court system. Sharp was astute enough to understand that Kawamura's written assurances were backed by his potential loss of face. Despite the fact that the side letters weren't public, the word of a top bureaucrat in the Japanese agency had to be respected. The silence lengthened. Arthur broke into a sweat. Sharp was still smiling. Boy, he'd hate to fight Sharp, Arthur decided.

"Arthur, I said this would be a first and I meant it. It's a first in every way. I've seen the contents of the side letter. I want you to know I accept Dr. Kawamura's assurances."

That night Arthur dialed Kondo's number. He knew that Kondo would be waiting beside the phone. He tried to imagine the light in his eyes when he heard the news. "Kondo-san," Arthur began, "I want to discuss the color of pink and the corporate game."

There was a deep laugh on the other end of the line. "Well done, Arthur-kun," Kondo said softly, "well done."

Analysis:

The Japanese are diligent about maintaining order by protecting the de facto structure of an institution. This often causes complex maneuvering behind the scenes. As a negotiation evolves, the relationship of each party to the other's institutions and, ultimately, to the negotiation changes.

For a negotiation to be successful, a real effort to understand the de facto situation initially is made. This is followed by a commitment to locate and develop a trusting working relationship with the apparent power and by an exchange of information in off-the-record meetings with that power. Finally, with a win/win situation in mind, the parties work together to negotiate a successful contract. Arthur's case illustrates this progression.

When the story opens, General Aviation has been through the "know me" phase and has established networks in Japan by doing business with both the Japanese government and other Japanese companies. Through this contract, both Japanese and Americans have come to respect one another and understand the importance of involvement in the research consortium.

The meeting the foreign companies have with MITI and its affili-

ated agencies NEDO and AIST typifies many characteristics of the "trust me" phase. The Japanese are still in an exploratory mode in terms of acquiring knowledge and building trust, and resent the presence of foreign lawyers at the meeting. They are not yet ready to engage the foreign companies in a conclusive exchange on the contract. The efforts of the British counsel, Williams, to debate the formula are counterproductive, not only because he choses a combative style but also because the Japanese are still trying to assess the people and the situation. This inquisitive stage is underscored by the tone of Arthur's dinner that same evening with Ikeda, a senior MITI official. Ikeda wants to seek an understanding of the options. Through Ikeda's attitude toward understanding General Aviation's financial system, Arthur understands that MITI wants the consortium to work. MITI will use this experience as a model for other endeavors with foreign companies.

In this spirit of learning, Ikeda agrees that General Aviation and other foreign companies write a letter of understanding of the contract. In the "trust me" phase, such a letter is an attempt to pinpoint the problems in a situation—not to solve them. Ikeda realizes the letter will not have conclusive results because by its very nature it is critical of the contract and the Japanese system. The Japanese are using the letter of understanding as a vehicle to gain knowledge of the problem areas and they expect the foreign companies to do the same.

However, even in this stage, there is an effort by the Japanese government to break into the "believe me" phase and to begin working together. This is shown by their proposal for General Aviation to join the Japanese research association, a team of technical experts who will assess the proposals from each company. From the Japanese point of view, although it involves a commitment of time and money, the research association is a fundamental part of the system where networks can be extended, state-of-the-art research will be assessed, and policy will be implemented. It is therefore a credible investment. General Aviation cannot immediately accept this offer, due to a lack of a short-term return.

The foreign companies finally enter into the "believe me" phase when they reveal their understanding of the contract and one another by creating their own system of demands. Japanese have great respect for the order and integrity of a system. Since there is an enormous emotional identification with one's group, there is also an assumption that there is equivalent pride on the part of others. Group thinking (shudan ishiki) is also highly regarded in the ethics of Japanese business. People are encouraged to put aside their individual demands and develop a point of view that takes the goals of the group into consideration. The demands by the foreign companies are simply a statement of their requirements, given the rules of their particular institutions, and do not constitute a criticism of the Japanese system or of the contract. Rather they represent a list of what the foreign companies require to bring the contract into line with their own system. The tone of the negotiations changes and there is more effort spent in off-the-record meetings trying to find a mutually satisfactory way around both the Japanese laws and the rules of the foreign companies.

Arthur responds to this more cooperative atmosphere. He learns to negotiate through the detailed documentation that explains General Aviation's financial system. In this way Arthur allows the system to make the statement and to bear the responsibility. For instance, Arthur lets Kondo know that General Aviation cannot give the Japanese government a royalty payment it does not offer its own government. Kondo finds these arguments logical. From Kondo's point of view, Arthur is merely giving him information about General Aviation's potential problem. By using this approach, Arthur gives Kondo the freedom to find loopholes in General Aviation's financial rules that will satisfy the Japanese law.

The importance of Kondo's personality is also apparent in the "believe me" stage. All the Japanese agencies respect Kondo's hard work and his perspective on complicated situations. Soon Arthur, like his Japanese colleagues, is using Kondo as a conduit for information and as a valued adviser. The importance of a sincere (makoto) individual cannot be underestimated, especially if that person is designated as an essential facilitator for a group. Kondo makes Arthur aware of the degree of interdependence of the Japanese agencies and the consultation (sodan) that occurs on every issue. Japanese use consultation routinely to determine the best course of action, as self-protection, and to increase and strengthen networks and obligation. Arthur also recognizes the personal commitment (giri) of Kondo, Ikeda, and Mori to their work.

The negotiation progresses to the "marry me" phase after the baseball game. The stage has been set in the sense that Arthur and Kondo have been working together in the "believe me" stage for some time. There is obvious trust in the relationship, to the point where they communicate constantly to find loopholes in each other's systems. From Kondo's point of view, Arthur's invitation to the baseball game with his son is Arthur's recognition of his love for Americana and an inclusion in the intimacies of family life. Japanese set great store by personal gestures that acknowledge feelings (ningo). Sometimes their emotional reaction is confusing to Westerners. Kondo's response is to form a partnership.

Kondo's idea of the side letter allows General Aviation's and the other foreign companies' financial and royalty systems to stay in place. It also gives full respect to Japanese law. To accomplish these aims, the side letter must be kept secret. Because the side letter interprets the language of the contract on issues that foreign companies find sensitive, the contract is never challenged but rather is manipulated to everyone's satisfaction. For instance, the idea of notional value— where the foreigners and Japanese work in concert to determine an acceptable substitute for the commercialization cost in the formula— reveals the side letter's cooperative approach. In the "marry me" phase, professionals work together to accomplish the common goal of a win/win situation.

Arthur's relationship with Kondo opens the door for more personalized relationships between General Aviation and NEDO. When General Aviation's management and their wives take a trip to Japan, they are entertained in an intimate manner that will, from the Japanese point of view, generate friendships as well as obligation (on). Japanese often extend this kind of hospitality in situations when they are obligated or when they perceive more personalized contact will yield better results.

Dr. Sharp realizes that, although the side letter might not hold up in court, the promise (yakusoku) in Dr. Kawamura's cover letter (that Dr. Sharp can "rely" on him) must be taken seriously. Japanese do not routinely resort to litigation in business. Often an issue will be settled verbally or by a letter that might not stand up in court. In this case Dr. Kawamura is in essence stating that he takes full responsibility (sekinin sha) for the side letter. Taking responsibility is an important statement in a culture where decisions tend to be made with tremendous consultation. Dr. Sharp accepts the side letter and Dr. Kawamura's assurances, with this understanding and with the knowledge that if litigation occurred, it would take place in Tokyo District Court. Dr. Sharp is aware that litigation in Japan is a long, drawn-out process. The unlikelihood that this scenario will evolve makes Dr. Sharp's decision considerably easier. In the "marry me" phase the Japanese government and General Aviation have formed a partnership to resolve the problem of the contract. Both expect that the trust that has developed between them will enable them to explore other business opportunities and facilitate deals with greater ease and commitment.

GLOSSARY

aisatsu—A polite greeting, habitually addressed to others both at the start of each day and at the start of a meeting. The practice of greeting in Japan is more formal than it is in the West.

amae—A sense of mutual dependence. This is a frequent phenomenon of group-oriented Japanese society.

bu—A section or department within an organization, larger than a *ka* (see below).

gaijin—Foreigner; literally, "people from outside." An abbreviation of *gaikokujin*.

gakubatsu—Old school clique. Alumni tend to club together within Japanese firms.

giri—A favor one is expected to return, which is perceived as very important in Japanese culture. (See also *on*.)

haji—Shame. More strongly felt on behalf of the group than on the part of an individual; the *haji* of one person is identified with by other members of the group.

hara—The abdomen, frequently used in describing a "gut feeling." The Japanese consider the abdomen to be the center of emotion.

honne—What a person actually believes, as opposed to what one might say to please another. (See also *tatemae*.)

jinji-bu (or **jinji-ka**)—The personnel department. Due to centralized hiring practices, personnel departments are powerful entities in Japanese companies. Also, at least once a year the *jinji-bu* will reshuffle personnel between departments; this is an integral part of Japanese management.

ka—The smallest operative unit of a Japanese company, several of which comprise a *bu* (see above). A *ka* may consist of several *kakaris*, adaptable units of up to three people each.

kacho—The section chief in a Japanese company. Owing to the "bottom-up" nature of Japanese business culture, this can be an influential position.

katagaki—Position or title. This is very important because of the hierarchical nature of Japanese society; a Japanese businessperson will pay careful attention to the *katagaki* of a guest or acquaintance.

keiretsu—Literally, "interrelated company group." Many Japanese companies are organized as conglomerates, usually with a bank at the center. *Keiretsu* companies hold a certain percentage of each other's stock and provide each other with goods and services.

kohai—A person junior to another within a group, according to seniority. (See *sempai*.)

-kun—Suffix usually used by men to other men of the same rank or to men and women of lower status; denotes belonging to the same group.

madoguchi—A person or department handling contact with an outside party.

nakama—"Inside" members of a group. The distinction between "insiders" and "outsiders" is keenly felt in Japan.

nemawashi—The process by which others are prepared in advance for a decision; planting the seeds for an idea before it is formally introduced.

nenko joretsu—The seniority-oriented promotion system and pay structure, still practiced by the majority of Japanese companies.

Nihon teki—Literally, "Japan-like"; or very Japanese. *Nihon teki* can have both positive and negative connotations.

Nihonjin ron—The theory that explains why the Japanese are physically and mentally a unique people.

ningen kankei—Human relations. The cliquish nature of Japanese companies makes *ningen kankei* an important factor in business culture; awareness of intracompany politics is especially crucial for personal success in smaller units.

nintai—Patience. Important in the process of appraising a proposal.

on—A sense of personal debt, or feeling of gratitude for a special favor.

onjo shugi—Paternalism displayed by Japanese employers in return for company and group loyalty.

ringi—Approval gained by means of a system of gathering consensus, achieved through the circulation of a proposal.

-san—The most common suffix attached to names, which is acceptable in both formal and informal situations.

sekinin—Responsibility, both group and individual. It is often the case in Japan that a sense of group responsibility is more developed than that of an individual's.

sekinin-sha—The person held accountable for an action, or in charge of a certain operation.

sempai—A person who is senior to another, both in terms of age and experience. (See *kohai*.)

sensei—"Teacher"; also master or mentor.

shacho—The president of a company, usually retaining more power than that which would be given to a Western chairman. CEO positions are almost always held by *shachos*, not chairmen.

shokai—Introductions. Personal introductions carry more weight in Japan than in the West; those with the appropriate *shokai* will be much more favorably received than those without.

sodan—Consultation. Considered very important, hence the profusion of meetings held in a Japanese business day.

tate shakai—Refers to the vertical, seniority-based structure of Japanese society. (Seniority is gauged by both age and rank.)

tatemae—An impression one constructs, as opposed to what one might actually think, given the circumstances of a particular situation. (See *honne*.)

tsukiai—The feeling that one must keep company with certain people. In order to maintain good *ningen kankei* (see page 239), much time is devoted to social activities. This includes socializing with colleagues and participating in company-organized excursions. Every employee feels obliged to "do *tsukiai*."

uchi no kaisha—"My company." Employees identify strongly with their companies, and in turn can exert great influence on company policy.

wa—An harmonious tone. *Wa* is integral to Japanese business relations.